THE EVERYTHING GROW YOUR OWN VEGETABLES BOOK

Dear Reader,

I was in my mid-twenties before I started my first vegetable garden. I had just moved into a new home with a great backyard and decided it would be fun to plant some veggies. I started planning what I would grow, turning over the grass to make a new garden spot, and then planted my first seeds. Once the seeds starting popping out of the soil I was hooked! Over the last fifteen years growing vegetables has become a full-time passion for me and has brought a huge amount of joy, friendship, and satisfaction to my life. I moved from growing a few veggies in my little backyard garden to growing on two acres of land and selling my veggies. I began teaching gardening workshops at my local community center when I realized people wanted to grow vegetables but were not sure how to get started. I then created a website (*www.your-vegetable-gardening-helper.com*) to help vegetable gardeners with practical and easy-to-follow steps and information. This book seemed like the perfect next step to reach even more of you who want to grow your own vegetables. Growing organic vegetables is a way of life I would recommend to everyone!

Happy gardening,

Catherine Abbott

Welcome to the EVERYTHING Series!

These handy, accessible books give you all you need to tackle a difficult project, gain a new hobby, comprehend a fascinating topic, prepare for an exam, or even brush up on something you learned back in school but have since forgotten.

You can choose to read an *Everything®* book from cover to cover or just pick out the information you want from our four useful boxes: e-questions, e-facts, e-alerts, and e-ssentials.

We give you everything you need to know on the subject, but throw in a lot of fun stuff along the way, too.

We now have more than 400 *Everything®* books in print, spanning such wide-ranging categories as weddings, pregnancy, cooking, music instruction, foreign language, crafts, pets, New Age, and so much more. When you're done reading them all, you can finally say you know *Everything®*!

QUESTION

Answers to
common questions

FACT

Important snippets
of information

ALERT

Urgent
warnings

ESSENTIAL

Quick
handy tips

PUBLISHER Karen Cooper

DIRECTOR OF ACQUISITIONS AND INNOVATION Paula Munier

MANAGING EDITOR, EVERYTHING® SERIES Lisa Laing

COPY CHIEF Casey Ebert

ACQUISITIONS EDITOR Katrina Schroeder

ASSOCIATE DEVELOPMENT EDITOR Elizabeth Kassab

SENIOR DEVELOPMENT EDITOR Brett Palana-Shanahan

EDITORIAL ASSISTANT Hillary Thompson

EVERYTHING® SERIES COVER DESIGNER Erin Alexander

LAYOUT DESIGNERS Colleen Cunningham, Elisabeth Lariviere, Ashley Vierra, Denise Wallace

Visit the entire Everything® series at *www.everything.com*

THE
EVERYTHING®
GROW YOUR OWN
VEGETABLES
BOOK

Your complete guide to planting, tending,
and harvesting vegetables

Catherine Abbott

Foreword by Meghan Shinn, Editor, *Horticulture* Magazine

JG
PRESS

This book is dedicated to every gardener who
is committed to enjoying a healthy lifestyle
by growing organic vegetables.

An Everything® Series Book.
Everything® and everything.com® are registered trademarks of F+W Media, Inc.

Published by World Publications Group, Inc.
140 Laurel Street, East Bridgewater, MA 02333
www.wrldpub.com

ISBN 10: 1-57215-761-5
ISBN 13: 978-1-57215-761-3

Printed and bound in China

10   9   8   7   6   5   4   3   2   1

Library of Congress Cataloging-in-Publication Data
is available from the publisher.

Illustrations by Barry Littmann and Eric Andrews.

Contents

Acknowledgments

I want to thank everyone who encouraged me to write this book. You are all very much loved and appreciated. I want to also acknowledge my local gardening community for the friendship, encouragement, and support you have all extended to me over the years. This is my way of thanking you and paying it forward.

Ten Steps to a Bountiful Vegetable Garden

1. Choose the best site you can to grow your veggies. A great site will have full exposure to the sun, great soil, and good drainage. It will also be easy to access from your house and near a good water source.

2. Start with good soil and keep improving on it. Keep your soil healthy by regularly adding in organic matter such as compost and aged animal manure. Use cover crops and mulches to help enhance the soil fertility.

3. Start planning your garden on paper. Planning what vegetables you want to grow, how much you will need, and where to plant the seeds or transplants will save you time, energy, and money in the long run.

4. Start with a small space. A vegetable garden takes time and effort, so start with a small garden site; as you gain confidence, you can gradually increase the size of your garden.

5. Grow what you and your family like to eat. You want to be able to enjoy the veggies you grow.

6. Select vegetable varieties wisely. Different vegetable plants and seeds need a variety of conditions to grow and produce well, so choose what grows best in your garden site.

7. A good water source is essential. You want your water source to be easily accessible. It is best to water deeply once or twice a week, preferably early in the day.

8. Take the time to observe your plants. You will be able to spot any problems early on, which will make it easier to prevent or control any damage.

9. Research any problems. Taking the time to research a problem before you start treating it will save you money, time, and energy.

10. Keep your garden clean. Having good garden practices is one of the best ways to prevent and control pests and diseases in your vegetable garden.

Foreword

WHEN WE WERE PLANNING content for *Horticulture* magazine's 2010 issues, one of our long-time columnists, generally a "flower guy," pitched several stories about food gardening. "It is the Year of the Vegetable, it seems," he quipped.

I had to agree with him. Interest in vegetable gardening gained much steam in 2009, following many years when American gardeners focused on perennials, flowers, lawns, and other aspects of the ornamental landscape.

In the '50s my grandfather tended a vegetable garden to help feed his growing family. It remained a favorite hobby, and years later he would send bags of tomatoes, beans, cukes, and carrots home with us grandkids.

My father also grew vegetables in the '70s and early '80s. "Everyone did," he tells me. "We had millions of zucchini we couldn't give away, because so did all our friends." A tattered recipe for Zucchini Pie in my mom's recipe box proves the point. (Interestingly, she and my grandmother both handled the flower gardening in their yards.)

Interest in veggie gardening seemed to wane in more recent decades, though; for instance, back issues of *Horticulture* rarely cover the topic after 1985, up until the past couple years, when we've increased coverage in response to readers' wishes.

So why is vegetable gardening suddenly back in the spotlight? With the risk of sounding a bit dramatic, I'll say that homegrown veggies are the antidote to the present day's complexities and the elixir for many contemporary fears.

Think about the worries and pressures that have built up for so many Americans recently, then realize how vegetables assuage these so handily, like tiny unassuming superheroes:

- Many of us are facing short personal budgets and rising costs, including at the supermarket. Growing vegetables can put nutritious, fresh food on the table for a minimum price.
- Our society is plagued by health concerns, including a rise in obesity and its complications. We're wary that commercially grown vegetables may carry sickening bacteria after several outbreaks in the past couple years. Homegrown vegetables are good for our bodies and waistlines, and it's comforting to know exactly where our food comes from and how it's handled.
- We're increasingly aware of the environment's fragility. Locally grown veggies (and what's more local than your own backyard?) don't depend on fuel-heavy long-distance shipping.
- Vegetable gardening allows you to control how much, if any, pesticides and fertilizers go into your own vegetable garden. You can produce 100 percent organic veggies if you like—for a fraction of the cost of store-bought organics.
- Nowadays e-mail, the Internet, and cell phones keep us in touch, available, and connected 24-7. That can be great for relationships and work advancements, but it can also distance us from the natural world, quiet time, and in-person interactions. Growing vegetables brings nature up close, with tasty rewards to share with family and friends.

Even if you haven't a care in the world, homegrown vegetables can be your heroes. They taste better than the store-bought kind, and seed catalogs offer infinite varieties to try.

So dig in and get growing! Catherine Abbott will tell you *Everything*® you need to know.

Meghan Shinn
Editor
Horticulture Magazine

Introduction

THERE IS A GREAT sense of accomplishment in planting a tiny seed, watching it grow, and then picking the vegetable and eating it. If you are new to vegetable gardening, this book will help you get started in having your first veggie garden. If you are an avid gardener, you'll find new tips and tricks to make your life easier. Wherever you are in your vegetable gardening process, you will find the information in this book helpful and easy to follow.

We all want to be healthier, and for most this means more exercise and eating more vegetables. Growing your own vegetables will help to solve both of these issues. Gardening is a great way to work a little more exercise into your regular routine. Digging, hoeing, weeding, and watering are all great activities and can be accomplished at any age or level of fitness if you take your time. As for eating more vegetables, there is nothing better than biting into a fresh tomato picked from the vine or hearing the crunch as you bite into a carrot you just pulled out of the ground.

For some people, starting a vegetable garden can be intimidating; there seems to be so much you need to know. This book will help to guide you in choosing the best site you can, planting the veggies you love, and then keeping them healthy and growing until they are ready to be harvested.

This book is divided into chapters focusing on specific topics, making it easy for you to find what you need quickly. Feel free to jump from chapter to chapter as you have questions during your vegetable growing season. There is specific information on how to plant and care for common vegetables that you may choose to grow. You will find the information to be useful no matter what climate or area you live in.

Vegetable plants need care and attention to grow well. It is important that you choose to grow vegetables in a way that works best for you. If you do not have access to a backyard, try growing vegetables in containers on your balcony or front porch. A vegetable garden can be as small or as large as you want or need it to be. Taking the time to plan what you want to grow and how you want to grow it is an important step to having a successful vegetable garden.

Be open to experimenting and trying new things. Do not be afraid to make mistakes. The temperature, the amount of sunlight, and the amount of rainfall can all have a huge effect on how well your vegetable plants grow. Because we have very little control over the weather, you may have new successes and new challenges every season.

Having a successful vegetable garden takes time, effort, and commitment. The feeling of accomplishment you get when you watch the seeds sprout and then turn into fabulous-tasting food is one of the great pleasures in life. Start out small, grow what you love to eat, have fun, relax, and enjoy healthy food on your table.

CHAPTER 1

Choosing a Garden Site

A vegetable garden can be as small or as large as you want or need; it can be in a few pots on your balcony, a large acreage in the country, or any size in between. Whether you are a gardening novice who wants to start your first vegetable garden or an experienced gardener who just wants some tips on how to enhance it, this chapter will offer the information you need to make the best choices.

Why Do You Want to Grow Vegetables?

The first thing to consider when deciding to start a vegetable garden is why you want to start one. What you want the vegetable garden to do for you can determine what size you may need and what you may want to grow.

You can save money on your grocery bill and feed your family healthy organic produce by growing your own vegetables. As a hobby, gardening is a wonderful way to connect with other gardeners, neighbors, and most of all with your family. Children love to get out into the garden planting, watching things grow, and eating the freshly picked vegetables. You may have many other reasons for wanting a vegetable garden. Whatever reason you choose to garden, it can be fun and it's a great way to stay active and enjoy the outdoors.

FACT

Gardening is good for your health! You can burn 150–250 calories per hour just by getting out into your vegetable garden. Exercise also releases endorphins into the bloodstream. Endorphins make you feel happy and give you a more positive outlook overall.

Planting a vegetable garden can be very rewarding. It is miraculous how a tiny little seed can produce enough vegetables to feed your family for several meals. By growing one or two vegetables for yourself, you can save on trips to the supermarket, know exactly what is in your food, and control how it was grown.

Whatever your reason for growing your own vegetables, it is important to consider that gardening does take time, money, and energy. Be realistic when you estimate how much time you have to devote to your garden. People will often start a huge garden in the spring only to tire of it and let the weeds take over by summer. If you are a first-time gardener, start small. Increase the size of your site every year as you become more familiar with growing your own vegetables.

If you only have a few minutes a day to spend on your vegetable garden, perhaps you can start with a few pots. If you have a few hours a week, you could manage a small garden spot or perhaps a raised bed. If you want to grow enough food to feed your family all year round, you may need to set aside at least one day a week to tend to a much larger garden. No matter where you live, you can find a spot to grow some of your own vegetables.

What Do You Want to Grow?

When choosing a garden site, it is important to know what you would like to grow. Some vegetables need warmth and lots of sunlight to grow, while others do well in a shadier spot.

Planning what you want to grow will save you time, money, and energy in the long run. It is important to grow what your family will eat. Write down a list of vegetables that you love to eat. Get your family involved so they can be part of the decision-making process. That way, they will feel a sense of ownership and just might be more willing to help plant and take care of the garden.

ALERT

Children love to garden. For young children, choose quick-growing veggies like radishes so they can watch them grow. Veggies that are fun to eat, like peas or corn, are also great. Let older children grow what they want in their own designated little garden. Teach them how to plant, weed, water, and take care of that area.

Some vegetables take a lot more of your time than others, so take that into account when you make your selections. Swiss chard and salad greens are easy to grow and can be harvested from just a few plants several times. A twenty-foot row of asparagus will take some time to plant initially, but you'll be able to look forward to enjoying asparagus in the spring for years to come. Some root crops such as carrots, beets, or radishes need to be thinned as they grow. This can be time consuming, especially if you have large rows of these vegetables. It is important to know how much time you want to put into gardening.

If you want to grow enough of certain vegetables so that you can preserve or freeze them for eating during the winter months, it is important to plant more than you would need for fresh eating alone. Plan ahead and decide what you want to do with your harvest.

If space is a consideration, research plants that give bigger yields but don't take up a lot of space. Root crops (except potatoes) and leafy greens will yield a lot for the space they use up. You can train tomatoes, cucumbers, and beans to grow vertically, giving you more of a harvest for the space used. Consider growing vegetables that have more than one edible part. For example, if you grow beets, you can eat the root and enjoy the leaves in a salad. If you grow onions, you can eat the greens in your salad and then wait until the bulbs are large enough to harvest to save on space as well.

Here is a list of ten common vegetables you can easily grow:

- Beans
- Cabbage
- Carrots
- Cucumbers
- Lettuce
- Onions
- Peas
- Potatoes
- Squash
- Tomatoes

Growing a vegetable garden will take effort and time, so it is important to grow what you or your family will eat. However, do not be afraid to try something new. A vegetable fresh from the garden has much more flavor than most veggies bought at the local grocery store, so you could be surprised by what you or your family may eat! If you find you do not like something or have an overabundance of certain veggies, give some away to friends, neighbors, or your community food bank.

Consider Your Climate

The United States and Canada are divided into plant hardiness zones that range from 1—the coldest areas such as Alaska—up to 11—the warmest areas such as southern California, southern Florida, and Hawaii. These zones are based on temperature variations and first and last frost dates, which give the gardener an idea of what plants will grow best in each zone.

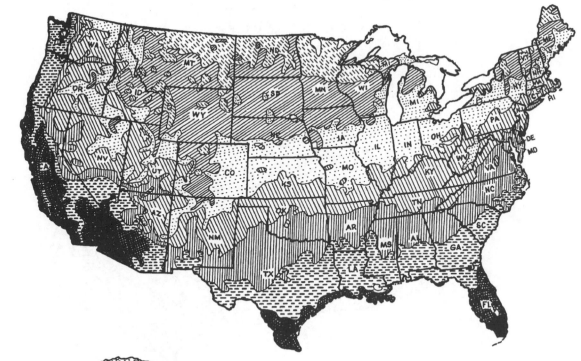

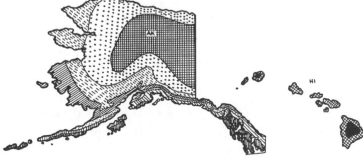

Range of average annual minimum temperatures for each zone

Zone 1	Below –50°F	
Zone 2	–50° to –40°	
Zone 3	–40° to –30°	
Zone 4	–30° to –20°	
Zone 5	–20° to –10°	
Zone 6	–10° to 0°	
Zone 7	0° to 10°	
Zone 8	10° to 20°	
Zone 9	20° to 30°	
Zone 10	30° to 40°	
Zone 11	Above 40°	

Planting zones in the United States

Planting zones in Canada

These zones can be important when choosing perennial plants, but most vegetable gardeners grow annuals within their area's growing seasons. Most areas in the United States and Canada also have four seasons—spring, summer, fall, and winter. The majority of gardeners grow vegetables in the spring and summer, although some gardeners in the southern United States can grow during the fall and winter months as well. Growing seasons can be extended by using greenhouses or other structures to give vegetable plants protection from inclement and unpredictable weather.

The length of your growing season will be pretty standard but can vary depending on the weather. You should also be aware of the average amount of rainfall in your area when choosing your site. The general climate of your area is important to consider, but each garden site will have specific issues.

Is the area protected from the wind? Does the site have lots of mature trees that will block out the sun or does it get full sun? Choosing different ways to grow on your site can help you control variables. For example, growing in raised beds or in a greenhouse can solve a multitude of site problems.

The Importance of Sunlight

Sunlight plays a big part in growing a successful vegetable garden. This is the one area you have the least control over. When choosing your garden site, you will need to consider the amount of sunlight these areas get throughout the day. Most vegetables need an average of six hours of sunlight in order to grow. But don't fret if you only have a shadier spot. There are a few plants that will grow in a bit of shade, and perhaps you can grow other vegetables in containers that can be moved around to follow the sun's path.

The sun alters its path throughout the seasons, so take the time to track its progress. Jot down the time when sunlight hits your area throughout the different seasons and record how long it stays there. It may not matter if your garden site is deprived of sunlight in the winter because you won't be growing anything at that time, but if you get no sun during the spring and summer, you will need to choose another site.

You also want to consider how the trees in the area affect the amount of sun your site will receive. You may get full sun in the winter months when the leaves are off the trees, but the site becomes shadier as the leaves come out. The solution is to find a sunnier spot if you will be growing your veggies during the spring and summer.

The following vegetables do well with four to six hours of sunlight a day:

- Carrots
- Lettuce
- Kale
- Peas
- Swiss chard

The following vegetables traditionally produce fruit and need more sunlight:

- Cucumbers
- Eggplants
- Peppers
- Squash
- Tomatoes

Consider whether your vegetable plants will have any competition for the soil's nutrients. Perennial shrubs aren't usually a problem, and they can even benefit your garden by attracting beneficial insects to the vegetable patch. But beware of planting your garden near large trees, which will take nutrients from your vegetable plants.

QUESTION

Which organic matter is best to use in your garden?
Choosing aged animal manures or compost or shredded leaves or seaweed does not really make a difference. What is most important is to add organic matter to your garden soil every year. Choose what is readily available and inexpensive so you can add large amounts to your beds.

Most gardeners do not have an ideal garden site; however, you can still grow a great vegetable garden with a little knowledge and a willingness to experiment with different vegetables. What books or seed catalogs say will or will not grow has been proven wrong in many garden sites.

The Water Source

The amount of rainfall your garden gets will vary from year to year, so a good water source near your garden site is essential. Most people will be less inclined to water if they have to carry it from a long distance away. Make sure your garden hose can easily reach across the full length of your garden site.

Most vegetable plants need one to two inches of water each week; some will need more if you live in an extremely hot climate. Containers and raised beds may also need more watering depending on the temperature in your area and how much rainfall you get. There are several different ways of watering your vegetable garden, including using sprinklers, a soaker hose, drip irrigation, and hand watering.

ALERT

Place small empty tuna cans in four different areas of your vegetable garden. Turn on the overhead sprinkler and leave it on for one hour. Measure the amount of water in each can. This will give you an indication of how much water various spots in your garden receive from the sprinkler in an hour.

If you live in an area that gets a lot of rainfall, consider investing in a rain gauge. It will help you keep track of the amount of water your vegetable garden receives. If you get too little water, the vegetable plant roots won't be able to grow deep enough to reach the reserves of water and nutrients in the soil. Too much water will saturate the soil, reducing the amount of air space needed for the vegetable roots to grow strong, deep, and healthy. Either is harmful to your vegetable plants, and stressed plants will not produce as much.

From Lawn to Garden

More and more people are replacing all or part of their lawns with vegetables and flowers. In a lot of areas, water restrictions mean you might have a brown lawn during the summer months. It's not very attractive, so why not put in a veggie garden instead?

If you are concerned about what your neighbors or community will say, take the time to tell them what you are planning to do. Make sure there are no restrictions; if there are, go to the town or neighborhood committee for permission. Growing your own food is important for all of us, and it has become fashionable as well.

If you choose to remove the sod from your front or backyard, start with one small area or build a raised bed to put over the sod. Removing sod can be time-consuming and hard work—and remember that you're inevitably removing some valuable soil when you remove the sod. One option is to turn the sod over, leaving it to decompose over several weeks. Another option is to use mulch to prevent the grass from getting sunlight so it will die back naturally. This option will take longer to make a bed, but it's easier on the back!

FACT

Save water by growing vegetables rather than having a green lawn. According to Environment Canada, a single lawn sprinkler spraying 19 liters per minute uses more water in just one hour than a combination of ten toilet flushes, two five-minute showers, two dishwasher loads, and a full load of laundry.

TURN YOUR LAWN INTO A VEGETABLE GARDEN

1. Cover the area you want to make into a vegetable garden with cardboard, overlapping the cardboard to make sure no area is left uncovered.
2. Moisten the cardboard by spraying it with water.
3. If you have any shredded leaves or grass clippings, put a one- to three-inch layer over the cardboard.
4. Place three to twelve inches of compost or garden soil on top of the whole area. If you can only put on a couple of inches, leave the site for a few weeks so the cardboard can decompose a bit. If you can add twelve inches of soil, you can start planting your seeds and transplants immediately.

You now have a garden site instead of a lawn. You can spruce up the area by adding trellises or other garden structures. If you are the first one in your neighborhood to turn your lawn into a vegetable garden, take the time to make it look great and share your harvest. Your neighbors may feel inspired to follow in your footsteps.

City Gardening

Living in a rural or suburban setting where land is more readily available to grow your own vegetables gives you an advantage when starting a garden. What do you do if you live in an apartment building or condominium?

Balcony or Porch Gardening

Balcony or porch gardening is becoming increasingly common as more people want to grow some of their own vegetables. If you have a sunny spot to put a few containers, you have a garden site. Even if the area does not get full sun all day, many varieties of vegetables grow well in containers. The balcony is a great place to grow your vegetables vertically (which takes up less space), so consider growing plants that do well trellised. Try cucumbers, peas, and beans.

Condominium Gardening

Many condominiums have common spaces or even rooftops that would be perfect for growing vegetables. Talk with your condo board and suggest starting a vegetable garden in these common areas. A garden makes a wonderful space for people to relax and get together, and fresh food is a great bonus for everyone in the complex.

FACT

Large cities are giving residents the opportunity to grow food. In Vancouver, a portion of the city hall lawn is to be converted into a community garden. In Washington, D.C., organic activists are calling on the president to turn part of the White House lawn into a community food garden.

Community Gardens

A community garden is a shared space where a group of people or residents of a certain area grow their vegetables. More and more city neighborhoods are starting community gardens on empty lots in the center of a city, in local parks, and on private properties that are donated for this purpose.

These gardens can be funded through local governments, community services, or specific groups. The main purpose is to make space available for growing food for everyone who wants to take part. If you are looking for a spot to grow on, check out your local area for an existing community garden or look into starting one in your neighborhood.

Community Shared Agricultural Garden (CSA)

A Community Shared Agricultural (CSA) garden is usually started by a farmer who decides to grow vegetables for a group of people who sign up to receive a certain amount of food each week during the growing season. Being a member of the CSA often means volunteering at the farm to help out with planting, weeding, and harvesting the vegetables. This is a great way for you and your family to spend a few days a month helping to grow the food you receive from the CSA every week. The website *www.localharvest.org/csa* allows you to find participating farms in your area.

CHAPTER 2

Your Garden Layout

Your garden layout is a visual plan of what you want your garden to look like; it can be as simple as a few boxes drawn on a piece of paper or as detailed as a thorough design made by a landscape designer. The layout of your garden site is used to mark the locations of your beds and pathways and show which vegetables are grown in each area. In this chapter you will receive advice on how to make your own garden layout and where to place your vegetables to get a great harvest.

What Is Your Style?

Before you start making plans, think about what you would like your vegetable garden to look like. Vegetable gardening takes time, energy, and money, so planning ahead can help you establish clear goals for your garden. When planning a vegetable garden—especially if you are a first-time gardener—it is important to take a look at your garden style so you can get a clear idea of your goals. Not sure what your style is? Go to your local bookstore or library and flip through books and magazines.

What jumps out at you? Is it the formal looking garden where all the vegetables are contained within specific areas and everything looks tidy? Is it the more natural looking garden that's more lush and full with a variety of vegetables and flowers? Do you like garden structures and lovely meandering pathways? Do you like stone or bark mulch? Get an idea of what you would like your garden site to look like; gardens are a work in progress, and it can take several years to get yours the way you want.

A formal garden has orderly rows and structural elements such as raised beds. It has clear boundaries, everything has its place, and the garden almost always looks manicured. A natural or rustic garden has a more naturalized look. Wild plants and vegetables grow in harmony, the boundaries are less clearly defined, and structures are often made from wooden posts, driftwood, and boulders. These are two fairly extreme styles, and one may appeal more than the other. Many people like something in between the two styles. Either way, it is important to have an idea of what you would like your garden to look like before planting your first vegetables. If you are not sure of how to begin, ask for advice. Talk to other gardeners, check out local community centers for gardening classes, join a gardening club, or hire a landscape designer. They can give you great tips and help you get started.

Be realistic with the amount of time you have to spend working in your garden. If you like the look of the huge formal garden and only have two hours a week to put toward your garden, it probably will not look and produce the way you expect. A rustic garden also needs work in order to keep weeds from taking over. It's usually best to start small and add to the garden each year.

Now that you are more familiar with your garden style, it is important to identify your goals. Is your garden's main goal to produce food for your family? If this is the case, you'll get the best results if you grow what you like to eat in the most practical, cost efficient way. Do you also want to use the vegetables to beautify your yard or patio? Choose attractive and colorful vegetables that will add texture and color to your garden. Rainbow or red Swiss chard and different varieties of colorful lettuce all accomplish this. Is your goal to have a space where you can put a great bench to sit, relax, and enjoy some privacy? Vegetables that grow best on trellises or along fences will give you that extra bit of privacy. Other vegetables will attract birds, butterflies, and ladybugs that are beautiful to watch.

ESSENTIAL

Vegetables have the same basic needs as humans; they need light, food, water, and warmth. How well these needs are met will determine how they will grow, mature, and produce healthy food. These four essentials need to be considered when choosing your garden site.

Asking yourself what you want from your vegetable garden will assist you in deciding what to plant, how to plant, and where to plant to get the best results. No matter why you want to grow vegetables or how small or large of a site you have, adding a vegetable garden will give you healthy food.

Design Decisions

It is now time to decide how you want to grow your vegetables. Take a look at your garden site. Knowing the kind of terrain, soil, and access to sunlight can help with your design decisions. If you have a large, fairly flat area, long rows may work well for you. If you have poor soil, a raised bed might be best. If you have a tiny porch or patio, you may only have enough space for a few pots. These are all great ways to grow a fabulous vegetable garden.

Row Gardening

Row gardening is best if you have a large, flat area to grow on. It is the design most often used by large conventional growers or market gardeners because it is the easiest for equipment such as tractors and rototillers.

Even though row gardening is used on larger plots, it can easily be applied to a flat, sunny yard. Try starting with a ten foot by ten foot area. Make sure you allow space for pathways between rows and at the ends of the rows to accommodate wheelbarrows and other equipment.

Row gardening

Rows can be as long and as wide as you want or need them to be. The width is often dependent on the type of equipment you will be using to till the beds. If you are going to be using a rototiller, measure the width of the tines to give you an idea of how wide your bed should be. Consider how long your reach is to decide on your garden's width; if you are weeding on one side, you should easily be able to reach across the bed without straining.

Growing in Raised Beds

Raised beds are structures that have four sides and hold soil. They are a great option for a small space, for areas with poor soil, or for hillside gardens. If you want to grow in a moist area that has poor drainage, the raised bed will allow for better drainage. If you have a sloped or terraced garden site, raised beds will help define these areas and make it easier to grow. If the formal garden style appeals to you, using raised beds is a great way to add structure, definition, and tidiness to your vegetable garden.

FACT

Save money by renting large equipment like rototillers, shredders, cultivators, and weed eaters. You usually only use these items a few days out of the year and they are expensive to purchase. Save yourself some money by renting them from your local nursery or an equipment rental company.

Raised beds can be made to any height, which can be a huge advantage if you have physical disabilities, have limited mobility, or cannot bend easily. Make sure it is built to the height that works best for you. Adding a ledge on the top will allow you to sit while gardening.

Container Gardening

If you live in the city and only have a balcony or porch, you can still grow a lovely vegetable garden. Containers come in various sizes and can sit or hang in your space. Some vegetables grow better in containers than others, so choose your vegetable plants carefully for the best possible results.

Pathways

Pathways allow easy movement between your garden rows, raised beds, or containers. They are often an afterthought, but they are necessary for a successful and healthy garden. You need pathways so that you can walk through your garden to observe, weed, and water your vegetables. You can also use them to move wheelbarrows and carts through your garden for ease in fertilizing and amending your garden soil.

Each pathway should be between twelve and sixteen inches wide so you can comfortably walk between rows and beds. If you plan to push a wheelbarrow or cart down a path, it will need to be a bit wider. By having enough space between rows, you will be less likely to walk on or damage your vegetable plants; plants do not grow well if crushed and will often attract pests and diseases as well.

Pathways are definitely functional, but they can also add to the beauty of your garden. Well-defined garden beds and pathways can be very inviting to walk on and aesthetically pleasing to look at. There are many different materials that can be used in the pathway to keep the weeds from taking over. Some nonorganic materials are crushed rock, stone, brick, black plastic, and landscape fabric. The crushed rock and stone can be attractive but also very costly. Black plastic and landscape fabric are not as attractive on their own and are often covered by something else, such as rock or bark mulch.

ALERT

After pulling weeds or removing diseased or damaged plants, do not leave them in your pathways. These can create a haven for other pests and diseases, which can spread very quickly. Use a bucket when weeding. Place diseased plants directly into a garbage bag when pulling them out so as not to spread the disease further.

Some organic materials that are great for your mulching are layers of newspaper, grass clipping, sawdust, bark mulch, straw, and leaves. Placing other garden waste such as grass clippings on pathways is a great way to recycle within your own yard. Leaving your pathway as grass is another option; however it is best used when planting in raised beds for ease of mowing. Make sure you have a path wide enough so your mower can easily go through.

Using mulches on your pathways keeps the weeds and grass from growing and getting into your vegetable beds. If the pathways are left bare, you will be fighting with the weeds all season. The weeds may get ahead of you and go to seed, which will create even more weeds in future years. Take the time in the spring to mulch the pathways and replenish the material in early summer and again in the fall. By doing this, you will save yourself a lot of time and heartache in trying to combat the weeds. If you choose to leave your pathways grass, make sure you mow regularly so the grass does not spread into your garden beds.

Choosing the Right Vegetables

It is important that the vegetables you choose will grow well in your climate and conditions. This is especially important for the novice gardener; it can be disheartening to plant something and watch it founder. Learn what your vegetable plants need to grow well.

Most vegetable plants need at least six hours of full sun to grow really well. If you have this type of sunlight, most common vegetables will grow well for you. However, most of us must garden in less than ideal conditions, so it is important to choose your vegetables wisely. If you have a shady garden site with only two to four hours of sunlight, choose the vegetables that will do best in these conditions.

The following vegetables like a shady, cooler garden site:

- Lettuce
- Spinach
- Cabbage
- Peas
- Salad greens

ALERT

In late spring and early summer, add an organic fertilizer such as kelp or fish emulsion to your vegetable plants. This will give them the boost they need to start growing, flowering, and producing fruits or pods for you to enjoy.

Growing your vegetables in a shadier site may produce smaller veggies that may take longer to grow, so make sure you provide them with nutrient-rich soil. A shadier garden site may have poorer drainage, so if this is the case, raised beds may be a good option.

If you have an area that gets a lot of sun—six hours or more—most vegetables will grow well. If your garden site gets a lot of heat, choose vegetables that grow best in hot conditions. These vegetables are often started indoors in the early spring and planted out in the end of May or June, depending on your climate.

The following are some warm season or heat-loving vegetables:

- Beans
- Corn
- Cucumbers
- Eggplants
- Okra
- Peppers
- Squash
- Sweet potatoes
- Tomatoes

The Length of your Growing Season

If you live in an area where you have a very short growing season—for example, from June to September—you must take that into account. There are some vegetables that grow very quickly from seed. Radishes and some salad greens mature in thirty to forty-five days. Other vegetables such as tomatoes, broccoli, and squash need three to four months to grow from seed to maturity. These vegetables are most often started from seed in greenhouses and transplanted once the weather is warm enough. This gives them the head start they need to mature, especially if you get your first frost in September.

If you have a long growing season where you can plant seeds in March and harvest as late as November and December, consider succession planting so you can eat your vegetables all through the year. If you live in this kind of climate, you can plant cool-season crops such as radishes, leeks, onions, salad greens, and spinach early in March, warm season crops at the end of May, and another round of cool-season crops of broccoli, Brussels sprouts, cabbage, and kale in late summer.

When choosing what vegetables you want to grow, take the time to learn more about your climate and garden conditions. This is an important step toward having a successful and bountiful vegetable harvest.

Consider What the Veggies Need

Sunlight and growing seasons are both important considerations, but you should also research the individual needs of the specific vegetable plants you have chosen to grow. Some vegetable plants grow best upright or vertical; others like to be protected from the hot sun, wind, or rain. All of these factors need to be considered when planning your vegetable garden layout.

Vertical Support

Growing plants vertically is great, especially if you are short on space or want the plants to give you some privacy. Vertical planting can also add structure and interest to your vegetable garden. It is crucial for the health of some plants. Tomatoes that are left to grow along the ground will become moldy, rot, and attract pests and diseases. Vertical planting also increases air circulation. Cucumbers like air around them. Keep in mind that you may need vertical supports for plants that want to grow upward.

The following is a list of vegetables that grow best with vertical supports:

- Beans, especially climbing and runner varieties
- Cucumbers
- Peas, especially snow and snap varieties
- Tomatoes

Protection from the Elements

Some vegetables need lots of sun and warmth to grow, while others like it a bit shadier and cooler. Depending on your garden conditions, you may need to protect some of your plants from the elements. Early in the spring, young plants need to be protected from the cold and some pests. This can be done by throwing a light blanket, sheet, or floating row cover over the plant at night or during the hottest part of the day. Later in the season when the temperature rises, cool-season plants like lettuce and salad greens may need protection so their outer leaves do not wilt and burn. A floating row cover will offer protection; you can also shelter plants with a slatted wooden structure. It is important to know your garden conditions so you can plan ahead and learn what your vegetable plants may need to produce great food.

ALERT

If you get an unexpected cold spell in April or early May, your young transplants or seedlings will need a little extra protection. Some common household items such as bed sheets, old towels, newspapers, and cardboard boxes are all great ways to keep your veggie plants protected.

You already know how important it is to have easy access to your water source. You must also take into consideration different plants' watering needs. Some plants love their leaves to be wet, but others do better if their leaves are never damp. Watering overhead is great for greens, spinach, and lettuces; it keeps them cool and the leaves fresh and crisp for harvesting. Tomatoes and carrots can easily get blight and other diseases if their leaves get wet, so it is best to water these vegetables at the base of the plant. Another consideration is the size of the vegetable plant's leaves. If you are overhead sprinkling broccoli, cabbage, or squash, the leaves will hog the water and very little will reach the roots, where it is most needed.

Placement of the Plants

Now is the time to get out graph paper, a ruler, and a pen. Planning ahead will save you money and time. With a detailed plan, you will purchase the seeds and transplants you need rather than wasting money by bringing home plants that you really do not want or have the space for. Uncertainty is one of the biggest hurdles novice gardeners struggle to overcome. If you don't know where to start, there's a good chance you might never get started at all. Having a garden plan layout will help you. It is easier to erase something on paper than it is to move around plants in your garden.

Use graph paper and a pencil to draw your garden site to scale, making a note of the directions north, south, east, and west. If possible, have your raised beds or rows facing north to south for best distribution of sunlight. Now divide your garden site into three sections—four if you are going to plant perennial vegetables. Label each section with a letter or number; this will help you plan your rotations year after year.

Vegetable rotation means you plant your vegetables in a different spot each year. By rotating where you plant your vegetables, you can prevent pests and diseases and create a healthier garden soil. Different vegetable plants require and use different amounts of nutrients and attract different pests and disease, so rotation will help you grow a more successful garden.

List the vegetables you are planning to grow and group them into three categories:

1. Root vegetables
2. Brassicas
3. Everything else

Beside each vegetable on your list, make a note of the amount of space it needs to grow to maturity. (You will find information in the chapters on specific vegetables later in this book.) Next, place the vegetables from the first category into the first section. Repeat with the other two categories. When marking where each vegetable will go, remember to use the correct spacing for each vegetable and put the taller plants to the north side so they do not shade out the sun for the smaller ones.

Sample Layout

Let's look at a 64-square-foot raised bed vegetable garden. This space can feed one to two people for a season. The following table shows you how many of each vegetable to plant across in the 4-foot wide bed. The number in inches is the width of each row or the total space needed for the plant to grow to maturity. The table is split into three columns: one represents the first raised bed, the second represents a 24-inch pathway between the beds, and the third represents the second raised bed.

▼   TABLE 2-1

Bed 1	24-inch Pathway	Bed 2
3 tomatoes with 6 basil in between		16 radishes
24-inch row		6-inch row
4 peppers		16 radishes
12-inch row		6-inch row
16 peas		8 beets
6-inch row		6-inch row
16 peas		8 beets
6-inch row		6-inch row
16 beans		16 carrots
6-inch row		6-inch row
16 beans		16 carrots
6-inch row		6-inch row
2 cabbages; 2 cauliflower		1 squash
16-inch row		24-inch row
2 broccoli; 2 Brussels sprouts		6 lettuce
16-inch row		12-inch row
4 marigolds		6 spinach
4-inch row		12-inch row
		8 onions
		12-inch row

FACT

Most vegetables are annual plants, which means they complete their life cycle within one year. They grow and produce pods, fruit, or tubers and then die back within one season. Perennial vegetables, such as asparagus and artichokes, are plants that grow and produce fruit or tubers each year without having to be reseeded.

Sample Planning Instructions

Let's look at the same 64-square-foot garden. The dates that follow are only guidelines; get to know your own garden site and climate.

Early March: Starting Seedlings

If you are starting your own seedlings, put them in flats indoors. This plan calls for extra just in case not all the seeds germinate.

▼ TABLE 2-2

Tomato	6 seeds
Basil	8 seeds
Peppers	6 seeds
Cabbage	2 seeds
Broccoli	2 seeds
Cauliflower	2 seeds
Brussels sprouts	2 seeds
Onions	12 seeds
Lettuce	3 seeds
Spinach	3 seeds
Marigolds	4 seeds

Late March: Plant Your Peas

You can plant your peas directly into your outdoor garden beds in late March. Make sure the soil is not too wet or too cold. If your soil isn't ready, plant these in early April. You may want to add a few extra seeds in case not all of them germinate.

▼ TABLE 2-3

Shelling peas	1 row of 16 seeds; seeds 3 inches apart
Snow peas	1 row of 16 seeds; seeds 3 inches apart

Early April: Direct Planting and Seedlings

You can plant the rest of your garden outdoors in early April. Again, make sure the soil is acceptable for new plants and add a few extra seeds.

▼ TABLE 2-4

Carrots	1 row of 24 seeds; seeds 2 inches apart
Beets	1 row of 16 seeds; seeds 3 inches apart
Radishes	1 row of 24 seeds; seeds 2 inches apart
Lettuce	½ row of 4 seeds; seeds 6 inches apart
Spinach	½ row of 4 seeds; seeds 6 inches apart

At the same time, you can start more seedlings in flats indoors.

▼ TABLE 2-5

Cabbage	2 seeds
Broccoli	2 seeds
Cauliflower	2 seeds
Brussels sprouts	2 seeds
Lettuce	3 seeds
Spinach	3 seeds
Squash	2 seeds

Late April: Set Out Seedlings to Your Garden

Choose your healthiest one or two transplants for each plant from the early March seeding. Give the others away.

▼ TABLE 2-6

Cabbage	1 plant
Broccoli	1 plant
Cauliflower	1 plant
Brussels sprouts	1 plant
Lettuce	2 plants
Spinach	2 plants

Wait until early May to set out your onions. Choose your eight healthiest onion plants and transfer them.

Early May: More Direct Planting

Plant more seeds directly into your garden in early May.

▼ **TABLE 2-7**

Carrots	1 row of 24 seeds; seeds 2 inches apart
Beets	1 row of 16 seeds; seeds 3 inches apart
Radishes	1 row of 24 seeds; seeds 2 inches apart

Late May: The Final Round

Choose your healthiest transplants from your early March seeding. Give any extra plants away.

▼ **TABLE 2-8**

Tomato	3 plants
Basil	6 plants
Peppers	4 plants
Squash	1 plant
Broccoli	1 plant
Cauliflower	1 plant
Brussels sprouts	1 plant
Lettuce	2 plants
Spinach	2 plants
Marigolds	4 plants

At the same time, plant your beans directly into the garden according to the following table.

▼ **TABLE 2-9**

Green beans	1 row of 16 seeds; seeds 3 inches apart
Yellow beans	1 row of 16 seeds; seeds 3 inches apart

CHAPTER 3

The Garden Soil

Soil is important because it supports your vegetable plants by providing them with nutrients, warmth, air circulation, and the moisture they need to grow to maturity. To grow great vegetables, it is important to get to know what your soil needs to stay healthy and rich in nutrients. If you are a first-time vegetable gardener or want to expand your existing garden, this chapter has great information on how to prepare your garden beds.

What Is Soil?

Soil is made up of soil particles, organic matter, water, and air. Soil particles are mineral materials that have been broken down into pieces smaller than pebbles. The organic matter is made from decaying organisms, mainly plants that are at various stages of decomposition. About half of soil is actually solid; the rest is filled with air and water.

Air space is needed so that oxygen and carbon dioxide can move freely in and out of the soil; both are needed for the vegetable plant roots to grow. If your soil is mostly clay, it is very hard, which does not allow much airflow. Soil can get compacted by machinery or even by being walked on, which can inhibit the air circulation as well. To avoid this, designate pathways so your garden beds will not be walked on.

Moisture is another very important aspect to soil. The water in the soil encases the soil particles and dissolves them; this enables the vegetable plant to absorb the nutrients through the water. If the soil gets too wet, it becomes saturated and does not leave any room for the oxygen and carbon dioxide to reach the plant roots or for the water to dissolve the soil particles, leaving your plants nutrient deficient.

Your soil needs a healthy balance of soil particles, organic material, and water and air circulation so your plants can get the oxygen, moisture, and nutrients they need to grow to maturity.

FACT

The types of weeds growing in your garden are a good indication of how good your soil is. Some common weeds that indicate you have rich soil are burdock, ground ivy, lamb's quarters, pigweed, and purslane. Some weeds that indicate you have poorly drained soil are curly dock, hedge bindweed, sheep sorrel, and smartweed.

Now that you know more about what soil is and what your plants need from it to grow well, you can get to know your own garden soil. Is it healthy?

What Is Your Soil Type?

The best soil is fertile. It is well drained but still holds moisture when it gets warm. It is not compacted, allowing air circulation and nutrient absorption. Most gardeners do not start out with ideal soil. However, over time you can have very healthy garden soil that will grow fabulous vegetables for you.

There are four basic types of soil—sandy, clay, silty, and loamy (sometimes called *humus*).

Sandy

Sandy soil is mostly made up of sand and is the opposite of clay soil. In this type of soil, the particles are large and do not hold together well. Sandy soil is often the warmest soil, which can benefit the heat-loving vegetables. This type of soil does have some drawbacks. It does not hold water; therefore, it does not have many of the nutrients your vegetables need. To tell if you have sandy soil, pick up a handful of soil and rub your fingers through it. If it falls apart and feels gritty, your soil is made of mostly sand.

The best ways to improve sandy soil is to add organic matter such as compost, rotted manures, and shredded leaves to your beds every year or even twice a year if you have enough material. Organic matter adds nutrients to the soil and helps to retain moisture in the soil. Both nutrients and moisture are needed to grow healthy vegetable plants.

Clay

Clay soil is the most challenging soil to have. The soil particles are very tiny and bind together to make the soil heavy and difficult to work with. Clay soil stays colder than other soils so plants often grow slower. This soil is richer in nutrients and it retains more moisture than sandy soil; however, it often gets waterlogged, which prevents oxygen from reaching the roots of your vegetables. Clay soil retains moisture, so you do not have to water your garden as often in the hot summer months. To check if you have clay soil, take a handful of soil and roll it between your hands. If it forms a small, elongated shape and does not fall apart, you have mostly clay in your soil.

To improve clay soil, you want to add as much organic matter as you can. Adding in compost, shredded leaves, and rotted manures such as horse, cow, or chicken manures will help enlarge the amount of space between the soil particles, making the soil lighter. This will increase air circulation, allowing the oxygen and nutrients to be absorbed by the plants.

ALERT

If you have really poor soil, perhaps growing your vegetables in raised beds or containers is a better option. Rather than struggling to get your garden started, there are some good packaged soil mixtures sold at nursery or landscape businesses. It may cost you a bit more to get started, but it will save time and energy in the long run.

Silty

Silt soil has medium-sized particles, larger than clay and smaller than sandy soils. Silt drains better than clay soil and holds nutrients better than sandy soils, so it is better than either of them. The disadvantage of silt soil is that it lacks organic matter. This type of soil is very rare and is really only found near rivers or in areas that were once under water. To test if you have silty soil, put a small amount of soil in your hand, add a bit of water, and rub it between your fingers. If it has a soapy feel, you have a silty soil. The best way to improve this type of soil is to add organic matter in the form of compost and rotted manures.

Loamy

Loamy soil has the ideal soil structure—a mixture of sand, clay, and silt. It holds the nutrients, retains moisture without getting soggy, and it is easy to work with. Gardeners who have been gardening for years usually have made what soil they started with into a rich, loamy soil. To test if your soil is loamy, take a handful of dry or slightly moist soil and poke it with your fingers. If it crumbles easily, you have a loam type soil.

Combination

Most soils are a combination of all these soil types; some just have a bit more sand or clay in them. No matter what your soil type, they all need to be replenished with healthy amendments (organic materials) and organic fertilizers on a regular basis. Your vegetable plants draw nutrients continuously while they grow. Rain and wind can wash or blow away nutrients as well, so it is important to know your soil and to take care of it in order to have healthy vegetable plants.

Soil Testing: Is It Important?

A soil test gives you a nutrient analysis and the pH level of your soil sample. It will also give you an indication of what nutrients your soil needs and the amounts needed to grow your vegetables. It is an important step, especially if you are starting a new garden, because it will tell you what kind of soil fertility you are starting with.

You can find fairly inexpensive soil testing kits in most gardening stores, hardware stores, and nurseries. This will give you a general idea of what nutrient deficiencies your soil may have. For more accurate and in-depth information, you can have your soil tested by testing laboratories found in most large cities. They cost more but give you very detailed information about your garden soil.

HOW TO COLLECT A SOIL SAMPLE
1. Have a clean bucket in which to place the soil.
2. Take a small amount of soil from six to eight different areas in your garden; plan where those will be ahead of time.
3. Remove any grass, plants, or debris from the areas you have chosen. Dig a hole 6 inches deep, then take a small amount of soil—½ cup will do— from the side of the hole and place it into your bucket. Do this for all the other sample areas in your garden.
4. If the soil is wet, allow it to dry by placing it on a clean piece of plastic or cloth. Leave it in a sheltered place for a few hours. Then mix it well and place it into a clean container. Usually two cups of soil is plenty for a lab

to test. If you are doing your own test, you need even less; check your soil test kit for instructions.

Take soil samples from your vegetable garden each year for the first two or three years so you can learn what your soil needs to remain healthy. After that, doing a soil test every four years is usually sufficient.

The soil test can also test your soil pH. Soil pH is a numerical symbol that indicates whether your soil is acidic or alkaline. The scale range is 0 to 14; a reading of 0 is extremely acidic, 14 is very alkaline, and 7 is neutral. Most vegetable plants grow best when the soil pH is between 6 and 7.

▼ **TABLE 3-1: VEGETABLE PH REQUIREMENTS**

pH level	Vegetable
Above 7	Asparagus
6–7	Broccoli, beets, cabbage, carrots, cauliflower, lettuce, onions, peas, peppers, spinach
5–6	Beans, cucumber, raspberries, rhubarb, squash, Swiss chard, tomatoes
4–5	Blueberries, potatoes, strawberries

If your soil is too acidic it becomes infertile, and if it is too alkaline it is toxic and will kill your vegetable plants. Climates with lots of rainfall usually have more acidic soils than areas with less rainfall. If you have an acidic soil, adding lime will make it more neutral. If you have alkaline soil, the addition of sulfur makes it more neutral. Both lime and sulfur are considered soil conditioners rather than fertilizers and therefore should be added separate from each other. The best times to add lime or sulfur to your garden beds is in the early spring. Wait at least a week before adding in any organic amendments and fertilizers.

Soil Nutrients

To produce vegetables that taste great, your garden soil needs three important elements: nitrogen, phosphorus, and potassium. Nitrogen is needed for leaf and stem growth and it gives the plant the green color. Phosphorus is needed for seed germination, flowering, and fruit and root growth. Potassium promotes the growth of buds and roots. It also gives your fruits and vegetables their flavor. A soil test will reveal your vegetable garden's nutrient levels.

Nitrogen

The element code for nitrogen is an N. The element code is a universal code displayed on bags of fertilizer and can be used as a quick reference when purchasing specific types of fertilizer. If your soil is deficient in nitrogen, you may see vegetable plant leaves turn yellow and fall off or plants whose growth appears stunted. On the other end of the scale, too much nitrogen in the soil may lead to leggy or spindly plants or plants that have lots of green leaves but do not produce any flowers or fruit.

So what do you do? If your soil is very low in nitrogen, you can add five pounds of fertilizer per 100 square feet of vegetable garden. Animal manures, blood meal, fish meal, and cocoa shells are organic sources of nitrogen. If it is just a bit low, add in two and a half pounds per 100 square feet. To maintain a consistent amount, add one pound per 100 square feet every year. Spreading the fertilizer gently around the base of the plant and watering it in can help a troubled plant fairly quickly. If you are going to plant a new crop, rake or till the fertilizer into the first six inches of the garden bed. If you find your soil has an excess of nitrogen, try planting vegetables that need a lot of nitrogen, such as leafy greens, and make a note to do a soil test the following year.

Phosphorus

The element code for phosphorus is a P. If your soil doesn't have enough phosphorus, you may see vegetable plants with dull looking leaves that have a purplish tint to them. Plants are often stunted and very slow growing. Few vegetable gardens have an excess of phosphorus in the soil, and too much phosphorus will not have an adverse affect on your vegetable plants.

If your garden is low in phosphorus, add in six pounds of fertilizer per 100 square feet. Bone meal, animal manures, fish emulsion, and rock phosphate are all common sources of phosphorus. If your plants are producing well, maintain a good amount of phosphorus in the soil by adding in one pound per 100 square feet each year.

Potassium

The element code for potassium is a K. If there isn't enough potassium in your soil, you'll see a loss of color in the veins of the leaves, brown spots on the undersides of the leaves, and plants that are often short and stocky. Like phosphorus, excessive levels of potassium are uncommon and do not adversely affect vegetable plants.

QUESTION

What do the numbers mean on the bags of fertilizer?
A bag with a listing of 8-10-5 will contain 8 percent nitrogen, 10 percent phosphorus, and 5 percent potassium. Always choose organic fertilizers; they are made from animal, vegetable, and mineral sources, not manmade chemicals that will be harmful to your plants and soil.

If your soil is low in potassium, add ten pounds of fertilizer per 100 square feet of some of the organic sources. Potash rock, wood ash, and greensand are all common sources of potassium. If you just want to maintain the amount you have in your soil, add two and a half pounds per 100 square feet each year.

Do You Fertilize?

Your garden soil fertility is always changing; nutrients are being used up by growing vegetables, tilling the soil disturbs the structure, nutrients are leached out by the rain, and the wind can strip away top soil and organic matter from the beds. If you want to grow great vegetables, it is important to fertilize your garden beds. With a soil test you can find out if your garden soil is deficient in any of the nutrients you need and how much you need to add to the soil.

There are two ways to fertilize. You can choose to feed either the plant or the soil. To feed the plant, you use fertilizers that are often soluble, which you dissolve in water and then use to water your plants. These are usually purchased at your local garden store. Feeding the soil involves amending your soil by adding different materials to it that will decompose over time, increasing the soil's fertility. Both of these methods benefit your vegetable plants.

There are two kinds of fertilizers you can purchase: organic and nonorganic. Organic fertilizer is better for your health because you are not touching or breathing in pesticides, and it's healthier for your soil, which is also a living thing. Liquid kelp, or liquid fish emulsion, is a soluble organic fertilizer. Nonsoluble fertilizers include cottonseed meal, blood meal, bone meal, greensand, and rock phosphate. Nonorganic fertilizers, also known as chemical fertilizers or pesticides, are manmade, often from petroleum products. When growing your own food, it is important to choose organic fertilizers, which are the healthier option. When purchasing liquid or bagged fertilizers, ask to ensure you are purchasing organic fertilizes whenever possible.

ESSENTIAL

There are eight common trace elements that are needed for good vegetable plant growth. They are calcium, sulfur, iron, boron, copper, manganese, molybdenum, and magnesium. There are usually sufficient amounts needed by the plants in garden soils, so you do not need to add them.

What Are Soil Amendments?

Soil amendments are used to improve soil texture and structure—and, therefore, fertility. Very few gardeners have an ideal soil type, so organic amendments such as animal manures, compost, seaweed, straw or hay, and green manures are added to the soil. Coffee grounds, grass clippings, fish fertilizer, kitchen scraps, and wood ash are all great organic soil amendments that can be used as mulch or added to a compost pile. Adding these organic materials to your soil will make a clay soil easier to work, help retain moisture in sandy soils, and supply some nutrients to the vegetable plants that all types of soil need on a regular basis.

To keep your soil fertile and rich in organic matter, add at least two inches of organic matter in both spring and fall. One way of adding it in is to cultivate it directly into your garden beds in the spring when you till the soil. You can make your own compost and add it to the beds when you plant or mulch the beds for the winter months. Another way to add in organic matter is to mulch your garden bed throughout the season. Using straw, hay, or leaves as mulch around your vegetable plants and allowing them to decompose over time will add more organic matter to your beds.

Animal Manures

Some common animal manures come from horses, cows, and poultry. Make sure any animal manure you add to your garden is well rotted for at least six months. Horse manure can be used for quick-growing vegetables like lettuce and brassicas. They do well when this manure is added to their beds prior to transplanting. Cow and poultry are the most nitrogen-rich animal manures and can be used for vegetables that need more nitrogen like leafy greens and spinach. Horse manure is usually already mixed with straw or wood chips, making it fairly light and easy to dig into your garden bed. Cow and poultry manures are often heavier, so mixing these with some straw or peat moss will make them lighter to use. Any animal manure is great to use, but stay away from cat and dog feces. Animal manure can be purchased from local farmers or in bags at your local garden center.

ALERT

Ruth Stout popularized the no-dig approach to gardening in *How to Have a Green Thumb Without an Aching Back*. This is a method of gardening where several inches of mulch are spread on garden beds and replenished every year. The mulch keeps the weeds under control and decomposes over time, enriching the garden soil. Vegetables are planted through or under the mulch.

Seaweed

If you are lucky enough to live near a beach, collecting fresh seaweed and adding it to your garden bed in the fall will add nitrogen, potassium, and other trace minerals to your soil. When using fresh seaweed, chop it up and dig it into the soil, use it as mulch, or put some into your compost every few weeks. If you do not live near a beach, you can find good dried seaweed products at garden centers and nurseries that will have the same benefit for your garden as the fresh stuff.

Straw, Hay, and Leaves

Straw is the hollow stalk that is left after grain has been harvested. Hay is dried grasses used for animal feed. Hay usually has more weeds in it but is often half the cost of straw, so you will need to see which works better for you. Straw and hay can be purchased in bales from local farmers or at garden centers. Any type of leaves can be collected in the fall and shredded with a lawn mower or weed eater. All of these organic materials can be used as mulch and left to decompose on the beds to add organic matter to your soil over time.

Green Manures

Green manures are plants grown in the fall or winter months after the harvest is completed and tilled under in the early spring. They are often referred to as a *cover crop*. Buckwheat, clover, fava beans, fall rye, vetch, and field peas are all common cover crops. These are grown during winter in warmer climates to protect the soil from being leached by the rain or blown away by strong winds. In the spring, the plant is mowed and tilled under, leaving it there to decompose and add organic matter and some nutrients to the soil.

Soil Preparation

Once you have your garden layout planned, it's time to prepare your garden beds. In early spring once the soil is dry enough, you start preparing your soil. If you are a first-time gardener and starting your first vegetable garden bed or a seasoned gardener looking for some easy tips, here are some steps to get you started.

Remove Any Grass

Remove any grass, rocks, or debris from the area you want to plant in. If you are a first-time gardener, prepare a ten-foot-square area for rows or one raised bed. If you start with a small area, you will less likely be overwhelmed and more likely to be successful with your plantings. You can always make the area larger each year as you get more experienced.

QUESTION

How do I know if my soil is ready to be worked?
To test your soil for wetness, take a handful of soil and squeeze it in your hand. If it forms a ball, it is too wet. If it crumbles, the soil is ready to work.

Turn the Soil

You can turn your soil with a spade or more sophisticated equipment such as a rototiller or tractor and plow; it all depends on how large of an area you have. If you are just starting out with a small area, a spade is probably the easiest and cheapest method—although it can be back-breaking work, so take your time. Before tilling or digging your soil, make sure the soil is ready to be worked. If it is too wet or too dry, the soil structure and particles can be damaged, as can other organisms and earthworms found in the soil.

After turning the soil, take time to break down any large clumps left with a rake or hand cultivator and remove any rocks larger than a marble. Most vegetables like a fairly clean, smooth soil to grow well.

ALERT

You can add lime or sulfur to your garden soil to increase or decrease the pH, but this needs to be done separately from your soil amendments and fertilizers. You should add them in at least one week apart so they can both benefit your garden soil.

Apply Soil Amendments and Organic Fertilizers

Once you have tilled the soil in the early spring, add in well-rotted manure and compost to your beds. Add at least ½" to give your soil a healthy structure and improve fertility. Dig these organic amendments into the top six to twelve inches of your garden soil.

Now is also the time to add extra nitrogen, phosphorus, potassium, or lime. All of these can be dug into the top few inches of your soil with either a spade or rake.

Rake the Bed

Once you have tilled and added in amendments and fertilizers, you want to make the bed ready for planting. Raking will make the bed smooth and level and you can pick out any debris or small rocks you missed before. A soil with a consistency of coarse bread crumbs is best for planting your vegetables, especially if you are seeding directly. Taking the time to prepare your soil well will give you great vegetables to enjoy.

CHAPTER 4

Veggies in Containers

Do you want to grow veggies but live in a condominium or apartment with only limited outdoor space? Is your garden the size of a postage stamp? Is your soil hardpan or rocky? Growing your vegetables in containers is the solution to all of these problems! In this chapter you will find great advice and information on everything you need to know about growing your vegetables in containers.

The Advantages

One of the great advantages to growing vegetables in containers is they take up very little space. Containers can be placed on a balcony, porch, or patio; they can sit on a windowsill, attach to balcony railings, or hang in baskets from the rafters. They can also be used in your backyard to grow veggies that may not do well in your soil or to enhance a spot in your existing garden. Whatever option you choose, containers will provide you with some great vegetables to enjoy.

Container vegetable gardening also takes less time to maintain than a backyard garden. You'll spend much less time weeding your vegetables if you grow them in containers because the vegetable plant usually fills the pot, leaving less room for the weeds to grow.

Growing in containers can save you a sore back. Bending, lifting, digging, and twisting are all regular activities for a vegetable gardener. Gardeners with physical disabilities or back problems often find it difficult to garden. Using containers is one way to make it easier to grow vegetables. Choose containers that are the height that works for you or place smaller containers on a table or bench to make them easier to reach and enjoy.

ESSENTIAL

Growing flowers among your vegetables has two advantages. They can add color and scent to your vegetable garden, which will attract beneficial insects, such as ladybugs, bees, and wasps, and repel the more harmful ones, such as aphids, slugs, and cutworms. Some great flowers to grow with vegetables are calendula, California poppies, and marigolds.

Growing vegetables in containers can add a decorative touch to your garden or patio. The containers themselves can be very attractive and the plants themselves can add color, texture, and interest to a dull or somewhat boring space. For example, Swiss chard comes in bright rainbow colors, and kale has a fabulous texture to its leaves. Peppers produce fruits that are green, red, yellow, and orange. There are many varieties of lettuce and salad greens that grow in various shades of greens and reds for you to enjoy all season long as well.

Growing your vegetables in containers allows you to be able to follow the movement of the sun. Sunlight is very important for the growth of your vegetable plants and it changes with the time of day and season. A container can be moved or turned so the plants get the amount of sunlight they need to grow well.

Heat-loving vegetables such as tomatoes and peppers are often more productive when grown in containers because the soil heats up more quickly and stays warmer. This is especially important if you live in a cool, damp climate or have unpredictable summer temperatures. These types of vegetables often need shelter from the wind and rain as well, so growing them in a container allows you the freedom to easily move them to a more sheltered area when necessary.

Growing your tomatoes in a hanging basket

Disadvantages to Container Growing

Your backyard garden often only needs watering once or twice a week because the plant roots can pull water from deep in the soil, but vegetable plants that are grown in containers do not have this option. Most containers need watering every day, but some need attention twice a day, especially during the summer months or in a hot climate. Because containers need watering so often, it is difficult to leave them unattended for any length of time.

Purchasing containers and the soil needed to fill them can also be expensive. The cost will depend on how many containers you need, and the sizes and types of containers you choose to purchase. If you are planning to grow your vegetables in a container for several years, choose a good quality one so it will last. Containers need to be cleaned on a regular basis to keep them free of pests and diseases, so choose a container that is easy to take care of.

In a garden bed you use the existing soil, but in a container you need to purchase the soil. Some or all of the soil needs to be replenished every year since the vegetable plants will use all the nutrients.

ESSENTIAL

Making a shopping list before you even enter the garden center will save you time and money. Before you go, decide what vegetables you want to grow, where you will put the containers, how many containers you will need, and what sizes you need to grow your veggies.

Even though there are a few disadvantages to growing your vegetables in containers, it is definitely worth growing this way, especially if you only have a small space to grow in. Be creative and have fun making your small space beautiful!

The Best Veggies for Containers

First and foremost, grow what you love to eat. The following tips are particularly important to keep in mind if you'll be growing in containers.

Choose Dwarf Varieties

Dwarf varieties are vegetable plants that are smaller in size and therefore need less space to grow. The root system usually needs less space, which makes them a great option for containers. Go to your local garden centers and check the free seed catalogs for dwarf varieties.

FACT

Herbs are a wonderful addition to any meal! Make room for growing parsley, cilantro, and basil in your vegetable containers or garden beds. If you enjoy oregano, thyme, and sage, place these in pots of their own or in the perennial area of your garden site; these perennial herbs can be left in the same container or area for several years.

Grow Vertical

If you want to grow a lot of vegetables on your balcony or patio, employ your vertical space by using trellises or fences. Select vegetables that can be trained to grow upright. Plants grown this way will often produce even more fruit or pods for you to enjoy. Snow peas, shelling peas, pole beans, cucumbers, and tomatoes can all be grown vertically. Choose attractive materials such as bamboo, metal, or wood to make trellises or stakes for your plants to grow on.

Grow Early and Late Veggies in the Same Pot

Some vegetable plants grow better in the cool of spring or fall, while others are best planted when the weather is warmer. Vegetables will mature and be harvested at different times of the year. To make the most of your containers, plant a crop of early maturing veggies such as radishes or baby salad greens in the early spring; once you've harvested them, plant your tomatoes or peppers in that same container. This way you will have a continuous supply of wonderful vegetables to harvest and enjoy. When planning your container garden layout, make a note of which vegetables can be planted early and which will do well later in the season and make sure the size of container will work for both.

Here is a list of the most common vegetables to grow in containers:

- Beans
- Beets
- Broccoli
- Carrots
- Cucumbers
- Lettuce
- Peas
- Peppers
- Radishes
- Spinach
- Tomatoes

The Containers

Some vegetables have a shallow root system; others have much deeper roots and need more space to grow. When choosing any container for your vegetables, there are three important rules to remember: first, the container must be deep enough to hold enough soil to accommodate the plant's root growth; second, it must be large enough for the plant to grow to maturity; and finally, water must be able to drain easily from the bottom of the container so the soil does not get waterlogged. The container can be any shape so long as it can fulfill these three essentials.

Small Containers

To grow lettuce, spinach, salad greens, radishes, and green onions, a container that is approximately eight to ten inches wide and at least six inches deep will be a sufficient size. In this size container you could grow two or three of your leafy greens and up to a dozen radishes or green onions.

Clay or plastic garden pots can be easily purchased at your local garden center or hardware store. Tin cans, bricks with a center opening, milk cartons, buckets, and old cooking pots also make great containers. Garden pots usually come with holes in the bottom of them, but if you are recycling a container make sure you make at least one good drainage hole so excess water can easily drain out.

FACT

An easy way to make holes in the bottom of a lightweight container is to use a hammer and nail. Make several holes from the outside in so the holes will stay clear when you put the container upright. A drill works well for making holes in wooden or metal containers.

Medium-Sized Containers

Medium-sized containers are approximately twelve to sixteen inches wide and at least ten inches deep. You can easily grow lovely carrots, beets, peas, and beans; just remember your peas and beans will produce a better harvest if they are grown on a trellis or supported in some way. If you choose a rectangular container, you can grow your peas and beans in the back and plant your root crops in front, making great use of the space.

You can easily purchase a medium-sized container made of clay or plastic at your local garden center, but you can also reuse Styrofoam coolers, wooden crates, plastic crates (which may need a liner such as landscape fabric in order to hold the soil), or plastic ice cream buckets (ask at your local ice cream parlor for their empties). Cedar, redwood, and teak are your best choices for wood if you choose to build your own box.

Large Containers

Larger vegetables such as tomatoes, cucumbers, cabbages, broccoli, peppers, potatoes, and dwarf corn need a container more than sixteen inches wide and at least eighteen inches deep to grow well. For best results, use transplants when growing these vegetables (except for potatoes and corn). Grow only one of these plants in each container. You can grow vegetables with shallow roots such as lettuce or salad greens around the base of these plants once they are established.

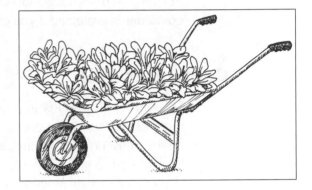

Use an old wheelbarrow as a container

There are many options for large garden pot at your garden center, but they can be expensive to purchase. Instead, reuse garbage cans, wooden barrels, metal washbasins, old wheelbarrows, or plastic clothes hampers.

When making a decision on what kind of container you want, take into account your climate and

Bathtub Garden

whether you will be leaving your containers outside all year long. In cold climates, the soil in your containers may freeze, which can split or break your container. If you get a lot of strong winds, lightweight containers can be blown around and damaged. If you choose not to grow anything in your containers during the off season, make sure you put them in a sheltered area such as a garage or shed so they will be protected. If you are growing your vegetables all year long, it is important that the soil does not get too waterlogged and the container is protected if you get a cold spell.

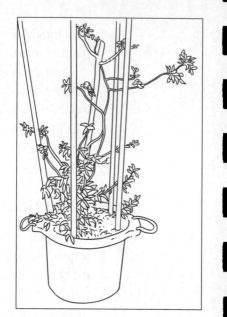

Plastic Tub Garden

Container Soil

Soil is probably the most important aspect of growing great vegetables in containers. The soil holds all the nutrients and retains all the moisture your plants need to grow. The soil needs to be rich but still lightweight enough that you can easily move your containers around. There are some excellent commercial soil mixes specifically made for container growing. Peat moss, vermiculite, and perlite make them lighter and well-rotted manures or compost keep them from drying out too quickly. These commercial mixes are sterile, which means they are free of any soil-borne diseases and they have the basic elements of nitrogen, potassium, and phosphorous.

You can make your own soil mix; just remember not to use your regular garden soil, because it is too heavy for containers and will become compacted. All container soils need to be light enough to allow good air circulation for the vegetable plants to get oxygen.

Here is a simple recipe for making your own container soil. All ingredients can easily be bought at your local garden center. Simply mix the following ingredients together:

- One cubic foot of peat moss
- One cubic foot of vermiculite
- Six ounces of lime

- Six ounces of bone meal
- One ounce of blood or alfalfa meal
- One ounce of langbeinite

One cubic foot is twelve inches in length, twelve inches in width, and twelve inches deep.

Before planting your containers, make sure the soil is well watered. The commercial soil mixes or your homemade container soil will absorb warm water more easily. When first seeding your containers, make sure they are kept in a fairly warm area but not in the direct sunlight. This will allow the seed to germinate without drying out too quickly. Seeds need to be moist in order to germinate and young transplants need more water so their shallow roots can reach the moisture. This means watering your containers often—at least once a day, sometimes twice.

ESSENTIAL

If you have young children, planting fast-growing vegetables is a great way for them to enjoy and learn about vegetable gardening. Try growing radishes, lettuce, spinach, and salad greens. Have your children help you plant the seeds, water them, and watch for the new growth to push through the soil within the week.

Radishes, beets, carrots, and lettuce will need to be thinned just like when they're grown in a garden bed. A single radish or beet seed can produce several plants, so they need to be thinned to leave room for the other plants to grow to maturity. Carrot and lettuce seeds are very tiny, so it's more difficult to plant them with the proper spacing. Thinning keeps the plants from being overcrowded, and thinning will create more room for vegetables to grow and flourish.

Watering and Fertilizing

The biggest disadvantage to growing your vegetables in containers is the amount of watering they need. The size of the container, the vegetables you are growing, and the weather all determine how often and how much you need to water. When your vegetable plants are young, they need to be watered more often because the soil dries out from the top down; since your young plants do not have a deep root system yet, they need more water nearer the top of the container. As your vegetable plants mature, the roots go deeper and therefore need less frequent watering.

How Much Water?

To see whether your container needs to be watered, stick your index finger into the soil up to the knuckle. If you can feel moisture, do not water. If the soil feels dry, give the container a good drink. The container has had enough water if you can feel the moisture two to three inches from the top after you've let it sit for a few minutes. If the container is quite dry, the water will drain quickly from the bottom, leaving very little water for the soil to absorb. If this is the case, keep giving the container a drink every few minutes until the water stops draining from the bottom. Overwatering is as big of a problem as underwatering, so make sure you check your containers regularly—as much as twice a day if the pots are small and it is a hot day.

Use mulch to help keep the moisture from evaporating from your container. Mulching the top of the soil with moss, leaves, grass clippings, or even shredded newspaper can prevent the moisture from evaporating too quickly, especially in hot weather. Mulching also works well when you are growing vegetable plants that prefer a cooler soil because it will keep the soil a bit cooler as well.

FACT

Growing plants that quickly spread and invade your garden can become a problem. By growing plants such as mint and peppermint in containers you can keep them under control. You can even bury the container in your garden beds; just make sure you leave about two inches of the container rim above ground. The container prevents the roots from spreading throughout your garden.

If you are going away on vacation, especially for an extended period during the summer months, make sure you have someone water your containers while you are gone. Using a drip system on a timer is an option if you are going to be gone for a short period of time; just make sure the hoses are secured in the containers so they get watered properly. If you only have a few pots, cut off the bottom of a soda bottle or plastic milk carton, place the top of the bottle securely into the soil, and then fill the container with water. If the container is well moistened to begin with, the water will slowly be released as it is needed. This is a great option if you are gone for only a day or two. Do not use a sprinkler when watering your containers because the container may not get enough water.

Fertilizing

Moisture is important for growing your vegetables, but so are nutrients. Plants that are grown in containers have a limited supply of soil and therefore a limited supply of nutrients. To make sure your plants produce great fruit and pods, fertilize the soil. Gardeners often think that buying a good commercial soil mix will be enough to sustain the needs of their vegetable plants all season, but plants need a little boost during the season.

There are some great organic fertilizers. One option is to use a combination of liquid kelp and liquid fish fertilizer every few days. Labels will tell you how often and how much to fertilize for different sizes of containers. You can also make your own fertilizer teas (see Chapter 13).

CHAPTER 5

Raised Beds

If you have poor garden soil, have a hillside garden, or just want to beautify your garden site, growing in raised beds is a great option for you. A raised bed can be made of a variety of materials, is usually enclosed to hold the soil, and has no bottom, which leaves lots of room for the plant roots to grow. This chapter is filled with useful information about raised beds—choosing the best materials, the mechanics of building one, and some tips for growing great vegetables.

The Benefits

Raised beds provide an easy way to use soil that is more fertile than what you now have. You can purchase soil from local nurseries and landscape companies. Building and filling the beds is more expensive than simply growing your vegetables in the soil you already have, but in the long run you will save yourself time and disappointment, especially if you have poor garden soil.

Space is another consideration. If your garden site is small or oddly configured, growing vegetables in a raised bed can help. If you have a long, narrow spot to garden, design your raised beds accordingly. A raised bed can be of any shape. If you have funny angles to contend with, make your beds triangle-shaped.

A raised bed can also be any height that works for you. Keep in mind that the higher the four sides, the more soil you will need to fill it. However, if you have difficulty bending, a bed that sits at waist height has advantages. When planning the size of your raised beds, make sure not to make them too wide. A width of four feet is probably the maximum you would want to go. You want to be able to easily reach the center of the bed if you have access to the bed from both sides. If you only have access from one side of your bed, make sure you can comfortably reach all the way across the bed. Gardening is much more enjoyable if you do not have to strain to reach the areas you are planting or weeding.

FACT

When you garden, it is important to take the time to stretch every fifteen to twenty minutes. Gardening often involves bending, lifting, hoeing, and digging, all of which require muscles that you may not use on a regular basis. Remembering to stretch or change positions while performing these tasks will reduce muscle soreness at the end of the day.

Fertile soil is necessary to grow great vegetables. A raised bed is an easy way to define the bed and pathway boundaries, which helps to keep you from walking on your garden soil. Walking on your garden soil will compact it; compacted soil has less space for air circulation and moisture, both of which are essential for your vegetable plant roots to absorb nutrients.

In a raised bed, moisture will drain away more quickly and the soil temperature will warm up faster in the spring. Both of these factors will allow you to plant your vegetables earlier in the spring. This is definitely a plus if you live in a rainy, cool climate or your garden site has poor drainage.

If a tidy and attractive vegetable garden is important to you, raised beds make a garden look neater and give definition and structure to a garden site. Different shapes can add interest if you have a particular look in mind. They can be used effectively to attract attention to some spots in your garden and downplay others. The beds keep the soil contained, leaving the pathways easier to mow or mulch and preventing weeds or grass from growing into your vegetable beds. This all contributes to a cleaner looking garden.

What to Consider

Choosing materials you want to use, calculating the cost of the supplies, and constructing the beds will take time, effort, and money. This is why a garden plan is so important. Raised beds are usually permanent structures in your garden, so take the time to decide on the design that will work for you now and in the future.

Any kind of structure takes time and money to build and maintain. Each spring and fall, take the time to make sure your raised beds are solid. Tighten loose screws, pound in exposed nails, and fix any areas that may be broken or cracked. A well-maintained raised bed is more attractive and functional.

Digging, fertilizing, and amending the soil in raised beds can be more difficult than in a traditional garden. In a row garden, you can easily use a tiller to cultivate your soil. This is not so easily done in a raised bed. You can use a smaller tiller, but most often gardeners turn over the soil in raised beds by hand, either with a spade or a rake. Neither is particularly easy, so you may want to consider this when choosing to use raised beds.

If you live in a warm climate, raised beds may need more watering than regular garden beds. Soil that is raised up will drain faster; this is usually an advantage, but during a hot, dry spell your soil will dry out more quickly and will need more frequent watering.

It's a good idea to start small. Plan your garden layout, decide on what style you want your boxes to be, and then start by building one or two. A great vegetable garden can take several years of planning, rearranging, and building to be just the way you want it to be. Most gardeners say their garden is never complete because there is always something new to consider each year.

QUESTION

What are the signs that your plants need watering?
Wilting or droopy leaves are sure signs your vegetable plants are in need of watering. Give your plants a slow, continuous drink for several minutes; this allows the plant to absorb some of the moisture before it drains away. The leaves should look normal again within a few hours.

Your Design

When choosing the design of your raised beds, consider your garden site and the style of garden you want to have. What is the main function of your raised beds? Is it mainly for growing food or are the aesthetics of your garden the main priority? If you want to grow great vegetables, think about the amount of sunlight the area gets, how close your water source is to your beds, and how much food you plan to grow. If growing vegetables is your first and only priority, choose materials that are functional and inexpensive and then spend more money on great soil, seeds, and plants.

If you want the raised beds to enhance the look of your yard, you want to have good soil, but you also want to consider what style of raised beds you want. Take into account the look of your home and other structures you may have now or plan for in the future. The type of material you choose is of much more importance and you will probably spend more money on it.

So what kind of material can you choose? Wood is inexpensive and easy to find and build with. Choose wood such as cedar and redwood that resist rot and insects. Stay away from pressure-treated wood, which is treated with heavy metals and poisons such as arsenic, copper, and chrome. Wood covered in creosote is also something to stay away from when building raised beds. The chemicals used to treat these pieces of wood can leach into your garden soil and ultimately into your food.

ESSENTIAL

Don't leave any areas unplanted or uncovered. Once a plant has been harvested and removed, replant another vegetable plant in its place. During the off-season, make sure your beds are covered with mulch or grow a green manure crop. Decomposing organic matter will make healthier soil and suppress the weeds.

If wood is not the look you want, small boulders or rocks are often easy to find and can be very attractive. Rocks will not provide the same barrier from weeds and grasses as solid wood sides, but some gardeners prefer the way they look. Using cement to fill in the crevices and cracks between the rocks will make a more solid barrier so weeds and grass do not grow into your beds.

If you want a more defined raised bed but do not want to use wood or stone, try using cement blocks, standard masonry bricks, or larger interlocking bricks. These come in various colors and sizes and can be easily stacked if you want to increase the height of your raised bed. You can use poured cement for a more involved and perhaps even more permanent option for your raised beds.

Building Your Raised Bed

This design is for a structure that is four feet by eight feet and 1 foot high, the size of the most common wooden raised beds. First, decide exactly where you want your raised bed to be. Then gather all your materials. Most building supply stores will cut the pieces of wood for a minimal charge, saving you time.

❑ 2 8'L × 2"H × 1" boards
❑ 2 4'L × 2"H × 1" boards
❑ 1 4'L × 2"H × 4", cut into 4 equal lengths

❑ 24 4" wood screws for full dimension wood or 3" wood screws for planed wood
❑ Drill
❑ Screwdriver to match the wood screw heads

Wooden raised beds

Once you have assembled all of your materials, follow these steps to build your raised bed:

1. Lay each 8-foot length on the ground. Place a 2 × 4 at each end. Use 3 screws to attach each 2 × 4 to each flat end of the board. Drilling a hole not quite the length of the screw will make it easier to screw the pieces together. Attach the 2 × 4 to the board to give the sides of your raised bed more support.
2. The 8-foot boards will be used as the sides of your box. The 4-foot lengths are the ends of your rectangular box. Attach each 4-foot length to the 2 × 4s by using 3 screws on each corner. You now have a four-sided raised bed.

Now that you have your raised box built, you need to fill it with great soil so you can grow fabulous veggies. You can purchase the soil from a local landscape company; if you have several beds, calculate what you need and have them deliver it. If you have made your beds in the fall and have all winter to fill them, you can take your time. Over the winter months, put down a layer of kitchen scraps or compost; cover this with a thin layer of shredded leaves or straw, a layer of rotted animal manure, and a layer of peat moss. Repeat the layers. Every few layers throw a handful of bone meal and alfalfa or blood meal into the mixture. In the spring, your raised bed should be filled with a rich humus soil. Do a soil test to check the pH. This should tell you whether you need to add lime or sulfur to your soil.

Remember to amend and fertilize your beds every year. A soil test can tell you what elements your soil may need.

FACT

Most vegetables need a pH between 6 and 7 to grow well. To raise the pH by one point, add 6 pounds of lime per 100 square feet of garden. To lower the pH by one point, add 1½ pounds of sulfur per 100 square feet.

Square Foot Gardening

In square foot gardening, you grow your vegetable in square foot sections. This method works well in raised beds. If you have a small garden area or limited time, the square foot method could be the perfect option for you.

Many beginner gardeners have grand ideas about what and how much they want to grow but have no idea of the amount of work it can take. By the time summer rolls around, they are exhausted from trying to keep up with everything, especially the weeding! The square foot method is a great method for the first-time gardener to try; it is intensive growing on a small scale.

If you want to grow your vegetables using the square foot gardening method, design your beds to be four feet by four feet. This makes it easy to divide the area into square foot blocks. In each one-foot square, you will grow one, four, nine, or sixteen vegetables depending on the size of the

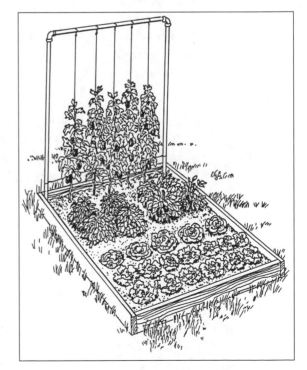

Square foot gardening

plants. Some vegetables are also grown vertically, so you will need a trellis at one end of your area. The side facing north is the best spot so that the trellised plants do not block the sunlight to the smaller plants.

▼ **TABLE 5-1**

Vegetable	Number Plants per Square Foot	Vertical
Beans, pole	8	Yes
Beets	9	No
Brassicas	1	No
Carrots	16	No
Cucumbers	2	Yes
Eggplants	1	No
Lettuce	9	No
Marigold flowers	4	No
Parsley	4	No
Peppers	1	No
Radishes	16	No
Spinach	9	No
Swiss chard	9	No
Tomatoes	1	Yes

One benefit of using the square foot method is the plants are grown close together, leaving less room for weeds to grow. This method also encourages growing flowers such as marigolds intermixed with your vegetables. The flowers repel harmful insects; this is called *companion planting*. Vegetable rotation is another essential component to square foot gardening. Vegetable rotation and companion planting are both discussed in more detail in Chapter 13.

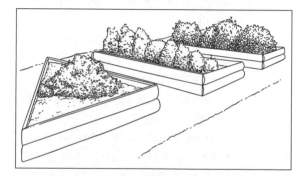

Raised beds can be made in any shape

Gardening with a Physical Disability

Do not let an aging back, arthritic aches, or limited mobility prevent you from the enjoyment of growing your own vegetables. You can design a garden that gives you easy access to your plants and the tools you want to use. Make sure doorways and pathways are wide enough to maneuver through without any difficulty. Whenever possible, make the pathways level.

Designing your raised beds at waist height will eliminate the need to bend. Having a small garden where plants are within easy reach for planting, watering, and weeding will also make gardening more fun and put less strain on your body. When building your raised beds, attach a board on the top of the bed for use as a sitting area or a place to rest your arms while working.

Using a lightweight commercial soil mix will make digging and planting easier. It will also limit the amount of energy you need to spend on preparing your soil. Having your tools the proper size and weight for your hands is important as well. Child-size gardening tools are lighter and smaller, making them a great option if you have limited mobility, especially in your hands. Store your tools in an easily accessible area like a rolling cart, which you can easily bring with you into the garden. Gardening should be accessible and enjoyable for everyone, so do not let an aging body or a disability stop you from growing your own veggies. Keeping your garden size small and easily manageable can make gardening more fun and enjoyable!

CHAPTER 6

Greenhouse Gardening

If you have a wet garden site, want to extend your growing season, or prefer not to work in unpredictable outdoor
weather, you can grow your vegetable garden in a greenhouse. Indoor gardening is also a great complement to
growing outdoors because you can give your vegetable
plants the head start or extra protection they may need. In
this chapter, you will learn about the advantages to growing your vegetables indoors and the various structures that
can be used for growing.

Extend Your Growing Season

Most gardeners would love to grow and eat their own fresh vegetables all year round, but most do not live in a climate where this is possible. Growing in a cold frame, plastic tunnel, or greenhouse allows you to start plants earlier in the spring and grow through the cooler and rainy fall months—and possibly during the cold winters. If you live in a climate that has a short growing season (early June to late August, for example), starting your seedlings indoors in early spring is necessary if you want to have a productive garden. Otherwise, vegetable plants such as tomatoes, peppers, and squash will not have enough warm days to mature if planted by seed.

For gardeners who want to have an early spring harvest of salad greens or baby carrots, growing indoors is a great place to start. Unpredictable weather during late winter and early spring can make outdoor planting nearly impossible. If you live in a hot climate, it's important to start vegetables such as spinach and brassicas early enough so they can be well established before the summer heat arrives. They need to be started in early spring when the weather is not cooperating, so starting your seedlings indoors is the answer.

FACT

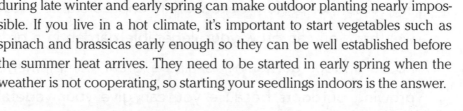

Humans have used the phases of the moon as a guide to identify the best times for planting since ancient times. According to this method, plant above-ground vegetables when the moon is increasing (waxing) and below-ground vegetables when the moon is decreasing (waning). *The Old Farmer's Almanac* website (*www.almanac.com*) and the gardening advice at *www.your-vegetable-gardening-helper.com* both have great information on the subject.

For harvesting vegetables in the fall and winter, plants usually need to be started in July. Cold or rainy weather often hits before they can mature, so growing them indoors is one solution. Another way to extend your growing season is to place a heater in your greenhouse, giving your veggies the extra warmth they need to grow and be harvested during the cooler fall and winter months. Start seedlings and grow through the shorter days of winter using a grow lamp or lights. This can give your vegetable plants that little extra light they need to do well.

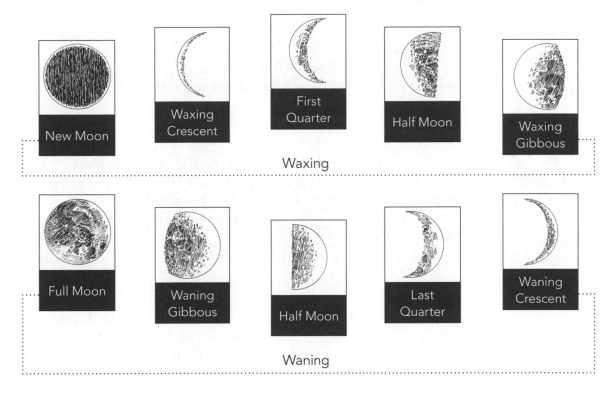

Moon cycles

Protect Your Plants

By growing your vegetables indoors, you'll have more control over the amount of heat, light, and water your vegetable plants get. You can add artificial light, control heat, and control your plants' access to water. In contrast, when you grow your vegetables outdoors, you have very little—if any—control over how much sunlight or rainfall your vegetable beds get.

Some vegetables, such as tomatoes, peppers, okra, and eggplants, need extra heat to grow their best. If you live in a cooler climate or your garden site is at a higher elevation with extreme temperature fluctuations, a greenhouse may be needed in order to grow these heat-loving vegetables. Other vegetable plants such as lettuce, spinach, and salad greens grow better when the weather is cooler and may need protection if the weather gets too hot.

Tomatoes and carrots can attract diseases and pests if their leaves become damp. It is very beneficial for these vegetable plants to be grown under cover where you can control how they are watered. Drip irrigation is often used in greenhouse settings and is a very effective way of watering your vegetables.

ESSENTIAL

Corn, trellised peas, and climbing beans are all great sun screeners for other vegetables. As they grow they will give smaller and more tender vegetable plants the shade and protection they need from the sun. Plant your lettuces and other salad greens around these taller plants during the hot summer months.

Growing indoors can help you prevent certain pests and diseases from reaching your vegetable plants. For example, flea beetles can devastate a bed of Oriental or salad greens. These little black beetles eat holes in the leaves and stunt the plants' growth. If your garden is susceptible to this pest, you have more control over it if you grow the affected crops indoors or under cover where the insect cannot reach them. Growing indoors can also prevent blight from ruining your tomato crop. Blight is caused by a fungus that spreads rapidly if the tomato plant's leaves get wet, especially during late July and early August.

Cold Frames

Cold frames work by capturing sunlight during the day and holding the heat inside through the night. There is no one standard size for cold frames, but the back is usually higher than the front, giving them a slanted top. They are usually built facing south in order to capture as much sunlight as possible. You want to position your cold frame in a sunny spot against a house, shed, or hillside for added protection from the wind. These structures are mainly used for overwintering tender plants and for growing trays of seedlings in the spring. It can also be used as a raised bed in the summer months if you simply leave the lid open or remove it altogether.

If you have access to an electric outlet, a cold frame can become a hot-house. You can bury an electric cable in the dirt or sand and then place trays of seedlings on top of the sand, allowing the seedling trays to be heated from the bottom. Some vegetable seedlings, such as tomatoes, peppers, and squash, need a high, consistent temperature to germinate and this type of hothouse is the perfect way to start them.

FACT

Winter gardening means planting vegetables in the summer and then harvesting during the winter. These plants usually reach maturity by the end of October and are eaten throughout the winter. Overwinter-ing means planting certain vegetables in late summer or early fall and harvesting them the following spring.

Plywood, cement, and stone bricks are the most common materials used in making cold frames. The roofing material is usually a clear prod-uct such as glass, plastic, or fiberglass. Old window frames or glass doors can be recycled to construct the roof. The bottom of the cold frame may be left uncovered or may have a variety of bottom coverings depending on what you use it for. If you are growing winter crops, you want to have a fer-tile, well-drained soil with amendments added every year. If you are using it for overwintering containers or starting seedlings, consider a floor of bricks, because they will retain heat longer and help maintain a consistent tem-perature in the structure. If you are making a hothouse for your heat-loving seedlings, you will want to bury your electric heating cable and cover it with an inch of sand. This will keep the bottom of the seedlings at the same tem-perature, which is what they need to germinate well.

Planning how you want to use your cold frame will help you determine your design and the materials you need to build it. A cold frame can be an inexpensive structure made from recycled or common materials that you have on hand or can easily get. It is easy to construct and can be used in a variety of ways all season long.

Plastic Tunnels

These structures are made of plastic or metal hoops with plastic sheeting secured over the hoops. Sizes vary depending on your needs. Your tunnel can be large enough to walk through or just the right size to protect your vegetables.

The plastic tunnel is used in much the same way as the cold frame, just on a larger scale. It is used to give young seedlings the protection they need in early spring, to grow heat-loving vegetables in the summer, and to grow winter crops for harvesting in the fall. It is usually unheated. It is not necessarily a permanent structure; in fact, it can be easily moved to different areas of your garden each season as you rotate your crops.

QUESTION

Why should you rotate your vegetables?
First, rotating vegetables within the same family will help prevent disease and insect damage to your garden. Second, different vegetables use different amounts of nutrients. By moving them to a different area each year, you help prevent the depletion of the essential nutrients in your garden soil.

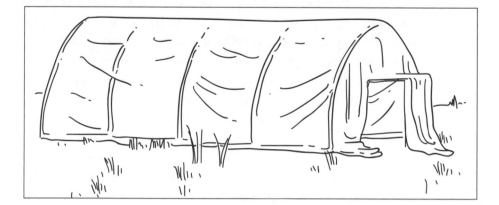

Plastic tunnel

The plastic tunnel is less expensive to construct than a glass greenhouse and can be just as effective. Plastic tunnels are often easier to vent than glass ones since the plastic is usually moveable. Some are even constructed to allow you to manually roll up the bottom sides, letting the cool air in and the excess heat out. You have to be aware that by opening the sides or ends you are also allowing pests to reach your veggie plants, so it is important to plan what you will be growing and why and vent accordingly.

One concern with the tunnels is that they can become too warm inside during the hot summer months. Too much heat can damage your plants just as much as too much cold, so it is important to have a way to ventilate your structure. You do not want your tunnel to get too much above 90°F for any length of time without allowing cool air in and excess hot air out. It is important to have a thermometer inside the tunnel at all times to monitor the temperature.

CONSTRUCT YOUR OWN PLASTIC TUNNEL
1. Decide the length and width you want your tunnel to be. Most tunnels are about 2–3 feet wide. It is best to space your hoops 3–5 feet apart so your structure is sturdy.
2. Choose a lightweight material if you are planning to move your tunnel. Try a plastic water pipe ½"–¾" in diameter works well for the hoops. The pipes can be purchased in various lengths and bend easily. Many seed catalogs have cloche pipe, which you can also use to construct your tunnel.
3. Sink two 2-foot lengths of rebar or a metal stake at least one foot into the ground. Place the plastic pipe over the exposed length; this will help keep the hoops in place.
4. Use greenhouse plastic to cover the frame you have constructed. Make sure you purchase an extra two feet of plastic so you can easily secure it to the end hoops.
5. Use garden clips to attach the plastic to the hoops. These anchor the plastic and can be purchased in many seed catalogs.
6. Drape plastic over each end and secure it with your clips. The ends can also be left open for ventilation; the decision will depend on what you want to use your tunnel for and what time of year it is.

Keep the plastic clear of snow and other objects that may weigh it down. Place a thermometer in the center of the tunnel so you can keep an eye on the temperature. A plastic tunnel with open ends usually has enough ventilation for a 10- to 20-foot tunnel. Anything longer may need additional ventilation on the sides, especially if you get hot weather during the summer months. The easiest way to ventilate the sides of your plastic tunnel is to lift the plastic from the ground and place a box or crate under it, leaving an open space on either side of the crate. Do this every ten feet on either side of the tunnel; this will allow cool air in and push the warmer air out the ends.

Glass Greenhouses

The glass greenhouse is a permanent and more expensive structure for your garden. It serves the same functions as a cold frame or plastic tunnel. The glass greenhouse is usually more attractive to look at and can be built to suit your garden style. Greenhouses come in all sizes and prices. If you are choosing to build a glass greenhouse, make sure you shop around and choose a quality product. They are often complicated and heavy to construct, so see if the price includes installation. Since greenhouses are permanent structures, it may be expensive to build one. Be sure you know what you are going to use it for and get one that works best for your needs.

Glass lasts longer than plastic, giving a greenhouse a clear advantage over cold frames and plastic tunnels. Plastic can easily be torn or punctured and has a life span of three to four years at the most. A properly installed and maintained glass greenhouse can last several decades. Plastic tunnels are often said to be easier to ventilate, but a glass greenhouse can be equipped with vents that automatically open and close when the inside temperature reaches a preset number. This means you don't have to do all the dirty work of checking the temperature and setting up manual vents yourself.

Some greenhouses are made of fiberglass rather than glass. Fiberglass is a strong yet lightweight manmade product that can easily be cut into shapes to fit your needs. It can be more desirable than glass because it lasts even longer, but it is often more expensive and can become scratched if it is not kept clean.

It's easier to add artificial heat and light to a permanent greenhouse structure than to a plastic tunnel. This allows you to extend your harvest, giving you fresh veggies all year long. However, a permanent structure may need more maintenance and can be more costly to repair than a cold frame or plastic tunnel.

ESSENTIAL

Amending and fertilizing your soil with manure is just as important in an indoor vegetable garden as it is for your outside garden beds. Bird and bat guano are the animal manures with the highest nitrogen content. The next highest are rabbit, poultry, and sheep manures. The animal manures with the least nitrogen are cow, pig, and horse.

Greenhouse Maintenance

When growing your vegetables indoors, it is important to have a balance of water, ventilation, and heat for your plants to grow well. It is best to water your plants from below and you must be careful not to overwater them. Temperatures can change drastically from day to night, so checking the temperature often will help you make decisions on when to ventilate or whether to add heat. Ventilation during the bright, sunny days is extremely important to maintain the temperature throughout the day and night. If you have automatic vents, make sure they are checked regularly and serviced if needed. Having a thermometer is essential in your cold frame, plastic tunnel, or greenhouse.

Keeping your greenhouse free of debris will help prevent disease and pests. Make sure to remove weeds from the structure. If you are removing diseased plants, make sure you place them into a plastic bag as soon as you pull them out or cut them so as not to spread the problem to other plants or your soil.

Fall or early spring are ideal times to wash and clean the glass in your greenhouse and the lid of your cold frame. A clean surface will allow more sunlight to reach your plants, so take the time to wash the glass inside and out. It is also important to clean and disinfect any shelving or tables you may have in your greenhouse to discourage the spread of disease. Organizing any items you may have stored and removing all old plants and debris will discourage pests from finding a home. Repair or replace anything that may be broken or in need of attention.

If you have a plastic tunnel, keep the plastic clean by sweeping off any debris and giving the outside a good spray with your hose. Look for tears or holes in the plastic. You can cover small tears with tape, but if you see larger tears or several holes it is best to replace the plastic altogether. Make sure the hoops and plastic are secure; if you live in a windy area, bury the plastic along the sides to make the structure more secure. If you will not be growing or using the tunnel over the winter, take it down and store the material. The materials will definitely last longer this way.

ESSENTIAL

Once you have pulled out harvested plants, sow a cover crop in their place. Once the cover crop has grown a few inches tall, till the crop under or pull it out and place it into your compost. Either way increases the organic matter in your soil.

A healthy, nutrient-rich soil is important for growing great-tasting vegetables. Amending your soil by adding in organic matter in the spring and fall will help keep your soil rich. Fertilizing with the three essential nutrients—nitrogen, phosphorus, and potassium—is also very important, so do a soil test every few years to give yourself an indication of what your soil may need. Knowing the pH level of your soil will help in planning what you want to grow and whether you need to increase or decrease the number.

Best Veggies for the Greenhouse

All vegetables can be grown indoors given the right conditions. Vegetable plants that are grown indoors need the same conditions as they do outdoors. They need fertile soil, the right amount of sun, and proper watering, fertilizing, and care. Some vegetables will do better indoors because the heat and moisture can be regulated. Just because plants are grown indoors does not mean they will grow or mature more quickly.

The best vegetables to grow indoors in the early spring include the following:

- Carrots
- Lettuce
- Radishes
- Salad greens
- Spinach
- Swiss chard

The heat of the summer months helps vegetables mature, but growing the following vegetables indoors gives them the extra heat they may need, especially if you live in a cooler climate:

- Beans
- Cucumbers
- Eggplant
- Okra
- Oriental vegetables
- Peppers
- Tomatoes

Fall brings cooler nights and often wetter weather, so planting some vegetables indoors protects them from excess water, lower temperatures, and snow. The best vegetables for growing indoors during the fall months include the following:

- Beets
- Carrots
- Lettuce
- Scallions
- Spinach

If you want to get a head start with your vegetable garden, starting your own seedlings can be very satisfying and easier on your pocketbook than purchasing them from your local garden store. The best plants to start as seedlings include the following:

- Brassicas
- Eggplants
- Onions
- Peppers
- Tomatoes

Growing your vegetables indoors in a cold frame, plastic tunnel, glass greenhouse, or a combination of any of these methods will allow you to extend your growing season. Any of these structures would be a great enhancement to your vegetable growing and your backyard.

Vegetable Seeds

A vegetable is a plant that is eaten whole or in part; often, the seed is eaten. The seed is also the part of the plant that produces a whole new vegetable plant. This chapter will provide you with great advice on how to choose your seeds, the best ways to start them indoors or outdoors, and how to care for the seedlings as they grow. You will also learn how to save money by saving your own seeds for growing next season.

Choosing Seeds

Hybrids. Genetically modified seeds. Open pollination. Looking at all the choices in a seed catalog can be quite overwhelming. What do all those terms mean, and why are there ten different varieties of cucumbers?

First Things First

When purchasing seeds you will want to buy from a reputable seed company or exchange with friends. Look for local companies that grow trials of the vegetable seeds they sell. Your vegetables will be grown in a similar climate, which means you can be sure the seeds will do well in your garden.

Deciding on a Variety

Different vegetable varieties are created when plants naturally cross within a species or when researchers intentionally crossbreed. Some have shorter or longer maturity dates, some grow larger than others, and some do better in different temperatures. Seed catalogs will indicate some of the benefits of each variety. Take the time to read and choose the variety that will work best for your situation.

A hybrid variety is made when seeds from two parent plants are crossed for the purpose of improving the plant's productivity. Vegetable plants are often hybridized in order to create disease resistant varieties and to increase vegetable size, color, and shape. Unfortunately, the seeds cannot be saved for future use. The seeds of a hybrid plant will not grow or will produce an inferior plant. If you are planning to save your own seeds, do not plant any hybrid varieties.

FACT

Genetically modified seeds (GMO) are produced by manipulating genetic components from unrelated organisms with the idea of producing a better product. There are many concerns and very little testing for the health ramifications of GMO seeds. Organic gardeners recommend against purchasing or planting these seeds.

An open pollinated seed is one where two parent plants from the same variety produce seeds, which produces a new plant just like the parent one. The male and female plants need to cross in order to create a new seed. Pollination is usually facilitated by insects, birds, or the wind, but it can be done by hand as well. If you choose open pollinating varieties, you'll be limited to a single variety of those particular vegetables. Cross-pollination may occur if you plant multiple varieties, and the resulting plants may look and taste inferior to the parent vegetables.

Starting Seeds Outdoors

There are two ways to plant your vegetable seeds: directly outdoors into the soil or indoors in seed trays to be transplanted to the garden later. Different vegetable seeds have different requirements for germination and maturing; some need heat and some do better in cool weather. You must know the best way to start each of your vegetables. Most vegetable seeds will do well either way, but some vegetables, such as root crops, need to be seeded directly because they do not grow well if their roots are disturbed.

Starting seeds indoors will give them a head start. This is beneficial, especially if you live in a cold climate where you cannot get into your garden until the end of May.

Vegetables best started by seeding directly into the soil include:

- Beans
- Beets
- Carrots
- Corn
- Garlic
- Peas
- Potatoes
- Radish
- Rutabagas
- Salad greens

When starting your seeds outdoors, make sure the conditions are right for your specific vegetable seed. If the soil is too wet and cold or too dry and hot, the seed may not germinate. Know what each variety of seed you are planting requires.

Here is a quick checklist for planting your seeds directly into your garden beds.

- ❏ Make sure the soil is moist.
- ❏ Mark the row using a stick, the edge of a hoe, or your finger. It should be the depth recommended for that particular seed.
- ❏ Sow the seed. If the seed is small, take a pinch of seed with your fingers and then gently spread the seed in the area you marked. Larger seeds can be dropped into the row. Place them an appropriate distance apart as you go.
- ❏ Cover the seed. Gently cover the seed with soil. You can do this by using your hand or the back side of a rake.
- ❏ Firm the soil down. This is done using your hand or the back of a hoe. This prevents the soil and seed from being blown away by wind or getting washed away when you water the bed.
- ❏ Water the bed. Seeds need to be moist to germinate, so gently spray the area you have just planted with water. Do not water too heavily or quickly or you may wash the seeds away. You will need to keep the area well moistened until you see the first green shoots coming through the soil, then water as needed. Do not let the bed dry out.
- ❏ Thin the plants. Once the first green shoots appear, some vegetable plants such as carrots, radishes, turnips, spinach, and salad greens need to be thinned. Thinning helps to make room for the vegetable plants to grow to maturity.

QUESTION

How deeply should the seeds be planted?
Vegetable seed packets give you valuable information, such as how deep to plant each variety. However, if you don't have the seed packet handy, a good rule of thumb is to plant the seed twice the depth of the size of the seed.

Some vegetables are difficult to start outdoors because the seed needs a very specific temperature to germinate. These are best started indoors so you have more control over their growing conditions. Some examples are tomatoes, peppers, and eggplants.

Transplants: Buy or Start Your Own?

Starting your own seedlings can be a very satisfying part of vegetable gardening. Its advantages are many. It can be more economical, especially if you have a large garden, and it gives you a head start with your growing season. You'll also know exactly how many plants you will have to transplant out, and you can prevent unwanted disease or pests from coming into your garden.

Buying Transplants

If you do not have the time or desire to start you own seedlings, check your local nursery or garden center for vegetable transplants. Make sure you purchase your seedlings from a reputable business and choose their healthiest seedlings. Unhealthy transplants can easily introduce insects and disease to your garden. A healthy transplant is bushy and compact, not spindly or leggy. The stems should be a healthy color and strong. Avoid plants whose roots are showing through the drain holes. These plants may be root bound, which may prevent them from growing to their full potential. Make sure you are ready to plant your transplants into the garden as soon as you bring them home.

Starting Your Own Seedlings

The process of starting your own seedlings can be intimidating, but it can be easily accomplished with a little know-how. Vegetables that do better started indoors and then transplanted to the garden include:

- Broccoli
- Cabbage
- Cauliflower
- Celery

- Eggplants
- Lettuce
- Onions
- Peppers
- Tomatoes

Start seeds indoors in flats

Many nurseries or garden stores sell seed starter kits. They come with all the components needed to start your own trans-plants—a tray, cells, labels, and a clear plastic lid. The two most common sizes are sheets that have seventy-two cells and sheets with twenty-four cells. The larger the vegetable plants at maturity, the larger the flat you should use for growing the seedling. For exam-ple, lettuce is usually planted in the seventy-two-cell sheets and brassicas or tomatoes are started in the twenty-four-cell sheets. The tray, cells, and lid can be reused from year to year, but make sure they are clean. Use one part bleach to ten parts water to clean them at the beginning of the season.

Some kits come with a starter mix, but you may have to purchase this separately. Use sterile potting soil made specifically for starting seeds; it is lighter weight than your garden soil.

ESSENTIAL

Make sure the water you use on your young seedlings is at room tem-perature. Water straight from a tap or outdoor water barrel may be too cold for the transplants. If the roots get too chilled, they will not grow well.

To start your seeds indoors, fill the cells with the starter mix, making sure they are filled to the top, and gently firm each hole down with your fingers. Place the cell sheet into the tray, which is used to support the sheet and hold any water that may drain out of the bottom of the cells. Make small indentations in each cell using the tip of your finger or a pencil-sized dowel, then place the seed inside it. Planting two seeds in each cell will give you a better chance of germination. If both germinate, cut the second seedling off with small scissors. Do not pull out the second seedling because this may damage the roots of the one you want to keep.

Once you have placed seeds in each cell, cover them with a light covering of the starter mix and gently firm the soil in each cell. Water gently and keep the soil moist until the seeds have pushed through the soil. Once they have sprouted, make sure your vegetable seedlings get full sunlight and the cells are watered regularly. Do not let the cells dry out; this is hard on the seedling and it will take a long time for the soil to absorb more water, which can stress the plant even more.

Some vegetables will need extra heat to germinate. You can purchase a heating pad from your local garden center or use a hotbed.

Caring for Your Seedlings

Now that you have your seeds planted in trays or directly in the ground, how do you care for them?

Common Quandaries

The seeds need to be kept moist to germinate, but the challenge of growing seeds outdoors is excessive rainfall. Too much moisture can saturate the soil, which can prevent the seeds from germinating or cause them to rot. If the temperature is too warm, the soil can become dry and hard, which prevents the sprouting seed from breaking through the soil. You will need to take extra care of your seeds and seedlings in the first few weeks after planting them; once they get established they will need less of your attention.

Growing indoors gives you more control over how much water the seeds get, but they need constant attention and often need to be watered at least twice a day if the weather is warm. If your seedlings are thin and breaking off at the base, this may be a sign of a soil-borne fungus called *dampening off.* If the seedlings are large enough to be transplanted, bury the stem as deep as possible. If the seedlings are still too young to go out into the garden, you will need to throw these in the garbage and start over again using clean cells.

Seeds do not need light to germinate, but once they have broken through the surface they need as much light as possible. Most seedlings need six hours of light to grow well. If you are starting them in late winter when the days are still short, grow lights may be necessary. Leggy and spindly look-ing seedlings may not be getting enough light. Another concern is extreme temperatures.

Young seedlings can burn and wilt very easily in the heat, and can die if they get too cold. Protecting them from extreme temperatures is necessary (see Chapter 13).

QUESTION

My seeds have not sprouted. What's wrong?
Some seeds, such as brassicas and lettuce, germinate quickly—some-times in as few as four days. Others, such as onions, can take up to twenty-one days to germinate. Check to see how long the seed is supposed to take before you start worrying. If your seeds should have sprouted by now, the seeds may be old and may not be viable any-more. Try planting again using fresher seeds.

Young seedlings are tender and tasty, making them more susceptible to some pests. One common concern for outdoor seedlings is slugs. If the leaves of your young lettuce or spinach plants are being eaten, you may have slugs. If the same thing is happening to your indoor seedlings, you may have a mouse problem. Part of caring for you seedlings is taking the time to observe them. If you find something wrong, investigate to determine what is happening to your plants.

Transplanting Your Indoor Seedlings

If you have decided to purchase your transplants, make sure you place them into the ground within a day or so of bringing them home from the nursery. If you started some of your own transplants, they will be ready to go into the garden after four to twelve weeks depending on the variety. The seedlings should have at least four true leaves before you set them out, and the outdoor soil temperature needs to be warm enough to support your vegetable plants.

It is important to transition some seedlings like tomatoes or peppers from inside to outside. They need to be set outside during the day and brought back in at night; gradually extend the time they are outside over several days. This is called *hardening off*.

Here is a checklist for setting out your transplants:

❑ Make sure the cells are moist before they are planted.
❑ Gently massage the seedling out of the cell, trying not to disturb the roots too much. Try not to tear the cell so you can reuse it next season.
❑ Make a hole the depth of the cell and place the transplant into it. Cover it with soil and firmly press the soil around the base of the plant.
❑ Water the transplant after planting. Remember the roots are tiny and close to the surface; water regularly so the soil does not dry out.
❑ Protect the plant from too much heat or cold so it can get a good start.

Choosing the right seed and making sure the seedling gets the best start it can will go a long way. A little care and attention in the beginning of a plant's life will give you a much healthier vegetable plant and a more abundant harvest.

Saving Seeds

When planning your garden layout, think about planting some vegetables for saving the seeds in the fall. This means you allow the plant to fully mature and then harvest the seed, saving it for planting next season. Some vegetable plants, such as peas and beans, produce pods with the seed inside. Others, such as tomatoes and cucumbers, produce fruit that contains the seeds. Still others, such as lettuce and onions, produce seeds after they flower. And with vegetables such as potatoes and garlic, the root becomes the seed.

Beware of Hybrids

Seeds that will not cross-pollinate with each other are easy to save. However, if you have two different varieties of the same vegetable plant growing in the same area, you risk cross-pollination. A home gardener does not want to raise hybrid varieties for seed because hybrid seeds will not produce vegetables that are as good as its parents' were. These plants need to be isolated if you want to harvest the seeds. The degree of isolation depends on the plants. Some, such as peppers and eggplants, only need to be about fifty feet apart so they do not cross-pollinate. Others, such as corn, spinach, squash, and radishes, need total isolation. You should only plant one variety of these vegetables if you are planning on saving the seeds.

Commercial growers like to plant hybrid seeds because they are specifically created to produce similar sized crops that mature at the same time. This is great if you are selling your produce, but for a home gardener who only wants one plant to be ready at a time, choosing nonhybrid is a better option. You want to make sure you collect the seed before they start dispersing naturally. You have to take the time to observe the plants to know when the seed is ripe enough for collecting, and you want to be sure you do it before they are blown away by the wind.

ALERT

Remember to label your seeds. Take the time to write down the vegetable type, variety, any special features, and the place and date you collected the seeds on the seed packet. The last thing you want to find is a whole box of unlabeled seeds.

Storing Your Seeds

The seeds must be thoroughly dry. Spread the seeds out on a plate or tray and place them in a warm location out of direct sunlight. Leave them for a couple of weeks to dry thoroughly. Before you put them into packets, make sure they are clean. Remove any chaff or dirt from the seed by placing the seeds into a kitchen sieve whose holes are tiny enough for just the chaff—not the seeds—to fall through. Try gently blowing on the seeds to remove any chaff.

Place your seeds in airtight containers. Plastic yogurt containers and paper envelopes work well. Keep them in a cool, dry spot such as a refrigerator or a cool, dry storage room. The main reason seeds do not last is because they become moldy or rot, both of which are caused by extreme changes in temperature or humidity.

Most seeds will last two to four years if saved and stored properly. If you are not sure if your seeds are still good, it's easy enough to test their viability. Spread ten seeds on a damp paper towel. Place the towel and the seeds into a resealable plastic bag and seal it. Put the closed bag in an area out of direct sunlight—the top of your refrigerator is a good spot. Check back in four to ten days to see how many seeds sprouted. This will give you an indication of the percentage of seed that will sprout if you plant them in your garden.

Whether or not you choose to save your own seeds, it is important to know how. There is more and more concern about how vegetable seeds are being grown and stored. If every home gardener chose to save only one variety of vegetable, it would make a difference. Start a seed bank in your community so you can support your fellow gardeners and the environment, and save yourself some money by sharing the seeds.

CHAPTER 8

Salad Stuff

Greens are plants that produce leaves quickly and are often harvested before the plant reaches maturity. They grow in various shades of greens and reds and have different flavors. You want your salad stuff to grow rapidly for best flavor, so they require a rich soil high in nitrogen and need to be well watered. In this chapter you will get information and easy growing tips for lettuce, celery, oriental vegetables, mixed salad greens, spinach, and Swiss chard.

Lettuce

Lettuce is one of the most common vegetables for the home gardener, and it's very easy to grow. There are several types and varieties of lettuce you can choose to grow, including leaf lettuce, Bibb lettuce, Romaine lettuce, and iceberg lettuce. With some leaf varieties, you can cut the outer leaves to eat, leaving the center to produce more new growth. You can also let the lettuce plant reach maturity and then cut the whole head at the base of the plant. Plan to plant several different varieties of lettuce in your garden so you can enjoy tasty and colorful salads.

Lettuce

Lettuce is a cool-season vegetable and can be planted as soon as you can get into your garden. It grows great in containers on a patio or balcony as well. All types of lettuce have the same growing requirements. You want your lettuce to grow rapidly for best flavor, so a nitrogen-rich soil is best. Add nitrogen-rich fertilizer such as blood meal, alfalfa meal, or aged chicken manure during the soil preparation. Lettuce plants have quite shallow roots, so you only need to add a few inches of compost or aged manure to the garden bed. You want the soil to be moist but well drained. Lettuce does not like soggy or saturated soil.

Lettuce can be planted almost anywhere in your garden. It is a fast-growing vegetable, so you get quick results. To have lettuce all season long, start a few plants indoors in early spring. When you transplant those out to the garden, plant more seeds. Do this every few weeks. A great way to get the most out of your garden space is to plant some lettuce seeds or transplants under slower growing vegetables such as cabbage, cauliflower, and broccoli. These larger plants will give the lettuce plants the shade they need during the summer months.

FACT

Overseeding is probably one of the biggest problems in growing lettuce. If seeds are broadcasted (sowed over a wide area by hand), they will need to be thinned. One of the best ways to do this is to treat your garden bed as a transplant bed. As plants come up, gently move the seedlings to other areas of your garden.

▼ **QUICK TIPS FOR GROWING LETTUCE**

Family name	Asteraceae (aster, daisy, or sunflower family).
Edible parts	Leaves and stems.
Location	Shady area with a cool temperature. Lettuce grows well in raised beds and containers.
Best soil	Loose, rich, well drained; pH 6.0–6.8.
When to Plant	For transplants sow indoors early March to mid-July; direct seed as soon as you can work your soil and plant more every few weeks.
How to plant	Can be transplanted or sown directly to the garden. Sow seeds ¼ inch deep, spacing them 8 to 10 inches apart in rows 12 to 24 inches apart.
How much to plant	10 to 15 plants per person each season
Companion plants	For a positive effect, plant with beets, cabbage, peas, clover, and radish. There are no plants that have a negative effect on lettuce plants.
Weeding	Keep the area around the plant well weeded.
Watering	Drip irrigation or overhead sprinkling will work well. Plants need 1 to 2 inches each week and may require more if the weather is hot. Sprinkling the leaves in the early morning will help to keep the plant cooler during the hot part of the day.
Care	Provide some shade in the heat of the summer. A floating row cover works well.
Fertilizing	Add compost tea or fish fertilizer around the base of the plant every 2 to 3 weeks after planting.
Pests and diseases	Use crop rotation as prevention. Some common pests and diseases include slugs, aphids, cabbage loopers, flea beetles, downy mildew, and fusarium wilt.
When to harvest	Lettuce plants reach maturity at between 50 to 75 days. Harvest leaf and Romaine lettuce when the plant is large enough to use. Harvest Bibb lettuce when a loose head is formed and iceberg lettuce when the head is firm.
How to harvest	Cut or pull off leaves of leaf lettuce. For head lettuce varieties, use a sharp knife to cut off the heads at the base of the plant.
Storage	Wash leaves, dry them in a salad spinner, and place them in a sealed plastic bag or container. They will store well for up to 1 week in the refrigerator.

Celery

Celery needs a three- to four-month growing season. It requires cool weather and likes a fairly consistent temperature through its growing season. Because of this, it can be a difficult plant for a backyard garden. If you really like eating celery, give it a try. It may need more of your attention, but it will be worth it in the end.

When preparing the celery bed, dig in at least twelve inches of compost or aged manure. To do this, dig a trench about a foot deep and fill it with your compost or manure. This gives you a nice deep bed in which to plant your celery transplants.

To get the stalks to remain light green like you see in the supermarket they will need to be blanched. If celery is not blanched the outer stalks can get brown spots and may become tough. This will give the stalks a milder flavor as well. About three to four weeks before you plan to harvest, tie the tops of the stalks together and mound soil around the plants to prevent the light from reaching them. You can also place a large coffee can with both ends removed around the whole plant.

▼ QUICK TIPS FOR GROWING CELERY

Family name	Umbelliferae or Apiaceae (carrot, celery, or parsley family).
Edible parts	Stalk and root.
Location	Level, open area.
Best soil	Celery is a heavy feeder and needs a rich, well-drained soil; pH 6.0–7.0.
When to plant	Start seedlings indoors in late February to April; transplant out in late spring when plants are about 4 or 5 inches tall.
How to plant	Celery can be transplanted or direct seeded. Space the plants 8 inches apart in rows at least 12 inches apart.
How much to plant	5 to 10 plants per person.
Companion plants	For a positive effect, plant with beans, brassicas, spinach, squash, tomatoes, and cucumbers. Stay away from carrots and parsnips.
Weeding	Keep well weeded.
Watering	Needs heavy watering, so keep soil moist.
Care	Blanch for best flavor and to get whitish stalks.
Fertilizing	Put compost around the base of the plant 3 weeks after planting and then again 6 weeks after planting.
Pests and diseases	Aphids, cabbage loopers, leafhoppers, damping off, and mildew.
When to harvest	Takes 90 to 110 days to mature.
How to harvest	Cut individual stalks as you need them or cut the whole bunch off at the base.
Storage	Will not store long once harvested. If you live in an area with mild winters, celery can be left in the garden over winter and harvested as needed.

Oriental Vegetables

Oriental vegetables are commonly used in oriental cooking. Some common varieties of oriental greens include mizuna, mibuna, pac choi, and leaf mustards. Chinese cabbage is another common oriental vegetable. These vegetables are cool-season vegetables that need rich soil to grow rapidly. They are easy to grow and it is best to succession plant them so they can be enjoyed all season long.

The seeds are often broadcasted, so you will want to have a fine, clean seedbed. Add in compost and aged manure when preparing the bed, making sure you rake out any clumps or rocks. If the seed is directly sown to the garden bed, the plants will need to be thinned.

FACT

Broadcasting means to scatter and spread widely. To plant seeds that you will be cutting as baby salad greens, use a hammer and small nails to punch holes the size of your seeds into the lid of a small jar. Fill the lid with your seeds and gently shake the seeds out onto your garden bed.

These vegetables are harvested either as young plants for use in salads or as larger mature plants, usually used for cooking.

▼ **QUICK TIPS FOR GROWING ORIENTAL VEGETABLES**

Family name	Brassicaceae (mustard family).
Edible parts	Leaves and stems.
Location	Will take a little shade; grows well in raised beds and containers.
Best soil	Loose, rich, loamy soil, clean seedbed; pH 6.0–6.8
When to plant	Cool-season. Plant directly to your garden bed in early spring or by transplant if you have a shorter growing season.
How to plant	Direct seed or transplant. Sow seeds ¼ to ½ inch deep, 8 inches apart in rows spaced at least 12 inches apart. If you are growing to use as salad greens the seed can be broadcasted.
How much to plant	10 to 15 plants per person.
Companion plants	For a positive effect, plant with beans, onions, and potatoes. Avoid planting near tomatoes or lettuce.
Weeding	Keep the area around the plant well weeded.

▼ **QUICK TIPS FOR GROWING ORIENTAL VEGETABLES—*continued***

Watering	Drip irrigation or overhead sprinkling will work well. Plants need 1 to 2 inches each week and may require more if the weather is hot. Sprinkling the leaves in the early morning will help keep the plants cooler during the hot part of the day.
Care	Provide some shade in the heat of the summer. A floating row cover works well.
Fertilizing	Add compost tea or fish fertilizer around the base of the plant every 2 to 3 weeks after planting.
Pests and diseases	Flea beetles, slugs, and fusarium wilt are common.
When to harvest	Plants mature in 21 to 45 days. These vegetables can be harvested starting when they are 3 to 4 inches high and continuing up to maturity. It is best to harvest the plant just before it goes to flower.
How to harvest	Snip young leaves with sharp scissors or a knife. Cut a mature plant off at the base. You may get a second growth if the roots are not pulled.
Storage	Wash leaves, dry them in a salad spinner, and place them in a sealed plastic bag or container. They will store well for up to 1 week in the refrigerator.

Salad Greens

There are many tasty green vegetables besides lettuce that can add flavor, color, and texture to your salad. Some common greens include arugula, corn salad, curly cress, sorrel, endive, and dandelion. You can also purchase mesclun blends, which are mixtures of different varieties of lettuces and other salad green seeds. The seeds are usually sowed by broadcasting to a garden bed and are cut as individual leaves when they are two to three inches high.

Arugula

ALERT

Enriching soil with chicken manure is a great way to add in organic matter and the nitrogen needed for growing great vegetables. Chicken manure can also burn plants due to the high nitrogen content. If you use chicken manure, let it age longer than other manures and mix it with shredded leaves or peat moss to spread out the nitrogen.

Salad greens are best grown during the cooler season in early spring. They require a fertile soil rich in nitrogen and are best grown quickly. Work in several inches of compost or aged animal manure to your garden bed in early spring. Make sure the garden bed is clean of any debris and rocks; these tiny seeds grow best in a fine seedbed. Plant the seeds by broadcasting and then lightly covering them with more fine soil.

▼ **QUICK TIPS FOR GROWING SALAD GREENS**

Family name	Arugula and Cress: Brassicaceae (mustard family).; Corn Salad: Valerianaceae (valerian family); Sorrel: Polygonaceae (knotweed family); Endive: Asteraceae (aster, daisy, or sunflower family).
Edible parts	Leaves and stems.
Location	Grows well in containers and raised beds; will handle a bit of shade.
Best soil	Fertile; a clean fine seedbed is best.
When to plant	Cool-season crops; seed every 3 weeks from March to September.
How to plant	Sow seeds ¼ inch deep, 2 inches apart. For mature plants space 6 inches apart. Can be seeded by broadcasting or can be transplanted.
How much to plant	10 to 15 feet per person each season.
Companion plants	For a positive effect, plant with beets, cabbage, peas, clover, and radish. There are no plants that have a negative effect on lettuce.
Weeding	Keep beds well weeded.
Watering	Keep soil moist.
Fertilizing	Fertilize after the first harvest is cut approximately 3 weeks after sowing. This will give the roots the boost they need to produce new leaves.
Pests and diseases	Flea beetles and slugs are common.
When to harvest	Plants mature in 30 to 50 days. Cut at 2 to 3 inches for baby greens or let the plant grow to maturity.
How to harvest	Cut individual leaves about 1 inch from the base of the plant with a sharp knife or scissors. Try not to disturb the roots so the plant will grow again.
Storage	Best eaten when freshly cut. They will store in the refrigerator for a few days. Wash leaves, dry them in a salad spinner, and place them in a sealed plastic bag or container.

Spinach

Spinach is another cool-season crop that does best grown in spring or fall when the temperatures are lower and the days are shorter. Spinach has one of the darkest colored leaves and because of this offers a wealth of vitamins and minerals.

Some common varieties for planting in spring and fall are Tyee and Olympia. For summer planting, try New Zealand spinach, a trailing perennial plant that produces thicker leaves. It does well in mild climates.

Spinach is easy to grow, but it bolts easily in warm weather, so it is best grown either early or late in the season. When a vegetable "bolts" it means it has grown too quickly and starts to produce seeds. The taste and flavor of the spinach is compromised once it begins to bolt. It needs a rich soil, so prepare your garden bed with several inches of compost or aged animal manure. Spinach does best in full sun, which is one of the reasons it is best grown early in the season when the sun is not too hot. Make sure the garden bed is well drained, especially if you live in a wet climate.

▼ QUICK TIPS FOR GROWING SPINACH

Family name	Chenopodiaceae (goose foot family).
Edible parts	Leaves and stems.
Location	Full sun.
Best soil	Rich soil abundant in nitrogen; pH 6.2–6.9.
When to plant	Low-temperature season. Start sowing indoors in April to July and transplant out every 4 weeks, or it can be direct seeded as soon as the soil is worked.
How to plant.	Can be direct seeded or transplanted. Plant ½ inch deep, 1 inch apart, and space 6 to 8 inches apart in rows at least 12 inches apart.
How much to plant	10–15 plants per person each season.
Companion plants	For a positive effect, plant with cabbage, celery, eggplants, onions, peas, and strawberries. There are no plants that have a negative effect on spinach.
Weeding	Keep beds well weeded.
Watering	Keep soil moist; sprinkling will keep the leaves cooler in warm weather.
Care	May need a little shade if the weather gets warm. A floating row cover works well.
Fertilizing	Give spinach plants a nitrogen-rich fertilizer once they are ⅓ grown, or approximately once every 10 to 14 days.
Pests and diseases	Aphids, slugs, cabbageworms, and leaf miners are common.
When to harvest	Can be harvested at any size from baby leaves to maturity, which ranges from 40 to 50 days.
How to harvest	Cut outer leaves as they grow or at the base of a mature plant.
Storage	Spinach does not store well. Wash leaves, dry them in a salad spinner, and place them in a sealed plastic bag or container. Spinach will keep in the refrigerator for a few days.

Swiss Chard

Swiss chard is an easy-to-grow vegetable and one of the best for a beginner. Swiss chard is related to the beet family, but it is grown for its leaves and stems instead of its roots. It will grow well in the spring, summer, and fall. It does well in containers and raised beds.

Swiss chard

Like most other greens, Swiss chard likes a well-drained, nitrogen-rich soil. Start planting in early spring. As you harvest the outer stems, the plant will keep producing more. A few plants will take you all the way through several weeks of harvesting.

FACT

Swiss chard is a power food with twelve of the main nutrients for a healthy diet. The best way to maximize the many nutrients in Swiss chard is to steam it for two to three minutes. A quick steaming will retain the bright color of this vegetable as well.

Swiss chard is one of the most colorful vegetables. It comes in a rainbow of colors—red, yellow, orange, green, and white. Some common varieties are fordhook giant, rhubarb, canary yellow, and perpetual.

▼ QUICK TIPS FOR GROWING SWISS CHARD

Family name	Chenopodiaceae (goose family).
Edible parts	Leaves and stems.
Location	Sunny area.
Best soil	Rich, loamy, well-drained soil; pH 6.5–6.8.
When to plant	Sow indoors in March or April and transplant out in 4 weeks or sow direct as soon as your soil is worked.
How to plant	Can be direct seeded or transplanted. Sow seeds ½ inch deep, 1 to 2 inches apart, in rows spaced at least 18 inches apart. Thin plants so they are 8 to 12 inches apart.
How much to plant	10 to 15 plants per person each season.
Companion plants	Plant with cabbage, celery, eggplants, onions, peas, and strawberries for a positive effect. There are no plants that have a negative effect on Swiss chard.

▼ **QUICK TIPS FOR GROWING SWISS CHARD—*continued***

Weeding	Keep area well weeded.
Watering	Keep soil moist. Drip irrigation or hand watering are recommended over sprinkling. As the leaves get larger they will impede overhead watering from reaching the plant roots.
Fertilizing	Use a nitrogen-rich fertilizer 2 to 3 weeks after transplanting or once the plants reach about 6 inches high.
Pests and diseases	Use crop rotation as prevention. Beware of cabbageworms, aphids, flea beetles, and leaf spot.
When to harvest	Plants mature in 45 to 50 days. Outer leaves can be eaten at any size; baby leaves are often used in salads.
How to harvest	Break off the outer leaves or cut them with a sharp knife.
Storage	Swiss chard will not store long. Wash leaves, dry them in a salad spinner, and place them in a sealed plastic bag or container. Will keep in the refrigerator for a few days.

CHAPTER 9

Brassicas

Also known as the cabbage family, this group of vegetables includes such favorites as broccoli, Brussels sprouts, cabbage, cauliflower, and kale. This chapter offers advice and growing tips for all of these wonderful veggies. They are cold, hardy vegetables that produce a lot of food for the space they use. They grow well in most soil types. Adding shredded leaves to the area where you will be planting the following year will help to produce fabulous brassicas for you.

Broccoli

Broccoli is a cool-season crop and is probably the easiest of all the brassica family to grow. Most varieties will produce one large head averaging about six to eight inches in diameter. Once this head is cut off, the plant will continue to produce side branches with smaller heads. Keep cutting these before they flower and you will be able to harvest broccoli from one plant for several weeks.

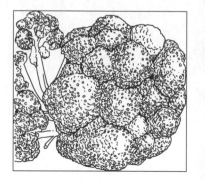

Broccoli

The broccoli plant may bolt if the weather gets hot. This means the plant will go to flower more quickly than it normally would in cooler weather. It is best to plant broccoli early in the spring (April) and then again in late summer if you have a mild fall and winter.

FACT

Broccoli is one of the most popular vegetables for the health-conscious eater. A half cup of cooked broccoli has 75 mg vitamin C, 1,300 IU beta-carotene, 3 grams protein, 5 grams dietary fiber, and only 40 calories, making it one of the top ten healthy foods to eat.

Broccoli often does best transplanted. This allows you to start your plants indoors so they get more growth before the heat of the summer arrives.

▼ QUICK TIPS FOR GROWING BROCCOLI

Family name	Brassicaceae (mustard family).
Edible parts	Flower buds and stems.
Location	Cool area.
Best soil	Rich, moist but well-drained loamy soil; pH 6.0–6.8.
When to plant	Start indoors April to mid-July, then transplant out after 6 to 8 weeks.
How to plant	Space transplants 16 to 24 inches apart in rows spaced 2 to 3 feet apart. Sow seeds ½ inch deep, 4 inches apart, then thin seedlings.
How much to plant	10 to 15 plants per person each season.

▼   QUICK TIPS FOR GROWING BROCCOLI—*continued*

Companion plants	For a positive effect, plant with beans, onions, potatoes, oregano, dill, sage, and nasturtiums. Planting with tomatoes and lettuce will have a negative effect on broccoli.
Weeding	Keep well weeded around the base of the plant.
Watering	Water deeply at least once a week around the base of the plant. Hand watering or drip irrigation are best. If an overhead sprinkler is used, the water is blocked from reaching the roots by the large leaves.
Fertilizing	Start to fertilize about 3 weeks after setting out the transplants and again when the bud starts to form on the plant.
Pests and diseases	Root maggots, cabbageworms, and club root are common. Crop rotation is essential to prevent pests and diseases.
When to harvest	Broccoli usually matures in 50 to 72 days. Cut the center head when it is about 5 to 6 inches in diameter or before the buds start to open.
How to harvest	Cut the center head with about 4 inches of stem using a sharp knife. The plant will form side branches off the main stem, which will produce smaller heads that need to be cut before they flower.
Storage	Broccoli will stay for a few weeks in your refrigerator. It is best to put it on ice or into the refrigerator as soon as it is harvested.

Brussels Sprouts

Brussels sprouts look like little palm trees with lumps growing from the plant stem, or trunk. The bumps, which are usually one to two inches in diameter, are the Brussels sprouts. They are often called *baby cabbages* because they look like miniature cabbages. Each plant should produce between 50 and 100 sprouts.

Brussels sprouts are a cool-season vegetable and the taste is improved by a light frost. Like most other brassicas, these vegetables like to have a fertile, well-drained soil to grow in. The plant is slow growing and is not often harvested until fall and early winter.

▼   QUICK TIPS FOR GROWING BRUSSELS SPROUTS

Family name	Brassicaceae (mustard family).
Edible parts	The sprouts, sometimes called the *bud*.
Location	Cool area.
Best soil	Fertile, moist, well-drained soil; pH 6.0–6.8.
When to plant	Sow April to July and then transplant out in 6 to 8 weeks.

▼ **QUICK TIPS FOR GROWING BRUSSELS SPROUTS—*continued***

How to plant	Set out transplants 16 to 24 inches apart in rows spaced 2 to 3 feet apart. For direct seeding, sow seeds ½ inch deep and every 4 inches and then thin to 16 to 24 inches apart.
How much to plant	5 to 10 plants per person.
Companion plants	For a positive effect, plant with beans, beets, onions, potatoes, and oregano. Avoid planting near tomatoes, lettuce, and strawberries, as they may have a negative effect.
Weeding	Keep area around base of plant well weeded.
Watering	Water deeply at least once a week around the base of the plant. Hand watering or drip irrigation are best. If an overhead sprinkler is used, the large leaves keep the water from reaching the roots.
Fertilizing	Start to fertilize about 3 weeks after setting out the transplants and again when the bud starts to form on the plant.
Pests and diseases	Root maggots, cabbageworms, and club root are common. Crop rotation is essential for prevention of pests and diseases.
When to harvest	When the big leaves start to turn yellow, it is a sign that the sprouts are ready to be harvested.
How to harvest	Harvest the sprouts from the bottom of the plant, moving upward until all the sprouts mature. The green sprouts should be 1 to 2 inches in diameter and will easily break off from the stem. Remove the bottom leaves as you harvest the sprouts.
Storage	Brussels sprouts can be kept for up to 1 week in the refrigerator. They can be frozen and used later.

Cabbage

Cabbage is another easy-to-grow vegetable in the brassica family. It grows well in most soils and is a cool-season crop. It is best to plant this vegetable in early spring for a summer harvest or in late summer for a fall harvest. The mature cabbage forms a head from a rosette of thickened leaves. The cabbage head can be round, pointy, or flatted depending on the variety. The leaves can be richly colored and textured. There are green varieties that produce light green leaves and red varieties with purplish red leaves. The Savoy cabbage has crinkly leaves. There are short season and long season varieties.

Cabbage

Cabbage can be eaten cooked or raw. Sauerkraut (cooked cabbage) and coleslaw (raw cabbage) are two of the most common cabbage dishes. Cabbage contains a good amount of vitamin C and some vitamin A. A medium head of cabbage will give approximately two pounds of cabbage or about twelve cups of shredded cabbage.

FACT

Cabbage is one of the oldest recorded vegetables. It was important for feeding people and animals more than 5,000 years ago. The exact point of origin is unknown, but it was once used in worship ceremonies in ancient Egypt. Cabbage was also important for American pioneers, who relied on the dependable crop as they traveled.

Cabbage, like all brassica vegetables, is susceptible to a variety of soil-borne diseases, so crop rotation is essential in order to keep your garden healthy. Once you have planted brassicas in an area, do not plant them in that spot again until at least four years after the first crop.

▼ QUICK TIPS FOR GROWING CABBAGE

Family name	Brassicaceae (mustard family).
Edible parts	Leaf heads.
Location	Cool area.
Best soil	Rich, moist but well-drained loamy soil; pH 6.0–6.8.
When to plant	Start indoors April to mid-July, then transplant out after 6 to 8 weeks.
How to plant	Space transplants 16 to 20 inches apart in rows 2 to 3 feet apart. Sow seeds ½ inch deep, 4 inches apart, then thin seedlings.
How much to plant	10 to 15 plants per person each season.
Companion plants	For a positive effect plant with beans, beets, onions, potatoes, and oregano. Planting with tomatoes and strawberries will have a negative effect on cabbage.
Weeding	Keep well weeded around the base of the plant.
Watering	Water deeply at least once a week around the base of the plant. Hand watering and drip irrigation are best; if an overhead sprinkler is used, the large leaves block the water from reaching the roots.
Fertilizing	Start to fertilize about 3 weeks after setting out the transplants and again when the bud starts to form on the plant.

▼ **QUICK TIPS FOR GROWING CABBAGE—*continued***

Pests and diseases	Root maggots, cabbageworms, and club root are common. Crop rotation is essential for prevention of pests and diseases.
When to harvest	Some varieties of cabbage will mature in 45 days; others can take several months to mature.
How to harvest	Cut the head of the cabbage off at the base of the plant using a sharp knife. The plant will form smaller heads if the roots of the plant have not been disturbed.
Storage	A head of a cabbage will last for a couple weeks in the refrigerator. If you live in a mild climate, the cabbage can be left out until you need it. Harvest before it gets large enough to split. Cabbage can be wrapped in newspaper, placed in boxes, and kept at zero degrees over the winter. It can also be frozen and used as you need it.

Cauliflower

Cauliflower is said to be the most difficult vegetable in the brassica family to grow. It is a cool-season vegetable, but it is also very sensitive to frost. Sunlight will turn the white head a darkish yellow color, so each head needs to be covered or blanched. This vegetable can be time consuming and not a sure thing for a home gardener, but it is worth a try.

There are several different varieties of cauliflower, some in bright colors of purple and orange! There are varieties that do not need to be blanched because the leaves grow in a certain way that covers the head and protects it from the sun.

Cauliflower

QUESTION

What does it mean to blanch a vegetable plant?
The sunlight needs to be prevented from reaching the plant in order for it to remain whitish in color. To make this happen, the plant is usually covered with its own leaves. If the white variety of cauliflower is not blanched, the sun may cause it to turn brownish. There are different varieties of cauliflower that are grown for their color; these do not need blanching.

Cauliflower needs a moderately rich soil. When preparing your garden bed, add in several inches of compost or aged animal manure as well as some fertilizer rich in phosphorus. This is a good area of your garden to put shredded leaves; cauliflower will do well with them decomposing in the bed. Cauliflower is also a great vegetable to mulch because the soil needs to be kept moist, especially if there is a long dry spell.

▼ **QUICK TIPS FOR GROWING CAULIFLOWER**

Family name	Brassicaceae (mustard family).
Edible parts	Heads.
Location	Cool, sunny area.
Best soil	Rich, moist but well-drained loamy soil; pH 6.0–6.8.
When to plant	Start indoors April to mid-July, then transplant out after 6 to 8 weeks.
How to plant	Space transplants 16 to 24 inches apart in rows 2 to 3 feet apart. Sow seeds ½ inch deep, 4 inches apart, then thin seedlings.
How much to plant	10 to 15 plants per person each season.
Companion plants	For a positive effect plant with beans, beets, onions, potatoes, and oregano. Planting with tomatoes and strawberries will have a negative effect on cauliflower.
Weeding	Keep well weeded around the base of the plant.
Watering	Water deeply at least once a week around the base of the plant. Hand watering or drip irrigation are best; if an overhead sprinkler is used, the large leaves block the water from the roots.
Care	Cauliflower heads need to be blanched if you want them to remain a whitish color. Start blanching 3 weeks before you plan to harvest.
Fertilizing	Start to fertilize about 3 weeks after setting out the transplants and again when the bud starts to form on the plant.
Pests and diseases	Root maggots, cabbageworms, and club root are common. Crop rotation is essential for prevention of pests and diseases.
When to harvest	Cauliflower usually matures in 55 to 100 days.
How to harvest	Cut the head of cauliflower off at the base of the plant using a sharp knife.
Storage	A head of cauliflower will last for a couple weeks in the refrigerator. Cauliflower can be frozen and used as you need it.

Collards

Collards are another cold, hardy vegetable in the brassica family. Their leaves look like cabbage leaves but do not form a head like a cabbage and are grown to be cooked rather than eaten raw. They are usually planted in the summer for harvesting in the fall and winter. The leaves of a mature plant are sweeter after a frost. The collard plant can also take the heat, so it is one of the few cooking greens that will do well all summer long.

Collards need a rich soil and a lot of water in order for the leaves to stay tender. When working the soil, add three inches of compost or aged manure to the garden bed. Collards also do best with regular fertilization. Use a nitrogen-rich fertilizer every few weeks, which will give them the nutrients they need to grow fast, develop a nice green color, and taste tender.

▼ QUICK TIPS FOR GROWING COLLARDS

Family name	Brassicaceae (mustard family).
Edible parts	Leaves and stems.
Location	Cool, sunny area.
Best soil	Rich, well drained; pH 5.5–6.8.
When to plant	Start indoors April to mid-July, then transplant out after 6 to 8 weeks.
How to plant	Space transplants 12 to 16 inches apart in rows 2 to 3 feet apart. Sow seeds ¼ inch deep, 1 to 2 inches apart, then thin seedlings.
How much to plant	5 to 10 plants per person each season
Companion plants	For a positive effect, plant with beans, onions, potatoes, and oregano. Planting with tomatoes and lettuce will have a negative effect on cauliflower.
Weeding	Keep well weeded around the base of the plant.
Watering	Water deeply at least once a week around the base of the plant. Water more in hot weather, less in the fall. Hand watering or drip irrigation are best; if an overhead sprinkler is used, the large leaves block the water from reaching the roots.
Fertilizing	Start to fertilize about 3 weeks after setting out the transplants and regularly until you harvest them.
Pests and diseases	Root maggots and cabbageworms are common. Crop rotation is essential for prevention of pests and diseases.
When to harvest	Collards usually mature in 60 to 80 days.
How to harvest	Cut off leaves as you need them, or cut the mature plant at the base.
Storage	Collards will not last long once they are harvested and will lose nutrients when stored, so it is best to use them as soon as they are harvested. They will stay in the refrigerator for up to 1 week.

Kale

Kale has high levels of vitamin C and calcium and the highest levels of beta-carotene of all the green vegetables. It is a hardy vegetable. Kale will survive over the winter and the leaves are more tender and sweet once they have been touched by frost. Kale will easily go to seed and spread throughout your garden, so pull the plants out before the seeds spread if you want to contain it.

There are several different varieties of kale, which are easily distinguishable because of their color and leaf. The most common are probably the green, curly leaf varieties. Some other varieties are Red Russian, which have gray-green leaves with a purplish stem; Lacinato, which has a dark blue-green leaf; Redbor, which has dark red leaves; and Improved Siberian, which has flat green leaves.

ALERT

Brassicas do best in soil with a pH that is more alkaline than acidic. Adding dolomite lime to the garden soil when preparing the beds will help to keep the soil at a good pH for these plants. Lime will also help prevent club root and other fungal diseases that brassicas are prone to.

▼ **QUICK TIPS FOR GROWING KALE**

Family name	Brassicaceae (mustard family).
Edible parts	Leaves and stems.
Location	Cool, sunny area.
Best soil	Rich, well drained; pH 6.5–6.8.
When to plant	Start indoors April to mid-July, then transplant out after 6 to 8 weeks.
How to plant	Space transplants 18 to 20 inches apart in rows 2 to 3 feet apart. Sow seeds ¼ inch deep, 2 to 4 inches apart, then thin seedlings.
How much to plant	5 to 10 plants per person each season.
Companion plants	For a positive effect, plant with beans, onions, potatoes, dill, sage, and oregano. Planting with tomatoes and lettuce will have a negative effect on cauliflower.
Weeding	Keep well weeded around the base of the plant.

▼ **QUICK TIPS FOR GROWING KALE—*continued***

Watering	Water deeply at least once a week around the base of the plant. Hand watering or drip irrigation are best; if an overhead sprinkler is used, the large leaves will block the water from the roots.
Fertilizing	Start to fertilize about 3 weeks after setting out the transplants and regularly until you harvest them.
Pests and diseases	Root maggots, cabbageworms, and club root are common. Crop rotation is essential for prevention of pests and disease.
When to harvest	Kale usually matures in 55 to 75 days.
How to harvest	Cut off leaves as you need them and the plant will keep producing for you all season long. Mature plants can be harvested at the base.
Storage	Eat the leaves as soon as possible after harvesting; they lose nutrients when stored. They will stay in the refrigerator for up to 1 week.

CHAPTER 10

Beans, Peas, and Perennial Vegetables

Freshly picked beans and peas are one of the tastiest of treats from the garden. They are easy to grow in pots or raised beds, can be trellised to add structure to your garden, and have lovely flowers that enhance your vegetable garden's appearance. The other vegetables that will be discussed in this chapter—artichokes, asparagus, and sun chokes—are all perennial veggies. They die back in the fall and emerge again in the spring.

Beans

Beans are one of the easiest vegetables to grow. You sow the seeds directly into the garden, where they will germinate quickly in the right temperature and grow vigorously. Considering the small amount of space they take up in your garden, they produce an awfully plentiful bounty. There are several different types of beans—bush beans (sometimes called *snap beans*), run-

ner beans, pole beans, shelling beans for drying, lima beans, soybeans, and fava beans (sometimes called *broad beans*). Most varieties need warm soil to germinate, so they are usually planted in the late spring. To tell whether it's time to plant your beans, walk barefoot on the soil at midday. If it feels cold, hold off for a while. If it doesn't feel cold, you're ready to go. The exception to this is fava beans, which are a cool-weather bean and best planted in early spring.

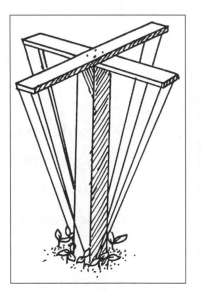

Beans grow at various heights. Bush beans grow to a height of sixteen inches; on the other end of the spectrum, pole and runner beans can grow up to eight feet tall. The type of beans you want to grow will determine whether they need support. Chapter 13 covers trellises and staking in greater detail.

Bean post

QUESTION

What is an inoculum?
An inoculum has beneficial microorganisms that allow crops of legumes (beans and peas) to increase the available nitrogen in the soil. You dip the seeds into the powder before planting them. The organisms attach to the legume roots and make swellings full of nitrogen, which is released into the soil when the roots decompose in the ground or in your compost.

Beans will grow in almost any reasonably good garden soil. They grow best in a sandy, loamy soil with a neutral pH. Beans do not like a lot of moisture before they germinate, but they need regular watering once they have sprouted to produce tender beans. They are best harvested young when they are the most tender and need to be picked every few days so the plant knows it needs to keep producing more. If you leave the pods on the plant, the plant will take it as a sign to stop producing.

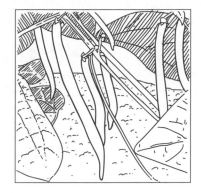

Yellow beans

▼ QUICK TIPS FOR GROWING BEANS

Family name	Papilionaceae (pea or bean family).
Edible parts	Seeds and pods.
Location	Open, sunny area.
Best soil	Sandy, loamy soil; neutral pH.
When to plant	Seeds need a temperature of 70–90°F.
How to plant	Bush beans: Sow 1 inch deep, 3 inches apart in rows 18 to 24 inches apart, then thin to every 6 inches. Pole or runner beans: Plant 5 to 8 seeds to each stake, thin to 3 to 4 plants. For other types check the seed packet for exact instructions.
How much to plant	Bush beans: 20 to 30 feet per person. Pole or runner beans: 20 to 25 feet per person. Dried beans: 100 feet per person.
Companion plants	Plant with beets, cabbage, carrots, corn, squash, and tomatoes. Plants that will have a negative effect are chives, fennel, garlic, and leeks.
Weeding	Keep well weeded, especially when the plants are small.
Watering	Do not water seeds until they have sprouted, then water regularly after that.
Care	Set up stakes for pole or runner beans at the time of planting. To prevent the spread of disease, try not to touch the plants when they are wet.
Fertilizing	Fertilize with fish fertilizer or compost tea after the first heavy bloom and again when the pods are starting to form.
Pests and diseases	Aphids, leafhoppers, Mexican beetles, mites, damping off, and downy mildew are some common pests and diseases.

When to harvest	Depending on the variety, beans will be mature between 50 and 100 days. Check the specific varieties you choose to grow for more information. For bush varieties, harvest when the pod is still small, about 4 to 6 inches long. For fava beans, pick when the pods begin to drop with the weight of the seeds. Shell these and cook them like peas. Runner or pole beans are harvested when the pod is 6 to 10 inches long and still flat. Dried varieties are harvested when the pod is fully mature.
How to harvest	When you pick the pods, gently tug the pod with one hand while holding the plant so as not to pull out the whole plant.
Storage	Fresh beans will last for only a week or so in the refrigerator. Beans can be blanched and then frozen and will keep in the freezer for several months. Dried beans will store for several years if harvested and dried properly.

Peas

Peas are a cool-weather vegetable. They do best when planted in the early spring; if you live in a climate that has mild winters, do a second planting in mid-August for a fall harvest. They can withstand a little frost. Peas like a rich, well-drained soil that is not too high in nitrogen. They like organic matter, so mix in several inches of compost or aged animal manure when preparing the garden bed.

Peas

ESSENTIAL

Using slender tree branches to support your pea plants as they grow adds a decorative touch to your garden. Stick several branches firmly into the ground in a circle, leaning them inward toward each other. Plant six seeds around the base of each branch. For best support, the branches should be approximately five feet high with one foot stuck into the ground.

There are three different types of peas. Shelling peas are grown for the seeds. Snow peas have a flat edible pod and are often used in stir-fries. Snap peas have an edible pod and seeds that are eaten together. There are several varieties within each of these types of peas. Some peas will need to be staked; snow peas and snap peas can grow up to five feet high.

Peas need moisture to germinate, and they often germinate faster if the seed is soaked overnight. Because peas are planted in the spring, it is important that the seed and plants do not get waterlogged, or they will most likely rot.

▼ QUICK TIPS FOR GROWING PEAS

Family name	Papilionaceae (pea and bean family).
Edible parts	Pods and seeds.
Location	Partial shade.
Best soil	Light, sandy, loamy soil, not too rich in nitrogen; pH 5.5–6.8.
When to plant	Requires moderate temperatures. Direct seed in early spring as soon as your soil can be worked for a early summer harvest. For a fall harvest, plant in mid-August.
How to plant	Sow seeds 1 to 2 inches deep, 1 inch apart in rows 18 to 24 inches apart.
How much to plant	50 to 100 feet per person.
Companion plants	For a positive effect plant with carrots, corn, cucumbers, eggplants, lettuce, radishes, and spinach. Plants that will have a negative effect are tomatoes, turnips, and rutabagas.
Weeding	Keep well weeded, especially while the plants are young.
Watering	Peas require regular watering.
Care	Put in stakes at the time of planting. They do not do well in the heat, so they may need some shelter once the warm weather comes.
Fertilizing	Fertilize with fish fertilizer or compost tea after the first heavy bloom and again once the pods start to form.
Pests and diseases	Use crop rotation to prevent pest and diseases. Aphids, cucumber beetles, and powdery mildew can cause problems.
When to harvest	Depending on the variety, peas will usually mature in 55 to 70 days. Pods need to be picked every few days so the plant knows to produce more. If the pods are not picked, the plant will stop producing. Shelling peas: harvest when pods are full, usually at about 2 to 3 inches long. Snow peas: harvest when the pods are still flat and about 3 inches long. Snap peas: harvest when pods are full and about 2 to 3 inches long.
How to harvest	Gently pull the pod from the plant.
Storage	Fresh peas will store in the refrigerator for up to 1 week. Peas can be frozen and kept in the freezer for several months. They can be dried and used for future plantings.

Artichokes

The globe artichoke is easy to grow, is relatively disease free, and can make a stunning addition to any garden. It grows rapidly and can grow up to six feet tall and just as wide. It is a cool-season perennial vegetable that will grow vigorously and produce for four to five years. Just a few plants will produce enough artichokes for a small family.

The globe artichoke is known as an exotic plant, and it's not a common vegetable for most home gardeners. However, it is definitely worth growing, especially if you are looking to plant something new. This stately plant has gray-green leaves and produces flower buds that resemble elongated pinecones. The cones are green and layered with edible bracts, but the heart of the cone is the true delicacy. If the plant is left to mature, a large bud opens to reveal a purple thistle flower. This flower can be dried and is often used in floral arrangements.

FACT

To cook an artichoke, cut the stem to one inch and snip off the leaf tips. To prevent discoloring, dip the cut edge of the leaves in lemon juice. After steaming or boiling for twenty minutes, test to see if they are soft by gently pulling out the center petal. If it pulls out easily, the artichoke is done.

Globe artichokes will produce some buds the first year but are best harvested in the second or third year after planting when they are producing between twelve to thirty buds on each plant. This is also about the time when they are becoming crowded and need to be divided. They require a cool period before they can flower but are sensitive to the cold and may only be grown as annuals if you live in a cold northern climate. Even if you live in a milder climate, it is best to cut the plants back to about six inches above the ground and protect the roots from freezing by using thick mulch.

▼ **QUICK TIPS FOR GROWING ARTICHOKES**

Family name	Asteraceae or Compositae. (aster, daisy, or sunflower family).
Edible parts	Flower bud, leaves (bracts), and the heart (base of the bud).
Location	Full sun, requiring a minimum of ten hours of sunlight.
Best soil	Rich, well-drained; pH 6.0.
When to plant	Start seeds indoors in January or early February and transplant them out 2 weeks after the last frost for your area.
How to plant	They can be started from seeds or root division. If you start them from seed, put them in individual pots so they can be transplanted with very little root disturbance. Space them 4 to 6 feet apart in rows 6 to 8 feet apart. Artichoke plants will need to be divided every 3 to 4 years.
How much to plant	1 or 2 plants per person
Companion plants	For positive results, grow this vegetable near your brassicas.
Weeding	Keep well weeded.
Watering	Water regularly during the growing season.
Care	In cooler climates, in late October cut the plant to about 6 inches from the ground and heavily mulch to protect the roots from freezing.
Fertilizing	Fertilize with liquid seaweed just before the buds start to form.
Pests and diseases	Common pests include aphids on the underside of leaves, slugs, and snails.
When to harvest	It can take between 85 and 150 days for artichokes to mature. Cut buds when they are 2 to 4 inches in diameter before the leaves or bracts start to open.
How to harvest	Cut 1½ inches below the base of the bud.
Storage	Store artichokes unwashed and dry in sealed plastic bags in the refrigerator. They will keep for up to 2 weeks.

Sun Chokes

Sun chokes, often known as Jerusalem artichokes, are not related to the globe artichoke in any way. The "Jerusalem" tag came from a misunderstanding of the Italian word *girasole*, meaning "sunflower." The term artichoke comes from an Arabic word meaning "thistle," which relates to the plant's appearance. It is a perennial vegetable that belongs to the sunflower family. The underground tuber is the part that is harvested and eaten.

Sun chokes will grow in any kind of soil and often grow quickly and prolifically. Plant tubers in the spring, giving them a large area to grow (they can grow up to 6 feet tall). They produce yellow flowers a little smaller in size than the common sunflower. When the leaves die back in the fall, the tubers can be harvested. They will overwinter in the ground and will taste sweeter after a frost. Sun chokes are a low-calorie alternative to potatoes.

▼ **QUICK TIPS FOR GROWING SUN CHOKES**

Family name	Asteraceae (aster, daisy, or sunflower family).
Edible parts	Tubers.
Location	Full sun.
Best soil	Will grow in any soil condition as long as it is well drained.
When to plant	Plant in early spring.
How to plant	Plant whole tuber or cut into pieces each with 1 or 2 eyes in each piece. Plant 4 inches deep, 24 inches apart, in rows 36 inches apart. Tubers left in the ground will produce a new crop each year.
How much to plant	5 to 15 feet per person.
Companion plants	For positive effects, plant near corn.
Weeding	Weed regularly.
Watering	Keep soil moist.
Fertilizing	No extra fertilization is needed if your soil is fertile.
Pests and diseases	Mites, cutworms, and root rot fungi can affect the tubers if soil is too wet.
When to harvest	In the fall, tubers taste sweeter after a frost. If you live in a cold climate, harvest before the ground freezes.
How to harvest	Dig up the tubers.
Storage	In mild climates, sun chokes can remain in the ground for most of the winter and harvested for fresh eating. If you need to harvest them, they can be stored in damp peat in a root cellar. They can be stored in airtight containers in the refrigerator for 3 to 4 weeks.

Asparagus

Asparagus is another perennial vegetable. Plant them in a permanent area; once planted, they will produce new shoots each spring and will do so for fifteen to twenty years without too much work on your part. It is best to buy one-year-old crowns or rhizomes as they take three years to grow from seed to harvest. In the first year of planting, resist cutting any of the spears so they can leaf out. The feathery foliage will nourish the roots, which in turn will give you more spears in the second year. In the second year, you can harvest the first few spears, but stop harvesting once the spears start to look spindly or have a diameter less than ¼ inch. In the third and following years, you will be able to harvest over a much longer season.

When preparing an asparagus bed, dig in generous amounts of compost or aged animal manure. This can be done by digging a trench one foot deep in your bed and then filling it with the three to four inches of organic material. Mix this with the existing soil. Lay the crowns in the trench and cover them with two inches of soil, but do not cover the tips of the shoots. As the plant grows, you can add more soil around the plant.

e! ALERT

When planting your garden, designate a specific area for your perennial vegetables. These vegetables do best if they are not disturbed by digging or tilling of the soil. A good spot for your perennial vegetables is around the edge of your garden site, where the plants can be left to grow without any disruption.

In the fall, cut back the fernlike foliage of the asparagus plant. This is also a great time to mulch the bed with aged animal manure to add nutrients to the soil as it decomposes over the winter. Leaves or straw can be added on top for more protection from the cold, but avoid mulching with sawdust, which is often too acidic for the plant.

▼ **QUICK TIPS FOR GROWING ASPARAGUS**

Family name	Asparagaceae (lily family).
Edible parts	Young shoots called *spears*.
Location	Full sun.
Best soil	Fertile, well-drained, sandy to clay loam soil; pH 6.0–6.7.
When to plant	Set out plants in early spring when any danger of frost is passed.
How to plant	Set out crowns 6 to 8 inches deep, 18 inches apart in rows spaced 3 to 5 feet apart. Cover the crown with 2 inches of soil and keep adding more soil as the plant grows.
How much to plant	10 plants per person.
Companion plants	There are no plants that have a positive effect, but avoid planting onions near your asparagus, as they can have a negative effect.
Weeding	Weed regularly.
Watering	Keep well watered.
Care	Cut back the foliage in the fall once it turns brown.

▼ **QUICK TIPS FOR GROWING ASPARAGUS—*continued***

Fertilizing	Apply a high-nitrogen fertilizer twice a year, once when the spears emerge and again at the end of harvest. If you have a soil that has a pH lower than 6.0, apply lime in the spring as well.
Pests and diseases	Aphids and asparagus beetles.
When to harvest	Do not harvest the first year of planting. From the second year onward, harvest the spears when they are about the thickness of the diameter of a pencil and 6 to 8 inches high. Stop harvesting once the spears are thinner than the diameter of a pencil.
How to harvest	Cut the spear ½ inch below the soil. This will help to prevent any diseases.
Storage	Asparagus is best eaten fresh. It will stay in the refrigerator for about a week.

CHAPTER 11

The Root Veggies

Root vegetables are grown for their edible roots. The veggies in this chapter are all easy to grow and have similar growing needs and soil conditions. They need a well-prepared garden bed with a light soil to grow their best. Here you'll find easy tips on how to grow some common root vegetables including beets, carrots, potatoes, radishes, and rutabagas. We will also discuss growing garlic, leeks, and onions, which are grown mainly for their roots but have some distinctive characteristics of their own.

Beets

Beets are a love or hate vegetable; either you love them or you have no desire to eat them at all. They are great addition to any home garden because they are easy to grow, have a long harvest, take up a small amount of space in your garden, and can be stored. They have more than one edible part and can be eaten raw or cooked, so they are a very versatile vegetable. The young leaves are used with other baby greens in popular salad mixes. The mature leaves can be steamed for a nutritious side dish to add to any meal. The roots can be harvested as sweet and tender baby beets or they can be left to grow to maturity to be harvested as you need them all summer and fall.

The many variety of beets give you more options than just a round red beet. You can buy seeds that will produce elongated roots, which have a milder taste. Beets can now be grown in a multitude of colors. There are white, yellow, orange, and striped varieties.

ALERT

Peeling beets can be messy and can stain your hands and cooking area, so leave the peel on. Once the beets are cooked, just plunge them into ice-cold water and the skins will just slip off. If you do get stains on your fingers, rub them with a fresh lemon and the red juice will easily wash off.

Beets like a fairly rich soil that is free of rocks and debris. Add in aged animal manure and lime if needed when preparing your garden bed. Make sure your bed is well prepared with at least a foot of loose tilled soil for the roots to grow. Remove any lumps, rocks, or sticks from the soil so they don't impede the growth of the root. Beets are usually direct seeded to your garden bed; however, they are slow to germinate, so mark the bed where they are planted. The seed can produce more than one plant; they will need to be thinned so there is only one plant for every three to four inches of garden soil as the seedlings start to grow.

▼ **QUICK TIPS FOR GROWING BEETS**

Botanical name	Chenopodiaceae (goose foot family).
Edible parts	Roots and tops.
Location	Sunny, open area.
Best soil	Fertile, well-drained soil, clean bed; pH 6.0–6.8.
When to plant	Sow April to mid-July for a continuous harvest.
How to plant	Sow seeds ½ inch deep and 1 inch apart in rows spaced 16 to 24 inches apart. Keep the soil moist until seeds have germinated; this can take from 14 to 21 days, so you need to be patient. Once the seedlings are a couple inches high, thin them so there is only 1 plant for every 3 inches of garden soil.
How much to plant	10 to 20 feet per person.
Companion plants	Cabbage has a positive effect on beets, so try to plant them near each other. Avoid planting beets near beans, because they can have a negative effect.
Weeding	Keep well weeded, especially when plants are small.
Watering	The soil needs to be kept moist when seeds are first planted. Once plants have sprouted, water regularly. If you are using an overhead sprinkler, make sure you leave it on long enough for the water to penetrate several inches into the soil in order to reach the roots.
Fertilizing	Dig in compost or aged animal manure and a balanced fertilizer when preparing the beds.
Pests and diseases	Leaf miners, beet web worms, flea beetles, wireworms, and leaf spot can affect your beet plants.
When to harvest	Beets mature in 45 to 65 days. You can start cutting the young leaves for salad when they are about 3 inches high. Start harvesting the roots once they reach the size of a golf ball. Harvest all your beets before the first frost in the fall.
How to harvest	Cut the leaves individually or harvest the whole plant by gently tugging it from the ground. Larger beets may require a garden fork to gently loosen the surrounding soil before you pull them out.
Storage	To store, cut off the greens, leaving 2 to 3 inches of stem. The greens can be stored separately for up to a week in a plastic bag in the refrigerator. The roots can be placed in a plastic bag and will keep in the refrigerator for up to 3 weeks. If you have a large amount to store, they can be packed in a box filled with peat moss and stored in a root cellar.

Carrots

Carrots are one of the most popular vegetables in the world. Pulling a baby carrot from the garden, wiping off a little dirt, and biting into it is an experience everyone should have. There is nothing better than a freshly picked carrot! Carrots are great to grow if you have children around because they grow fairly quickly and can be picked at any size—and children love to pull them out of the ground.

The time-consuming part of growing carrots is the bed preparation. Carrots need a deep, loose sandy soil that is free of debris to grow their best. They are a great vegetable to grow in raised beds because the soil texture is often lighter than in a regular garden bed. If you have a heavy soil, it is important to dig in compost or aged animal manure to lighten the soil; however, if the soil is too fertile the carrots may get hairy and misshapen and they may not taste as good. It can take a few years to get your soil to the proper consistency to grow fabulous carrots. If there are any obstructions in the soil, the carrot will grow around them, producing oddly shaped roots. It is important to take the time to break up any lumps of soil and pick out rocks that are larger than very small pebbles before planting your carrot seeds.

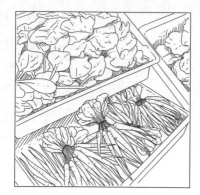

Carrots

QUESTION

Does eating carrots really help your eyesight?
Carrots are rich in phytonutrients called *carotenoids*, which are good for your eyesight, especially for seeing in poor light. It is best to eat carrots juiced or cooked because this makes the nutrients more available for the body to absorb.

Carrots are a cool-season crop and are best planted in the early spring to be harvested in the summer. If you live in an area where you get mild winters, plant another crop in late summer for a fall harvest. The carrot has its best flavor when grown in the full sun with cool nights. Carrots are direct seeded and need to be kept moist in order to germinate, so you may have to water the garden bed two to three times a day until they germinate. Water carefully so as not to wash the seeds away. It is important to keep the soil moistened because the seeds may not be able to break through the hard and crusty soil if the soil dries out.

To harvest large carrots so they do not break off, gently push the carrot downward into the round and then pull it upward. This breaks the roots and makes it easier to pull up.

▼ **QUICK TIPS FOR GROWING CARROTS**

Family name	Umbelliferae or Apiaceae (carrot, celery, or parsley family).
Edible parts	Roots.
Location	Sunny location.
Best soil	Fertile, sandy, loamy soil, free of debris; pH 5.5–6.8.
When to plant	Sow direct starting in April up to mid-July. Plant a row every few weeks so you will be able to eat carrots all season long.
How to plant	Sow seeds ¼ inch deep, ½ inch apart, in rows spaced 12 to 24 inches apart. Seeds can take from 7 to 21 days to germinate and need to be kept moist until then. Once they are a few inches tall, thin them so plants are 2 to 4 inches apart.
How much to plant	25 to 30 feet per person each season.
Companion plants	For a positive effect, plant with beans, leeks, onions, peas, and radishes.
Weeding	Carrots need to be kept free of weeds in order to grow well.
Watering	Water regularly, preferably with a drip irrigation system; carrots grow best if the leaves are not wet.
Fertilizing	It is best to add compost or manure in the fall to the area where you will be growing your carrots the following spring.
Pests and diseases	Carrot flies, aphids, leafhoppers, and nematodes are some common pests that affect carrots.
When to harvest	Carrots will mature in 30 to 80 days, depending on whether you want to harvest baby carrots or fully mature ones. You can start harvesting carrots once they are about the size of your finger.
How to harvest	Gently pull the carrot out of the ground. For mature carrots, push them gently downward to break the roots, then pull them out. This will prevent them from breaking off under ground.
Storage	When storing carrots, remove the tops. They will keep in a plastic bag in the refrigerator for several weeks or they can be frozen or canned. If you have a large amount, leave them in the ground covered with several inches of mulch and harvest as you need them.

Potatoes

Potatoes are the most used vegetable in the world. They are nutritious, versatile, easy to grow, and ideal for storage. Potatoes are closely related to tomatoes; like tomato plants, they produce sprawling and bushy vines above ground. However, potatoes produce tubers under ground. They need a long growing season—approximately four months with continuous cool weather for best production. When preparing your potato bed, make sure the soil is well tilled with compost or aged animal manure added to it. Potatoes need a more acidic soil, so never lime in the area where they will be planted.

Potatoes

Potatoes are planted as early as you can get into your garden. They are grown from stem cuttings, which are also called *seed pieces* or *seed eyes*. When planting, you can cut the seed potato into pieces; just make sure each section has at least three eyes. The potato plant can take up a lot of room and several plants will be needed for a small family to eat them fresh. You'll want even more if you want to store them for use during the winter months.

ALERT

If you like your baked potatoes crispy, do not wrap them in tinfoil when you bake them. The tinfoil will cause the potatoes to steam and become soft. Instead, brush the skin with some oil just before baking and bake at 500°F, not the usual 350°F.

The potato seed does not need much water until it has sprouted above ground. After the vine starts to grow, keep mounding soil up against the new growth; this is called *hilling*. This allows the tuber to grow without being exposed to the sun; too much sun exposure will cause the potato to turn green. You can harvest young potatoes after the plant has flowered by digging around the base of the plant with your hands. The tubers are mature and ready to be harvested once the vine has turned brown and died back.

▼ **QUICK TIPS FOR GROWING POTATOES**

Family name	Solanaceae (nightshade family).
Edible parts	Tubers.
Location	Sunny area.
Best soil	Fertile, slightly acidic, sandy loam soil, moist but well drained; pH 4.8–6.0.
When to plant	Seed them as soon as you can work your garden bed in the spring; potatoes thrive in cool weather.
How to plant	Cut seed potatoes into pieces, making sure each piece has at least 3 eyes. Plant 4 inches deep, 12 to 16 inches apart, in rows spaced 36 to 48 inches apart.
How much to plant	30 to 50 feet per person.
Companion plants	For positive effects, plant with beans, cabbage, corn, lettuce, onions, marigolds, and radish. Do not plant near pumpkins or tomatoes, which can both have a negative effect on your potato plants.
Weeding	Keep well weeded when the plant is small.
Watering	Water regularly from the time the vine first emerges above ground until the plant flowers. After flowering, the plant needs less water and rainfall is usually sufficient if the plants are mulched.
Care	Keep mounding (hilling) soil up around the vine as it grows; this helps keep the potatoes covered.
Fertilizing	Fertilize with compost tea once the flowers start to emerge.
Pests and diseases	Wireworms, Colorado beetles, scab, aphids, and flea beetles are some common pests and diseases.
When to harvest	Potatoes mature 90 to 120 days after being planted. New or small potatoes can be harvested once the plant has flowered. When the vine turns brown and dies back, the tubers are fully mature.
How to harvest	Harvest in the morning when the temperature is cool. For new potatoes, you can just dig around under the vine and pull out a few potatoes for your dinner. Once the vine has died back, pull the vine out and gently use a garden fork to dig up the larger tubers.
Storage	Potatoes are a great vegetable for storing and will keep for several months if stored properly. Make sure they are dry before storing them in a cool, dark area.

Radishes

Radishes are one of the fastest growing veggies. If they have fertile soil and lots of water you can be picking fresh radishes within thirty days after planting the seed. They love the cool weather in early spring. It is best to plant a row every few weeks so that you have a continuous harvest all spring long.

Radishes will grow well in raised beds and containers if you make sure they are well watered.

The most common radish is small, round, and red with a white inside. There many radish varieties to choose from in many different colors; some even form roots that resemble the shape of a carrot, miniature cucumber, or turnip. This is a great vegetable for children to grow because it grows quickly, is bright colored, and can be easily picked.

▼ **QUICK TIPS FOR GROWING RADISHES**

Family name	Brassicaceae (mustard family).
Edible parts	Roots.
Location	Sunny area.
Best soil	Fertile, well-drained, light, sandy loam soil; pH 5.5–6.8.
When to plant	Cool-season. Plant starting in April and every few weeks until mid-June.
How to plant	Sow seeds ½ inch deep, 2 inches apart, in rows spaced 12 to 16 inches apart.
How much to plant	15 to 25 feet per person each season.
Companion plants	For a positive effect, plant with beans, cabbage, cauliflower, cucumbers, lettuce, and peas. Squash and tomatoes have a negative effect, so avoid planting your radishes near them.
Weeding	Keep well weeded.
Watering	Keep the soil moist; radishes require lots of water so they do not become bitter and spicy tasting.
Fertilizing	It is best to add in compost or aged animal manure when preparing the beds before planting.
Pests and diseases	Cabbage root maggots and flea beetles are common pests.
When to harvest	Radishes mature 22 to 70 days after planting. Start harvesting when the root is ½ inch in diameter.
How to harvest	Gently pull the root out of the ground.
Storage	Radishes will keep in the refrigerator for about 1 week.

Rutabagas and Turnips

The rutabaga and turnip are closely related cousins. They are both cool-season crops, and they like fertile, well-drained soil that is well tilled so the roots have a lot of space to grow. The young greens make a great addition to a salad mix or can be steamed as a healthy green vegetable. They are filled with calcium and other nutrients. The roots from both vegetables can be eaten raw but are most often cooked in soups or stews or mashed as a side dish.

The rutabaga has large yellow roots and is often called a *winter turnip* or *Swedes*. The young leaves can be eaten, but they get coarse once they mature. The rutabaga is a hardy, slow-growing root vegetable that is normally planted in early to midsummer and harvested in the fall. They are hardy enough to remain in the garden all winter and can be harvested as you need them. They need a fair amount of space because the roots can grow quite large, weighing two to three pounds each.

ESSENTIAL

A well-tilled garden bed is essential to growing root crops. If you are starting a new garden, use a rotary tiller to till the area. If you are preparing beds in an existing garden, you can often simply loosen the soil with a spade, garden fork, or hoe. Root crops need a loose soil with a depth of eight to twelve inches.

The turnip has a small, white, round root with a purple skin. It grows like a large radish. The greens can be eaten young or as mature leaves; turnips are sometime grown just for the leaves. Turnip seeds are planted in early spring and are best harvested before hot weather arrives. They can be grown during the fall as well but need more protection from the frost than the rutabaga does. Turnips are not a fussy vegetable and will grow in most soil conditions.

▼ QUICK TIPS FOR GROWING RUTABAGAS AND TURNIPS

Family name	Brassicaceae (mustard family).
Edible parts	Roots and leaves.
Location	Sunny area
Best soil	Fertile; pH 5.5–6.8.
When to plant	Rutabaga: Plant in midsummer for a fall harvest. Turnip: Plant in early spring for an early summer harvest.
How to plant	Rutabagas: Sow seeds ½ inch deep, 4 to 6 inches apart in rows spaced 24 to 36 inches apart. Thin to 1 plant every 12 inches. Turnips: Sow seeds ½ inch deep, 2 to 4 inches apart in rows spaced 18 to 36 inches apart. Thin to 1 plant every 6 to 8 inches.
How much to plant	10 to 20 feet per person.

Companion plants	For a positive effect, plant with peas.
Weeding	Keep well weeded.
Watering	Keep soil moist until seeds have germinated. Water regularly after sprouts appear. If you use an overhead sprinkler, make sure it is long enough to moisten the soil several inches deep to ensure the water reaches the plant roots.
Fertilizing	It is best to add in compost or aged animal manure when preparing the beds before planting.
Pests and diseases	Armyworms, cabbage root maggots, and flea beetles are some common pests that can affect your rutabagas and turnips.
When to harvest	Rutabagas will mature in 90 to 100 days; harvest when the roots reach about 3 inches in diameter. Greens can be harvested when young. Turnips will mature in 30 to 60 days; harvest when roots are about 2 inches in diameter. Start harvesting greens once they are about 3 inches high.
How to harvest	Young leaves can be cut for using in salads; however, if you want the root to mature, do not cut off all the leaves. Gently pull the roots from the ground. If the larger rutabagas are hard to pull out, push downward on them to break the roots. This should make them easy to pull out.
Storage	Both will store for a long period of time if kept in a cool, dark place.

Garlic

Garlic is a cool-season crop grown mainly for its bulb, although the flower stem is also edible and very tasty. Garlic is a fairly hardy vegetable. It needs a sunny, well-drained area. Garlic is usually planted in the fall, either in October or early November at the latest, and is harvested the following June.

Choose the biggest cloves to plant and mulch the beds after they are planted. Garlic will grow slowly over the winter and will shoot up quickly once the days start to get longer in January and February. In the spring, keep the plants well weeded and give them more mulch and regular watering if you do not get any rain. In early spring, the garlic plants will produce

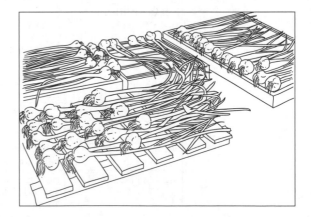

Garlic

flower stalks, which are called *garlic scapes*. They can be eaten like garlic cloves. Removing the stem before it fully flowers will allow the plant to put more energy into producing a larger bulb.

FACT

Garlic has been renowned for its powerful medicinal qualities for centuries. Hieroglyphs of garlic were engraved on the Great Pyramid of Giza to protect the builders. Doctors in ancient Greece and Rome believed garlic was a cure-all for many ailments and diseases. Today, people consume garlic and garlic supplements for their antioxidants.

The garlic bulbs are ready to be harvested once the garlic tops start to turn brown and die back. When harvesting your garlic, use a garden fork to loosen the soil so the bulbs do not break off. Garlic needs to be dried in order for it to keep properly; leave the bulbs in the sun to cure for up to three weeks. Protect them from the rain by covering them or bringing them indoors in bad weather.

▼ QUICK TIPS FOR GROWING GARLIC

Family name	Alliaceae (onion family).
Edible parts	Bulb (cloves) and flower stem.
Location	Sunny, dry area.
Best soil	Rich, well drained; pH 6.0–6.8.
When to plant	Plant bulbs in the fall if you live in a warmer climate or in the early spring if you live in an extremely cold climate where the ground freezes in early fall.
How to plant	Set out cloves of garlic 2 inches deep, 6 to 8 inches apart in rows spaced 16 to 24 inches apart. Plant the cloves with the pointed end up.
How much to plant	5 to 10 feet per person.
Companion plants	For a positive effect, plant near carrots and tomatoes. Beans, peas, and strawberries can have a negative effect, so avoid planting them near garlic.
Weeding	Keep well weeded.
Watering	Needs regular watering in the spring if there is very little rainfall.
Care	Mulch with straw or hay in the fall and again in the spring when the plants are 1 foot high to prevent weeds and keep the soil from drying out.

▼ **QUICK TIPS FOR GROWING GARLIC—*continued***

Fertilizing	Fertilize with compost tea or fish fertilizer after the flower stalks have started to form.
Pests and diseases	Aphids and thrips can be a problem. Using crop rotation will prevent most pests and disease.
When to harvest	Garlic takes 6 to 10 months to fully mature. When the tops start to turn brown and die back, garlic is ready to be harvested.
How to harvest	Loosen the soil around your plants with a garden fork and then gently pull out the bulbs, trying to keep the stem and bulb intact. The bulb will dry better if it is not broken off.
Storage	If dried and stored properly, garlic will keep for several months. Once cured in the sun for a few weeks, clean off any dirt remaining on the bulb and store it in a paper bag or box in a cool, dry storage area. Garlic can be braided and hung in a cool, dark area.

Leeks

Leeks, like garlic, are part of the onion family and therefore require similar growing conditions—rich soil, a sunny area, and cool temperatures. Leeks are a biennial vegetable, which means they do not produce seeds until the second year of growth. If you are planning to save your leek seeds, this is something you will need to take into consideration.

Leeks

Leeks can take four to eight months to grow to prime size, which is usually about 1½ inches in diameter. They will produce tender young plants in the first year, but growing them into the second year will give you a longer harvest. Plant them on the edge of your garden or mixed in with your asparagus patch so they are not disturbed. Keep mounding the soil up around the plant as it grows to keep the bottom part of the leek a nice white color.

When harvesting your leeks, gently lift them from the ground using a garden fork. If you are going to leave them in your garden over the winter, make sure they are mounded with soil and mulched with a good covering of chopped leaves or straw. The following spring, you will have a super early vegetable to harvest and enjoy. To prepare leeks for cooking, wash them thoroughly to get the soil out from between the leaves.

FACT

The allium group of vegetables, including garlic, leeks, and onions, has an internal clock. The duration of the light and darkness determines when they mature. They stop growing when the days get shorter and start growing again when the days start to get longer.

▼ QUICK TIPS FOR GROWING LEEKS

Family name	Alliaceae (onion family).
Edible parts	Stems.
Location	Sunny area.
Best soil	Rich, loamy soil, free of debris and well drained; pH 6.0–6.8.
When to plant	Requires cool temperatures. Sow indoors in March. Transplant to a permanent bed when they are the size of a pencil.
How to plant	Sow seeds ¼ inch deep in potting soil. Set out transplants every 4 to 6 inches in rows spaced 12 to 24 inches apart. Plant in furrows about 5 inches deep and then mound the soil around the plant as it grows.
How much to plant	10 feet per person.
Companion plants	For a positive effect, plant near asparagus, carrots, and celery. Beans, peas, and strawberries can have a negative effect, so avoid planting them near leeks.
Weeding	Keep well weeded.
Watering	An abundance of water is needed in the early stages of growth; less is needed when the plants are maturing.
Care	Mound soil around the plant to keep the bottom part of the stem white.
Fertilizing	Fertilize with compost tea or fish fertilizer when the plant is about 12 inches high.
Pests and diseases	Very few pests or diseases will affect leeks, but using crop rotation will help prevent problems.
When to harvest	You can start harvesting stalks once they are about 1 inch in diameter and continue throughout the winter months.
How to harvest	Gently loosen the soil around the plant with a garden fork and then pull the stalk.
Storage	They will store for a few weeks in an airtight plastic bag in the refrigerator. It is best to leave them in the ground covered with mulch and harvest as you need them.

Onions

Anyone who cooks for their family knows the onion is a common ingredient in many entrée recipes. Onions can be temperamental vegetables to grow. They like cool temperatures when they first start growing and then need heat in order to produce their bulbs. They require a rich, well-drained soil that is free of debris. Onions are most commonly planted in the spring and harvested in the fall, but they can be planted in the fall and harvested early in the spring in areas with mild winters.

Red onion

There are three ways of starting onions: by seed, with sets, or with transplants. Planting by seed is the slowest way; these need to be started as early as possible and they need ten to twelve weeks to grow before they can be put into your garden. Sets are actually miniature, dormant onions that are raised for propagation. Sets will produce green onions within three or four weeks but will often bolt in warm weather before they produce a nice-sized bulb. They can be planted in the fall and will be less likely to bolt in the cooler temperatures. Transplants are less likely than sets to bolt once the weather turns warm. You can grow you own transplants from seed or purchase them at a garden center in the spring.

QUESTION

How do I peel an onion without crying?
There are two ways to prevent tears. The first is to put a piece of bread on the point of your knife while cutting the onion. The bread will absorb some of the onion smell. The second way is to peel the onion under running water before you start chopping it.

Once the tops start to turn brown, your onions are nearing maturity. When the tops start to fall over, take a garden rake and gently bend all the browning tops over so they all are lying down. Leave them this way for a few weeks and then start to pull onions as you need them. If the season is coming to an end and all of your onions need to be pulled, make sure you allow them to dry so they will store well. You can place the onions on a newspaper or a screen or drape them over the edge of a pail with the green end hanging inside so they can dry. Leave the bulbs in sunny, dry spot for about ten days before storing them so they are thoroughly dry.

▼ QUICK TIPS FOR GROWING ONIONS

Family name	Alliaceae (onion family).
Edible parts	Bulbs and leaves.
Location	Sunny area.
Best soil	Rich, moist but well-drained light soil, free of debris; pH 5.6–6.5.
When to plant	For summer harvest, start seeds in January or February for transplanting in the early spring or place sets out in the spring. If you live in a mild climate, set out transplants or onion sets again in late summer for harvesting the following spring.
How to plant	Sow seeds ½ inch deep in pots indoors. Plant sets or set out transplants 4 to 6 inches apart in rows spaced 16 to 24 inches apart.
How much to plant	50 to 100 feet per person if you want to store them.
Companion plants	For a positive effect, plant with beets, cabbage, carrots, lettuce, potatoes, and tomatoes. Beans and peas have a negative effect, so avoid planting them near your onions.
Weeding	Keep well weeded.
Watering	In the early stage of growth, onions need lots of water. Keep the soil moist. Stop watering once the leaves begin to turn brown.
Care	Onions like rich soil, so add in several inches of compost or aged animal manure when preparing the garden bed.
Fertilizing	Side dress with compost (place around the base of the plant) when the bulb first starts to swell and again when the leaves are about 1 foot tall.
Pests and diseases	Very few pests or diseases affect onions. Crop rotation is the best way to prevent them.
When to harvest	Once the leaves have turned brown and died back, the bulbs are ready to be harvested. When growing sets for green onions, harvest once the greens are about 12 inches tall.
How to harvest	Gently loosen soil around the plant and then pull out the bulb.
Storage	Onions will store for several months if dried properly. Once the onions are harvested, lay them on a newspaper or a mesh screen in a sunny, dry area. Let them dry for seven to ten days, turning them a few times each day. Make sure they are protected from any moisture or dampness.

CHAPTER 12

Heat-Loving Veggies

In this chapter you will learn tips on how to grow corn, cucumbers, eggplants, peppers, squash, and tomatoes. These heat-loving veggies are mainly known as semi-tropical vegetables and need a lot of heat and warm soil to grow well. Soil temperatures must be warm for the seeds to germinate and the plants cannot handle any cold weather, especially during the seedling stage. In northern climates, these vegetables usually need to be started indoors in early spring and then transplanted out once the weather is warm enough.

Corn

Freshly picked corn dropped into a pot of boiling water is sweeter than anything you can buy in the supermarket because the sugar within the kernels has not yet turned to starch. Corn is a vegetable that can be planted in a newly cultivated garden area. It is hardy and tough, giving it the ability to grow and survive where many other vegetables would not. Corn does take up a fair amount of garden space, but it is definitely worth finding a place for it in your backyard garden.

There are many different varieties of corn. For any of them to be successful, they need lots of space, warm weather, fertile soil, and water. Each corn stalk will produce one or two cobs, so you need a large garden area to plant your corn in order to get a good quantity of cobs. Corn likes a rich, warm soil (above 50°F) and needs at least eight hours of sunlight a day to germinate. It is best planted on the northern side of your garden so it does not block the sun from reaching your other vegetables.

FACT

To tell if your corn on the cob is ready to be harvested, pull off some of the husk and then prick the kernels with your fingernail. If the juice looks like milk, the corn is ready to be picked and enjoyed!

Corn needs to be pollinated, meaning the male flowers from the tassels need to reach the female flowers, which is the silk on the ears. This is usually done by the wind. It is best to plant corn in blocks; that way, the corn pollen from the tassels can easily spread to other plants. When choosing your varieties, make sure they cannot cross-pollinate. It is best to choose only one variety of corn if you have a small garden. If you have a larger garden and choose to grow different varieties, make sure there is some distance between each variety or choose to plant varieties that will mature at different times.

▼ **QUICK TIPS FOR GROWING CORN**

Botanical name	Poaceae (grass family).
Edible parts	Seeds (kernels).
Location	Sunny area.
Best soil	Fertile, well-drained loamy soil; pH 5.8–6.8.
When to plant	Plant in the spring once the soil temperature is at least 50°F. In southern areas, corn can be planted in the fall as well.
How to plant	Corn is usually planted from seeds, although it can be transplanted as well if you have a very short growing season. Sow seeds 1 inch deep, 4 to 6 inches apart in rows of 30 to 36 inches apart. Plant at least 2 rows of corn so the plants will pollinate each other.
How much to plant	50 to 100 feet per person if you are planning to freeze some.
Companion plants	Plant with beans, peas, and squash. There are no plants that have a negative effect on corn.
Weeding	Keep well weeded until the plants are knee high; then weed occasionally.
Watering	Corn needs lots of moisture, so water regularly. If you are sprinkling, make sure the water reaches the roots. Do not let the soil dry out, especially when the ears start to form their silk.
Fertilizing	Apply a high-nitrogen fertilizer around the base of the plants once they have reached 8 to 10 inches high and again when the first silk appears.
Pests and diseases	Use a four-year rotation and compost stalks rather than leaving them on the ground to prevent disease. Common pests include aphids, armyworms, corn borers, flea beetles, and corn earworms.
When to harvest	Corn can mature at between 60 and 100 days. The first sign your corn is ready is when the silk on the ears starts to turn brown. You can then pull back the husk and gently prick the kernels; if they squirt a milky white juice, they are ready to be harvested.
How to harvest	Gently twist the ripe ears off the stalk.
Storage	It is best to eat corn when first harvested, as it is sweeter before the sugar turns to starch. Cobs will keep for a few days in the refrigerator and the kernels can be frozen and will keep for several months in the freezer.

Cucumbers

There are a wide variety of cucumbers to choose from. They are easy to grow, so cucumbers are a great choice for any gardener. They are a perfect vegetable for growing in containers. The three most common types of cucumbers are the long English varieties, which have an edible peel; the slicing varieties, which have a harder peel that is usually not eaten; and small cucumbers used for pickling. Cucumbers are a climbing vegetable plant; they do best if grown on a trellis. This allows air to circulate around the plant and light to reach the fruit, which will help to prevent pests and diseases. If the fruit is touching the ground, it will often rot before it matures.

Cucumber

When preparing your garden bed, add two to three inches of compost or aged animal manure, as this vegetable needs a fertile soil to grow its best. Cucumber seeds need a warm soil to germinate, so they are often started indoors and then transplanted out once the weather warms up. This is especially important if you live in a cooler climate. Cucumber plants grow quickly and can be harvested at various sizes depending on the variety. The fruit needs to be picked regularly so more will grow.

QUESTION

Why do my cucumbers taste bitter?
To grow tasty, nonbitter cucumbers, you need to have a soil that is not too acidic, so add lime to your garden bed in the spring. Inconsistent watering or large temperature differences can stress the plant, which can also cause the bitter taste. To avoid this, water regularly and protect the plant from the cold.

Cucumbers need to be pollinated, so it is important to know if the variety you choose is a hybrid or standard. Standard varieties have both male and female flowers on the same vine; insects or the wind will do the pollinating for you. The male flower comes out first and looks like a miniature cucumber. The female flower is identified by a swollen ovary just behind the male flower. Hybrid varieties have separate female and male plants and will need to be pollinated by hand. If you have saved cucumber seeds from the past or a friend has given them to you and you are not sure of the variety, check the plant as it grows to see what kind of flowers it is producing. If there is only a male or female flower, no fruit will form. Go to your garden center and purchase another plant that will pollinate the first one for you.

▼ **QUICK TIPS FOR GROWING CUCUMBERS**

Family name	Cucurbitaceae (gourd family).
Edible parts	Fruit.
Location	Cucumbers are great veggies for growing in greenhouses or containers.
Best soil	Rich, warm, well-drained, sandy soil; pH 5.5–6.8
When to plant	Plant in the spring once the soil temperature reaches 60°F.
How to plant	Can be direct seeded or transplanted. Sow seeds 1 inch deep 6 inches apart, in rows 4 to 6 feet apart. This is the best way if you are trellising the cucumber plant.
How much to plant	5 to 20 feet per person depending on whether you are going to be pickling any of them.
Companion plants	Plant with beans, broccoli, cabbage, lettuce, peas, radishes, and tomatoes. Sage can have a negative effect on cucumber plants, so keep them apart.
Weeding	Keep well weeded, especially when the plants are small.
Watering	Cucumbers need lots of water. Deep watering at the roots is better than using a sprinkler. If the weather is warm, water the plants every second day, especially if they are growing in a greenhouse or container.
Care	Cucumbers are best grown on a trellis so the plant gets good air circulation and light.
Fertilizing	Fertilize with manure tea or fish fertilizer 1 week after the plant blooms and then again 3 weeks later.
Pests and diseases	Aphids, cucumber beetles, flea beetles, mites, squash bugs, downy mildew, and powdery mildew can all affect the cucumber plant. Make sure you do not compost diseased plants!
When to harvest	Harvest the fruit when it is 6 to 12 inches long; this may vary depending on the variety. The cucumber will keep longer if harvested in the early morning when it is cooler. Pick the fruit regularly so that new fruit will keep forming.
How to harvest	Cut the fruit from the plant rather than twisting or pulling it off, which can damage the plant.
Storage	Cucumbers are best wrapped in plastic and stored in the refrigerator. They will keep for up to 1 week.

Eggplants

Eggplants need hot weather and rich soil to grow their best. This vegetable is much more common in Europe than it is in North America; however, if you enjoy a great moussaka, try growing eggplants in your backyard or in a container on the patio. Eggplants are in the same family as tomatoes and peppers, so if you plant them in the same area it is easier to do your vegetable rotation.

The most common eggplant variety produces a large, purple, oval-shaped fruit. You can also find varieties that have yellow, green, and white colored fruit and others that form rounded or cylindrical fruit. These can all add color to your garden and are definitely fun to show off to your guests.

Eggplant

If you live in a cool climate, it is best to start your eggplants from seed indoors in early spring and then transplant them out when warmer weather arrives. Eggplants need full sun and lots of heat, so they are an ideal candidate for a greenhouse or a more sheltered but sunny spot in your garden. Each plant will produce between eight to ten fruits.

ESSENTIAL

Eggplant is a versatile fruit used in common dishes such as caponata, lasagna, and ratatouille. They absorb lots of moisture, either water or oil depending on how you prepare them. Soak them in a bowl of salty water and dry them on a paper towel before cooking with them so they will absorb less of the moisture and remain firmer.

▼ QUICK TIPS FOR GROWING EGGPLANTS

Family name	Solanaceae (nightshade family).
Edible parts	Fruit.
Location	Sunny and warm area.
Best soil	Fertile, well drained; pH 5.5–6.8
When to plant	Sow indoors in April and transplant approximately 10 weeks later in late May or early June
How to plant	Set out transplants 24 inches apart in rows 36 inches apart.
How much to plant	1 or 2 plants per person.
Companion plants	Plant with peas, thyme, and tarragon. There are no plants that have a negative effect on eggplants.
Weeding	Keep weeded, especially when the plant is small.
Watering	Keep soil moist. This is most important when the plants are young.

▼ **QUICK TIPS FOR GROWING EGGPLANTS—*continued***

Fertilizing	Fertilize with compost tea or fish fertilizer after the first bloom and again when the fruit starts to form.
Pests and diseases	Flea beetles, lace bugs, aphids, Colorado flea beetles, and red spiders are some common pests that affect the eggplant.
When to harvest	Fruit matures in 60 to 95 days. Harvest when the fruit is firm to touch, fully colored, and has a glossy look to it. Harvest regularly so the plant will produce more fruit.
How to harvest	Cut the fruit off with scissors, leaving a ½-inch stem on the fruit. Do not twist or break off the fruit; this may damage the plant.
Storage	Store eggplants in a plastic bag in the warmer section of your refrigerator. They will keep for up to 5 days.

Okra

Okra is an annual vegetable grown for its tasty seedpods. It is an edible cousin of cotton. It is more popular in southern cooking and is a staple in a spicy Cajun stew called *gumbo*. It is also delicious battered and fried. The inside of the fruit is often used as a thickening agent for stews.

Okra is a tropical shrub that needs a warm climate to grow. A greenhouse would work if you live in a cooler climate. This plant will tolerate almost any type of soil as long as it is well drained. The okra plant can grow up to six feet tall and produces funnel-shaped yellow blooms.

Seeds are best started indoors and then transplanted out once the soil temperature reaches 70°F. The okra seed is tough, so nicking the seed with a file and soaking it overnight will help it germinate faster.

▼ **QUICK TIPS FOR GROWING OKRA**

Family name	Malvaceae (mallow family).
Edible parts	Pods.
Location	Sunny, hot area.
Best soil	Fertile, well drained; pH 6.0–6.8.
When to plant	Sow seeds in spring and transplant out when the soil temperature reaches 70°F.
How to plant	Set out plants 12 to 18 inches apart in rows 30 to 48 inches apart.
How much to plant	1 or 2 plants per person.
Weeding	Keep young plants well weeded.
Watering	Water deeply once a week.

▼ **QUICK TIPS FOR GROWING OKRA—*continued***

Care	Once the plant reaches 6 inches tall, mulch to conserve the moisture in the soil and to prevent weeds from growing.
Fertilizing	Fertilize with a high-potassium fertilizer when you first plant them and then side dress the plant with compost when they are 1 month old.
Pests and diseases	Aphids, corn earworms, mites, and nematodes can cause problems for the okra plant.
When to harvest	Pods are best harvested when young, about 2 to 4 inches long. Once you start harvesting, you will need to pick every few days so the plant keeps producing more fruit.
How to harvest	Use gloves when harvesting the pods and clip them from the plant using pruning shears or a sharp knife.
Storage	Okra will keep for up to 1 week in the refrigerator.

Peppers

Peppers come in various shapes, from chunky to long and skinny and round to conical. You'll find them in shades of green, red, and yellow. Their flavors range from mild and sweet to sizzling hot. Sweet peppers are also known as bell peppers because of the shape of the fruit. They are often harvested when green; that way, the plant produces more fruit. When left on the plant to mature, bell peppers will turn either yellow, orange, or red depending on the variety. Hot pepper plants grow taller and have narrower leaves than the bell varieties and their fruit can range in size from about one to seven inches long.

Bell pepper

Peppers are a little touchy to grow. They need lots of full sun, warm daytime temperatures, cool nighttime temperatures, fertile soil, and lots of water. Sweet peppers need a little less heat than hot pepper varieties. When preparing your garden bed, add compost or aged animal manure. Peppers can then be seeded directly if you have a long growing season; however, they often do better started indoors in early spring and transplanted out once the temperature reaches 65°F.

Peppers are a very popular vegetable, either cooked by themselves or with other foods. They are also eaten raw in salads or as appetizers. When preparing to use your pepper, cut it in half, remove the stem, and rinse away the seeds. Fresh or dried hot peppers need to be handled carefully because the oils in the skin can burn your skin or eyes. It is suggested that you use rubber gloves and hold the hot pepper under water when preparing it. Remove the seeds from a hot pepper if you want to cut down the heat; the seeds add to the hot taste.

ESSENTIAL

Transplant your vegetables on a cloudy day or later in the day when the sun is not so hot. The hot sun can wilt or scorch the young leaves, leaving them stressed. Make sure the transplants are moist before you plant them and gently water them after they have been placed in the ground. Watering the plant will help the roots become established.

▼ QUICK TIPS FOR GROWING PEPPERS

Family name	Solanaceae (nightshade family).
Edible parts	Fruits.
Location	Very sunny area.
Best Soil	Fertile, well-drained soil that does not have an excess of nitrogen; soil that is too rich will form leaves but poor fruiting; pH 5.5–6.8.
When to plant	Sow seeds indoors 6 to 8 weeks before you plan to put them into your garden. Transplant them when the temperature is 65°F.
How to plant	Set out plants 18 inches apart in rows spaced 30 to 36 inches apart.
How much to plant	5 to 10 plants per person.
Companion plants	Plant with basil, carrots, onions, oregano, and marjoram. Fennel will have a negative effect on peppers, so avoid planting peppers near them.
Weeding	Keep well weeded when plants are small.
Watering	Water regularly and keep soil moist when the plant is flowering and fruiting.
Fertilizing	Use fish fertilizer or compost tea after the first bloom and then after the fruit starts to form.
Pests and diseases	Aphids, armyworms, Colorado potato beetles, corn borers, mites, and cutworms are some common pests.

▼ **QUICK TIPS FOR GROWING PEPPERS—***continued*

When to harvest	Peppers mature between 60 and 95 days after planting depending on the variety. Harvest sweet peppers when they are firm and full sized. You can harvest them when they are green or leave them to turn red orange, or yellow. Harvest hot peppers when they are full size and have turned yellow, red, or dark green depending on the variety.
How to harvest	Cut or gently pull the pepper from the plant, leaving a stem of ½ inch.
Storage	Fresh peppers will last 1 to 2 weeks in the refrigerator if not washed and placed in a sealed plastic bag. Peppers can be frozen, dried, and preserved by pickling or canning them.

Squash

Squash is an easy vegetable to grow, and each plant can produce a large number of fruits. There are two types of squash—summer and winter. The main differences between these are the amount of time they take to mature and how well they will store once harvested. Summer squash is a warm weather vegetable that is eaten before the fruit has fully matured. The skin and seeds are eaten as part of the whole fruit. The winter squash takes longer to mature and are usually harvested in the late summer or fall. They usually have a larger fruit than summer varieties and the skin is tough and inedible. The seeds are often removed before cooking as well. Some varieties, such as pumpkin, produce lovely edible seeds that are delicious when roasted.

Squash likes a rich soil that has plenty of organic matter. They often grow best in the compost pile! They are a vine vegetable that can spread six to eight feet across, so make sure you give them lots of room when planning your garden layout. Squash can be direct seeded or put out as transplants, which is usually dependent on the length of your growing season. Each plant—especially the summer zucchini squash—can produce lots of fruit seemingly overnight, so one or two plants are usually enough for any family. Winter squash can also produce several fruits from

Zucchini flower

one plant, but if cured properly they will store for several months so you can enjoy them over time.

FACT

Competitions for giant pumpkins are very popular. During the fall you can find different pumpkin festivals all over the world. The world record for the largest pumpkin was recorded in September 2007, weighing in at 1,689 pounds. Imagine having that pumpkin in your backyard!

Squash plants require lots of water. Since the leaves become very large, it is best to water the plant by hand or with drip irrigation around the base of the plant so the water reaches the roots. Squash leaves are more susceptible to mildew if they get wet.

▼ QUICK TIPS FOR GROWING SQUASH

Family name	Cucurbitaceae (gourd family).
Edible parts	Fruits and some seeds.
Location	Sunny area.
Best Soil	Fertile, well-drained, light soil. If you have clay soil, add lots of organic matter to lighten it; pH 5.5–6.8.
When to plant	Sow seeds directly when the soil temperature is 60°F. You can start transplants in April and transplant them out approximately 6 weeks later, making sure the soil temperature is warm enough.
How to plant	Sow seeds 2 to 3 inches deep, 16 inches apart in rows 3 to 5 feet apart.
How much to plant	For summer squash, plant 1 to 2 plants for the family. For winter squash, plant 4 to 10 plants per family.
Companion plants	Plant with beans, corn, radishes, mint, and nasturtiums. Potatoes can have a negative effect, especially on summer squash varieties, so avoid planting them near each other.
Weeding	Keep well weeded when the plant is young.
Watering	Squash requires regular watering. Watering at the base of the plant rather than overhead is better for the plant.
Care	Plants need a large amount of space to grow.
Fertilizing	Give the plants fish fertilizer or compost tea once they have reached about 1 foot tall and are just starting to spread.
Pests and diseases	Aphids, cucumber beetles, mites, nematodes, squash bugs, squash vine borers, and powdery mildew can affect squash plants.

▼ **QUICK TIPS FOR GROWING SQUASH—*continued***

When to harvest	Summer squash will mature in 50 to 65 days. Winter squash takes 60 to 110 days to grow to maturity. For summer squash, harvest once fruits start to form and pick every few days when the fruit is still fairly small (6 to 8 inches); they are tastier when young. For winter squash, harvest when the skin is hard. Gently use your fingernail to pierce the skin. If it leaves a mark, it is not ready to be harvested; if there is no mark, it is ready for harvesting.
How to harvest	Cut from the plant, leaving a small stem on each fruit.
Storage	Summer squash will store for up to 1 week in the refrigerator. If cured properly, winter squash will store for several months. Cure winter varieties by leaving the cut fruit in the sun for several days. Turn the fruit every few hours so all sides will be exposed to the sun. Cover them if they will be left out at night.

Tomatoes

There is nothing tastier than a ripe tomato that you have just picked off the vine. Tomatoes are one of the most popular vegetables eaten in North America and most gardeners love to grow them. Most people think of a tomato being round and red, but there are several varieties that produce yellow and orange fruit and others that produce a fruit that is pear or plum shaped. The size of the tomato can rage from one to six inches in diameter, depending on the variety you choose. One plant will produce an abundance of fruit for you to enjoy.

Tomatoes

Tomatoes will grow well in any backyard as long as it is sunny and hot. They do well in containers and in greenhouses, especially if you live in a cooler climate.

Tomatoes are best started indoors, where you can regulate the temperature so they will germinate. Tomato seeds need ten to twelve weeks of growth before they are ready to be transplanted into the garden or a container. It is important that you introduce the plant to the cool outdoors gradually over several days when you are ready to transplant your tomato plants; this is called *hardening off.*

Unlike most plants, tomato plants like to be planted deep. Bury at least half of the stem underground to give the plant a strong root base. Tomatoes are best grown upright on supports. This allows the stem of the plant to grow tall without breaking from the weight of the fruit. It also keeps the fruit from touching the ground and allows air circulation around the plant.

Gardeners often give tomato plants either too much or too little water. When you first transplant a tomato plant, water it every few days until it is well established. Once the plant reaches two to three feet tall, the roots are probably just as deep; a little water each day will not reach where the roots need it the most. Tomatoes need a deep watering once a week or every ten days. Fruit that starts to split is one sign that the plant is not getting enough water.

If you are planning to grow your tomato plants in containers, it is best to choose dwarf or hanging varieties unless you have a very large container. A standard tomato needs a container at least eighteen inches deep.

QUESTION

What is the difference between determinate and indeterminate tomato plants?
Determinate plants are bush types that stop growing once they have reached three to five feet. The fruit ripens over a shorter period of time. Indeterminate vines keep growing until frost kills them, and they can reach up to twelve feet They produce larger crops over a longer period of time.

▼ **QUICK TIPS FOR GROWING TOMATOES**

Family name	Solanaceae (nightshade family).
Edible parts	Fruit.
Location	Sunny and warm area.
Best soil	Fertile, well drained; pH 5.5–6.8.
When to plant	Sow seeds early in spring; they can take 10 to 12 weeks before they are ready to go into the garden bed. Make sure the weather is 65°F before you put them outside.
How to plant	Set out transplants 12 to 18 inches apart in rows spaced 36 to 48 inches apart. Bury at least half of the stem underground when setting them out.
How much to plant	10 to 20 plants per person, depending on whether you want to can or preserve any fruit.

▼ **QUICK TIPS FOR GROWING TOMATOES—*continued***

Companion plants	Plant with asparagus, basil, cabbage, carrot, onion, parsley, peas, and sage. Potatoes and fennel can have a negative effect, so avoiding planting tomatoes near them.
Weeding	Keep well weeded, especially when the plant is young.
Watering	Water deeply once a week or every 10 days when the weather is hot.
Care	In cooler climates, tomatoes may need protection to grow their best. In the Pacific Northwest, the rain is also a concern because tomato plants do not like their leaves to get wet. In this climate, it is best to grow them under a plastic or glass shelter. If the temperature reaches above 100°F, the plant will stop producing fruit, so make sure there is good ventilation if it is grown under cover.
Fertilizing	Fertilize with fish fertilizer or compost tea 2 weeks before and again 2 weeks after the first picking.
Pests and diseases	Aphids, cutworms, tomato hornworms, flea beetles, leaf miners, nematodes, whiteflies, fusarium wilt, verticillium wilt, and blossom end rot can all affect your tomato plants.
When to harvest	Most varieties will mature 50 to 90 days after they have been transplanted into the garden or container. Harvest all your tomatoes—even the green ones—before the first frost. Green tomatoes will ripen if left in a warm area.
How to harvest	Gently pluck the tomato from the vine.
Storage	A ripe tomato will keep for up to 1 week on your kitchen counter. If you have lots of green tomatoes, you can wrap them in newspaper and place them in a cardboard box in a warm room. Check them regularly, pulling them out when they have ripened. Tomatoes can be frozen whole or chopped. They can be canned whole or diced, or made into sauces or chutney to be enjoyed all winter long.

CHAPTER 13

Tips for Raising Happy, Healthy Veggies

There are many aspects to vegetable gardening. First you have to plan your garden, decide what you want to plant, and plant the seed. Then comes caring for the seed so it will germinate. And finally, you must keep your veggies happy all season long. In this chapter you will learn about a number of measures that can go a long way toward providing you with a successful vegetable harvest.

Crop Rotation

Crop rotation is a process that is used to ensure you do not plant the same vegetable or family of vegetables in the same spot in successive years. By moving your vegetables to a new spot each year, you will be able to keep the soil more fertile, reduce the amounts of pests and diseases in your garden, and ultimately have a healthier and more productive vegetable harvest. Crop or vegetable rotation may seem complicated when you first learn about it, but it can be easy.

Different vegetable plants use varying amounts of nutrients from the soil to grow well. You already know that you should add organic matter and fertilizer to your soil every year, but it is also important to move your plants around so you don't deplete the soil's nutrients. One year you may grow a vegetable that uses a lot of nitrogen, and the following year you may plant a crop that uses more phosphorus. Rotating the crops gives the soil time to rebuild the nitrogen in that area.

Crop rotation also helps you cut down on pests and diseases in your garden. A few of these little guys can wreak havoc on your vegetable patch, so it's in your best interest to keep them out. Certain vegetable plants will attract certain pests and diseases, which often live in the soil where the plant grows. By moving these vegetable plants to another area of the garden, you deprive the pests or diseases of their food. On the other hand, some plants repel certain pests and diseases, which will also help keep them at bay.

QUESTION

Are some flowers edible?
Flowers are a great way to add beauty to your vegetable garden and attract beneficial insects—and some are indeed edible. Bee balm, pansies, nasturtiums, geraniums, tulips, violas, lavender, hollyhock, dianthus, day lilies, and roses are all edible and easy to grow. Harvest blooms just before using them.

To implement crop rotation in your garden, first divide your garden site into four fairly equal areas—five if you are planning to grow some perennial vegetables like asparagus or artichokes. You will plant a certain family of vegetables in each spot one year and move it clockwise to the next spot the following year. This will give you a four-year crop rotation. It is important to write down or draw a sketch of your garden so you have something to refer back to when planning for next season.

▼ **TABLE 13-1**

	Year 1	Year 2	Year 3	Year 4
Bed 1	Brassicas: broccoli, cauliflower, Brussels sprouts, kale	Heat-loving veggies: tomatoes, cucumbers, peppers, eggplants, basil	Root crops: carrots, potatoes, beets	Other crops: lettuce, peas, beans, chard, Oriental vegetables
Bed 2	Heat-loving veggies: tomatoes, cucumbers, peppers, eggplants, basil	Root crops: carrots, potatoes, beets	Other crops: lettuce, peas, beans, chard, Oriental vegetables	Brassicas: broccoli, cauliflower, Brussels sprouts, kale
Bed 3	Root crops: carrots, potatoes, beets	Other crops: lettuce, peas, beans, chard, Oriental vegetables	Brassicas: broccoli, cauliflower, Brussels sprouts, kale	Heat-loving veggies: tomatoes, cucumbers, peppers, eggplants, basil
Bed 4	Other crops: lettuce, peas, beans, chard, Oriental vegetables	Brassicas: broccoli, cauliflower, Brussels sprouts, kale	Heat-loving veggies: tomatoes, cucumbers, peppers, eggplants, basil	Root crops: carrots, potatoes, beets

If you are growing your veggies in containers, either wash the container and change the soil each year or plant the veggie in a different pot each year. This will keep your container vegetables healthier.

Companion Planting

Certain vegetables have a positive effect on each other, and planting them close together can help you maximize the benefit. On the other hand, beware of plants that negatively affect each other; be sure to plant these in different parts of your garden.

Planting a certain group of vegetables with another can create a habitat for beneficial insects or pests, which will help control the more harmful ones. Some vegetable scents will mask or hide a certain vegetable so pests will not be able to find it. Another plant may produce an odor that will repel certain pests or diseases. Certain plants are not affected by a particular pest or disease but will draw it away from a plant that is.

▼ TABLE 13-2: COMPANION PLANTING CHART

Vegetable	Positive Effect	Negative Effect
Asparagus	Parsley, tomatoes	Onions
Beans	Beets, borage, cabbage, carrots, cauliflower, corn, marigolds, squash, tomatoes, strawberries	Chives, fennel, garlic, leeks
Beets	Cabbage, kohlrabi	Runner beans
Broccoli	Beans, celery, dill, onions, oregano, potatoes, sage, rosemary, nasturtiums	Lettuce, strawberries, tomatoes
Brussels sprouts	Beans, celery, dill, nasturtiums, potatoes, sage, rosemary	Strawberries
Cabbage	Beans, beets, celery, dill, nasturtiums, onions, oregano, potatoes, sage, rosemary	Grapes, strawberries, tomatoes
Carrots	Beans, leeks, onions, peas, radishes, rosemary, sage, tomatoes	Dill
Cauliflower	Beans, beets, celery, dill, nasturtiums, onions, oregano, potatoes, sage, radishes	Strawberries, tomatoes
Celery	Beans, cabbage, leeks, onions, tomatoes	Carrots, parsnips
Corn	Beans, melon, peas, squash	
Cucumbers	Beans, broccoli, celery, Chinese cabbage, lettuce, peas, radishes, tomatoes	Sage, rue
Eggplants	Peas, tarragon, thyme	
Kohlrabi	Beets, onions	Beans, peppers, tomatoes
Leeks	Carrots, celery	Broad beans, broccoli
Lettuce	Beets, cabbage, clovers, peas, radishes, strawberries	
Onions	Beets, cabbage, carrots, lettuce, potatoes, strawberries, tomatoes	Beans, peas
Peas	Carrots, corn, cucumbers, eggplants, lettuce, radishes, spinach	Tomatoes, turnips, rutabagas

▼   **TABLE 13-2: COMPANION PLANTING CHART—*continued***

Peppers	Basil, carrots, lovage, marjoram, onions, oregano	Fennel, kohlrabi
Potatoes	Beans, cabbage, corn, lettuce, onions, petunias, marigolds, radishes	Apples, pumpkins, tomatoes
Pumpkins	Beans, corn, nasturtiums, radishes	Potatoes
Radishes	Beans, cabbage, cauliflower, cucumbers, lettuce, peas, squash, tomatoes	Grapes, hyssop
Spinach	Cabbage, celery, eggplants, onions, peas, strawberries	
Summer squash	Beans, corn, mint, nasturtiums, radishes	Potatoes
Tomatoes	Asparagus, basil, cabbage, carrots, onions, parsley, peas, sage	Fennel, potatoes
Turnips	Peas	
Winter squash	Beans, corn, mint, nasturtiums, radishes	
Zucchini	Beans, corn, mint, nasturtiums, radishes	Potatoes

Protecting Your Plants

Some vegetable plants need more care than others. Young seedlings or transplants are often the most vulnerable to weather extremes and pests. Different plants at various stages of their growth may need protection from the cold, frost, heat, excessive rain, or pests. A change in temperature—even if it's only a drop of a few degrees—can be harmful to your veggie plants. Cold weather, pests, or disease can kill a whole row of veggies in one night, so protecting them is important.

To have a successful garden, you need to take time to observe your veggie plants and be aware of the weather, especially in the spring when the temperature can vary widely from day to night. Most vegetable plants do not like the cold weather, and young plants can be quite fragile. To complicate matters, cold soil is more susceptible to fungi and disease, so it is important to protect the soil and plants if you live in a cold climate. Excessive heat can also kill your vegetable plants. The heat or dryness can make them wilt, which can cause them to become stunted or die if they are not attended to fairly quickly. Too much water can actually prevent your vegetable plants from getting the nutrients they need to grow well. For all of these reasons, you should always have materials near your garden so you can quickly cover or shield your plants.

FACT

When "chewing pests" like slugs have assaulted your vegetable plants, the plants can generally handle up to 20 percent damage without a huge loss of yield or the negative impact on the quality of the harvest. The only exceptions are plants that are grown for their leaves, such as spinach or cabbage.

You probably already have all the materials you need to protect your vegetable plants from cold, heat, wind, bugs, birds, and other pests. The following list includes common items and how you can use them:

- **Cardboard box.** Place the box over a plant to keep it from getting too cold at night.
- **Metal cans.** Large tomato cans or coffee cans are ideal to protect a plant from the cold or pests. Remove both ends of the can and place it gently over the plant. You can leave the can on during the day; the sun will still be able to reach the plant.
- **Wooden boards.** Pieces of wood can be used to block excessive wind or sun.
- **Paper bags.** Place a paper bag over a young seedling to protect it from the cold. Wind can blow a bag away and rain can cause it to disintegrate, so only use this method on cold, clear nights.
- **Plastic containers.** Yogurt containers, milk jugs, and large water bottles can protect young seedlings from the cold or even from slugs. Remove both ends of the container and firmly place it into the soil around the young plant to prevent slugs from reaching the plant. A clear plastic container can be used as a mini greenhouse for plants that like a little extra warmth; just be careful not to let the plants get too hot.

- **Sheets.** Throw your old bed sheets over your vegetable patch on a cold spring night. They are light enough that they won't damage the plant, yet they will still provide adequate protection.
- **Plastic sheeting.** Plastic sheeting is best used over a structure of either wood or plastic hoops to protect your plants. Create a greenhouse or cold frame to protect your plants. Chapter 6 has specific information.
- **Floating row covers.** This material can be easily purchased at any garden center or from most seed catalogs. It is lightweight and will let in some light and water while it protects your plants from the heat, cold, and pests. It is light enough to be laid directly over your plants or it can be attached to plastic or wooden poles to make a shelter.
- **Fencing.** A fence is one way of protecting your whole garden from animals such as cats, dogs, deer, raccoons, and bears. If you live in an area where these animals are common, investing in a good fence will save you a lot of heartache. Different types of fencing are used for different types of animals.

Trellis and Staking

Some vegetable plants need support to grow and produce healthy fruits or pods. Tomatoes and cucumbers do best if they can grow upright so that the fruit is not lying on the ground and the plant can receive both light and air circulation. Some varieties of peas and beans can grow up to six feet high or more and need support. These climbing vegetables have vines that need to be able to attach to a structure of some sort in order to continue to grow taller. Some common vine and sprawling vegetables include the following:

- Climbing and runner beans
- Cucumbers
- Snow and snap peas
- Summer squash
- Tomatoes

It is important to know which plants will need staking or a trellis so that you can put these up just before you plant the seed or set out your transplants. If you wait, you can disturb the roots, which can cause stress, and the vines of different plants can grow into each other, making it difficult to place a stake or trellis without damaging the plant.

FACT

If you have a small garden site, save space by growing a climbing vegetable next to a plant that has a sturdier stalk. Cornstalks make a great support for pole beans. You save space by growing them together and you save money by not having to make a support structure.

Growing vertically can save a lot of space, especially if you have a tiny garden site or grow in containers on your balcony. The plants are often healthier because they don't touch the wet or cold ground, and therefore attract fewer pests and diseases. Mildew and rot are common problems for many fruiting vegetables, so it's to your advantage to keep the fruit off the ground. When your plants grow upright, you can easily see the fruit to harvest. Gardening can be backbreaking work, but harvesting off an upright structure is easier on your body!

Trellis and staking material can be purchased at most garden centers or from seed catalogs. You can also make structures of your own out of materials you have on hand. The following is a list of some common types of trellis and stakes:

- **Plastic or nylon netting.** The plant's tendrils wind around the netting and move upward as they grow taller. The netting material is soft and easy to work with and will not decay. It can be cut to any size and is easily washed and stored. White nylon netting has large six-inch openings and is used mainly for larger plants like cucumbers and zucchini. Green plastic mesh netting has smaller openings, making it a better option for peas or beans. These trellis materials need to be supported by some kind of frame.
- **Wooden frame.** You can use scrap pieces of wood, bamboo, small tree branches, or even an old window frame to build a support for your netting. Make sure the frame is secure in the ground and attach the netting to the top and bottom of the frame with string, nails, or sta-

ples. Make sure the netting is fairly tight so it will support the weight of your plant when it starts to fruit.

- **Wire cages.** Wire cages are used to help keep your tomato plants upright. These are made of thin wire and are cone-shaped. Stick the narrow end securely into the ground around the base of your tomato plant. The plant will grow upright, using the wire cage for support. Wire cages are about four feet high, but some tomato plants can grow in excess of six feet. A stake may be a better option if your tomato plant is expected to grow higher than four feet.

Tomato growing in a wire cage

- **Wooden stakes.** Wood, bamboo, or even small cut trees will all work well as sturdy stakes. The stakes must be secured far enough into the ground to give enough support. One foot in the ground for every three feet above ground is a good rule of thumb. Tie tomato plants to the stakes with string, pieces of cloth, or even old pantyhose.

- **Teepee structure.** You can use pieces of wood, bamboo, or sturdy tree branches to make your teepee. Take six stakes of equal length. Push each stake securely into the ground in a small circle, angling them all inward toward each other. The top of each stake should touch the others. Tie them together with a piece of string or twine. This is a great way to grow climbing beans and peas; just plant four to six seeds around the base of each pole and watch them grow.

Compost and Manure Teas

Organic fertilizer teas are a great way to replace nutrients in the soil so your vegetable plant roots can absorb and use them. These teas can also deter some pests if the plant's leaves are sprayed with a diluted mixture; just remember to wash the plant thoroughly before you eat it.

Most plants do better with an extra boost of nutrients at some point in their growth. Giving your young transplants some fertilizer tea when they are first set out in the garden will help reduce the shock of any root disturbance. Other vegetable plants need an extra boost of nutrients when they start to flower to encourage them to produce lots of fruits or pods.

Compost, animal manure, and comfrey are all great organic materials for making your fertilizer tea. Gardeners often have limited amounts of compost and animal manure, so they really do not have enough to put on all their garden beds.

ESSENTIAL

Write it down! When it comes to fertilizing your veggies, make sure you keep records. Keep a journal or notebook and jot down when you gave your plant fertilizer and how much was given. If you do not write it down, you may forget some plants and fertilize others too often.

Regularly fertilizing your plants and replenishing nutrients in your soil helps keep them healthier. This reduces the risk that your plants will succumb to pests and diseases.

Make Your Own Compost or Manure Tea

You'll need a bucket or garbage can with a lid, hot animal manure or compost, and water. Follow these steps to make your tea:

1. Fill your bucket or garbage can one-third full with compost or manure and then fill it the rest of the way with water.
2. Mix well, cover, and let it sit at least overnight; letting it sit for a few days can make it stronger.
3. Put the tea directly around your plants or fill your watering can with half tea and half water to dilute it. If you dilute your tea, strain the tea with a piece of cheesecloth so you won't plug the nozzle on your watering can. This mixture can also be used to spray your plant leaves to deter pests.
4. Keep refilling your bucket or garbage can with more water until the water no longer turns dark brown. Once this happens, put the sludge into your compost and make a new batch of tea with fresh manure or compost.

Make Your Own Green Tea

Comfrey contains high levels of nitrogen, phosphorus, and potassium, which are essential nutrients for your vegetables. It can be invasive, but if you have a patch of it in your garden, cut it before it flowers and then put the leaves into a container to make tea. Follow these steps to make a green tea:

1. Fill your bucket one-third full with comfrey. Press it down firmly. Then fill the bucket the rest of the way with water and secure the lid.
2. In about a week, the liquid will turn a rich brownish-yellow color. It's ready to use! Keep adding more water as you use the liquid until the color fades. Put the sludge into your compost and start a new batch of tea.

Green Manures and Cover Crops

You can grow certain green plants, usually in the fall, and then cut and till them into the soil the following spring. These plants are usually called a *cover crop*. Green manure is an easy and economical way of adding organic matter to the soil. As the green matter decomposes, it adds texture and nutrients back into your soil. A cover crop will:

- Enhance the soil structure and drainage
- Protect bare soil from being blown away by the wind
- Keep important nutrients from being leached away by rain
- Loosen the soil
- Help control weeds
- Help break pest cycles
- Provide you with your own mulch and compost material

Vetch, fava beans, winter field peas, clover, and fall rye can be grown to increase the nitrogen content in your soil. They are called *nitrogen fixers*, which means their roots will hold nitrogen and then release it into the soil once the plant is tilled under. Buckwheat and phacelias are often used to suppress weeds and are great to plant if you are just starting a new garden site or your old site has gotten overgrown with weeds.

You can plant a cover crop at any time, but most gardeners plant theirs after they have harvested their main crop. Before planting, make sure the bed is clean. Roughly rake over the area in order to break up the first few inches of soil. Then broadcast the seed and keep it well watered if the weather is warm and dry.

It is easiest to turn over a cover crop if the plants are not too high, so dig them in once they reach six to eight inches high. If they grow taller, cut the plant a few inches from the soil and use the material as mulch or put it into your compost. Till the crop under and leave it to decompose for a few weeks before you begin to plant any vegetables.

CHAPTER 14

Composting Basics

Making a compost pile is a great way to turn your organic kitchen waste and your garden debris into a rich amendment for your garden beds. There are many benefits to composting, and it is easy to do, inexpensive to make, and environmentally friendly. In this chapter, you will get advice on choosing a bin, what materials to put into the bin, and problem solving to help you make compost, often called *black gold*.

The Benefits of Composting

Composting is a biological process in which organic waste is reduced to a humuslike material. When a plant dies, the remains are attacked by microorganisms in the soil. They eventually turn the material into an earthlike substance that other plants can use to grow. In nature, compost is more than just a fertilizer or a soil conditioner; it is a symbol of new life. You just have to walk in the woods to see fallen leaves and other debris made into compost that helps sustain many lives.

Making compost is an important part of a successful vegetable garden. It does take some time and effort, but the rewards are great! It is a constructive way to use your kitchen waste, which would otherwise go into the garbage, and an excellent spot to place your weeds and other garden debris. Having a compost pile is a great way to keep your garden clean, which is important to keeping your garden free of unwanted pests and diseases.

FACT

Good storage is important to making great compost. Certain materials come available all at once, usually in early spring and in the fall. This is the time you can accumulate leaves, grass clippings, or garden waste. There is often too much to put directly into your compost bin, so it's valuable to have a place to store them to use later.

Adding compost to your garden soil will help to:

- Build soil texture and structure.
- Retain the soil's nutrients.
- Lighten a heavy soil to make it drain more effectively or add organic matter to light, sandy soil to help it retain moisture.
- Control the erosion of your soil.
- Recycle what would most likely go into the landfill and turn it into something that food will grow in.
- Protect vegetable plants against drought.
- Support the essential bacteria in your soil.
- Provide healthy conditions for soil organisms such as earthworms.
- Control a good pH level in your soil.

- Release nutrients to your vegetable plants' roots.
- Prevent leaching.
- Control weeds.

If you do not have a compost heap, start one today. If you have a backyard, find a space to build a compost bin or just start making a pile. You can purchase bins that are very compact if you only have a small space to use. Do you live in an apartment or condo? Composting with earthworms may be the answer for you. It is an easy way to compost your vegetable waste when you do not have any outdoor space; a worm composting bin can be stored in a cupboard or on a small balcony.

Choosing a Bin

Composting has experienced a surge in popularity, so the home gardener has many choices of bins. The type of bin you choose will depend on where you will be putting it, how much waste you will have, and how much time and energy you want to put toward making compost.

Constructing your own bin can save you money. You can use recycled materials, and you can make the bin the size that will fit your needs. One common construction is a three-bin wood and

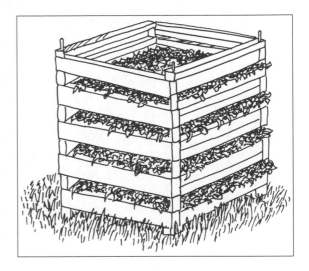

Compost bin

wire system. It is designed to provide good air circulation and each bin is usually three feet by three feet—the minimum size you need to make good compost. The first bin is used to collect debris, the second bin is where you start your pile, and the third bin is where you put the pile when it is nearly finished. This kind of structure will last a long time if you use rot-resistant wood like cedar or redwood.

You can easily build a simple three-sided bin with stacking concrete blocks, railroad ties, wooden boards, bales of straw, or pallets. Make sure the walls are about four feet high and the area is a minimum of three feet by three feet.

QUESTION

What tools do I need to make compost?
First, you need a bin of some sort. You will need a good quality garden fork to turn your pile, a thermometer to tell if the compost is heating up, and a tarp or plastic sheet to keep your pile covered unless you are using a commercial bin that already has a cover.

Wire fencing or wire mesh can be used to make a compost bin as long as the holes are small enough to hold the materials you have. Bending the wire into a circular shape is often the easiest and the sturdiest way to set it up. You can also purchase wire bins that are made from galvanized metal mesh. They come in several shapes and sizes and are easy to set up.

There are many different types of plastic compost bins on the market. Plastic bins are easier to move around, last longer than wooden bins, and protect your compost from the rain and sun. They come in round or square shapes; some have solid sides, and others have removable and stackable sides. Most have a capacity of twelve cubic feet, which is the size needed for your compost to heat up, but you can also find larger bins.

Another option is to purchase a compost tumbler. Tumblers are convenient because every time you rotate the drum, you turn the material, which will make it decompose faster. However, compost material can become very heavy and it can be difficult to turn the barrel when it is full. Tumblers can also keep the material too wet, so you need to be aware of how much moisture you are adding to the bin.

Composting Materials

The materials you add to your pile need to be biological so they will decompose. Wood, paper, vegetable waste, plant material, weeds, and animal manures are commonly composted materials. It's the mixture of the raw material that's important. You want to have a balance of green material, brown material, and manures or good soil. Too much green material will attract flies and give your compost a strong odor, and too much brown material will slow down the decomposition of the pile.

The green material adds nitrogen to your pile. Here is a list of some common items you can use:

- Cut grass
- Vegetable kitchen waste
- Animal or human hair
- Weeds that have not gone to seed
- Green garden debris
- Seaweed

The brown material adds carbon to your pile. Here is a list of some common items you can use:

- Thick vegetable stems such as broccoli stems and corn stalks
- Coffee grounds
- Shredded dried leaves
- Vacuum cleaner bag contents
- Small wood shavings
- Straw
- Hay
- Twigs
- Wood ashes
- Sawdust

Most of these materials are found in your own yard. If you do not have enough material to get started, sort the different materials into two piles and check out your neighborhood. Do your neighbors have leaves you can rake up and use? Do they use their grass clippings? Be careful not to use grass clippings where pesticides have been used! If you live near a beach, go foraging for seaweed. Coffee shops will often give coffee grounds away for free (they most often go into the garbage), so use them. Accumulate these items and then build your pile all at once.

Smaller materials will break down more quickly, so avoid putting large pieces of wood or cardboard into the pile. Shred large twigs, leaves, corn stalks, and broccoli stalks first or they will take a long time to decompose. Using a variety of materials with different textures will give your pile better air circulation, which will make better compost. A pile with only one or two materials in it will take longer to decompose.

ALERT

If you have no desire to make a compost pile but do not want your kitchen waste to go into the garbage, there is a practical solution. In the fall and winter, dig trenches about one foot deep in your garden beds, place the vegetable kitchen waste into the bottoms of the trenches, and cover them with soil.

There are certain materials that should never be put in your compost pile because they will not decompose or they may carry diseases that you do not want in the final product. Do not include the following items in your compost:

- Dog, cat, or human feces
- Animal urine
- Large amounts of oil
- Pine needles
- Meat products or bones
- Oak leaves
- Toxic materials or materials treated with pesticides

It is not usually necessary to add organic fertilizers to your compost because the green and brown matter will make rich compost on its own. But if you know your soil is deficient in a certain element, then by all means add a little to your compost pile. You can add the following fertilizers to increase the nutrient level and to correct the pH if it is needed:

- Rock powder
- Blood meal

- Bone meal
- Cottonseed meal
- Kelp
- Greensand
- Peat moss

Simply add a handful of any of these in between your green and brown layers. You can also add lime to neutralize the acidity in your compost. Dolomite lime is the best form to add because it has a combination of calcium and magnesium in it.

Making Compost

The best time to make a new compost pile is in the spring or fall. The extreme temperatures of summer and winter can slow down the decomposition process. A pile will most likely take between three to six months to make good compost. The final result should be a rich, dark-colored earthlike material that smells earthy and easily crumbles in your hands.

To make your compost pile:

1. Lay down six inches of carbon material—for example, straw or small sticks.
2. Cover that with six inches of green material—for example, leaves, grass, and green material.
3. Place your kitchen waste over this material.
4. Add in a handful of organic fertilizer if you want.
5. Cover with a thin layer of soil or manure to keep the flies and odor down.
6. Repeat until your pile reaches approximately three to four feet in height.

For best results, make the pile at least three feet high by three feet wide. Temperature is an important factor in making compost. The larger the pile, the easier it is to get it to the high temperatures needed to kill any weed seeds or diseased plant material that may be in your pile. The temperature of the pile usually starts out cool and gradually increases as material starts to decompose. Once your compost pile has reached approximately three feet by three feet, let it sit and start a new pile.

ESSENTIAL

Horse manure is known to help heat up a compost pile. If you do not have access to animal manure, seaweed and crab shells also make excellent heat generators. These are all excellent materials to use, especially in the winter when your pile may need a boost of heat.

Moisture is another important aspect to consider when making compost. The moisture in the pile will allow air to filter into it, which is needed in the decomposing process. The amount of moisture needs to be high—but not too high. Never let your compost pile dry out. Make sure you add water to your compost regularly, especially in the summer months. Keeping the pile covered will keep the sun from drying out the pile and prevent the rain from making it too wet. To check to see if your pile is moist enough, take a handful of compost from the middle of the pile. If it is crumbling and slightly moist to the touch, there is enough moisture. If it forms a hard ball, the pile is too wet. Turn your pile to allow more air circulation. Many gardeners never turn their compost and it does work, but taking the time to regularly turn over your pile will hasten the decomposition process.

Composting with Earthworms

If you live in an apartment or a condominium and do not have access to a backyard, composting with earthworms can be an easy way to turn your kitchen waste into a nutrient-rich compost you can add to your vegetable containers. An earthworm has the ability to consume its own weight in soil and organic matter each day. It leaves behind castings that form a rich compost. A pound of earthworms will generally compost one pound of kitchen waste and make one pound of compost each day.

To make a container to hold your earthworms, construct a wooden box two feet wide by two feet long and one foot high. If you do not want to go to this trouble, drill at least six holes into the bottom of a sturdy fifty-six liter plastic bin.

Here are the steps to making your earthworm compost:

1. Prepare the bedding by filling a bucket with one-third peat moss; one-third a combination of good garden soil, dried straw or leaves, and manure; and one-third water. Soak this mixture overnight.
2. The next day, squeeze out any excess water.
3. Cover the bottom of the bin with small pebbles.
4. Lay four inches of the bedding mixture over the pebbles. Leave the bin to stand one day; the mixture may heat up too much and kill the earthworms if they are put in right away.
5. The next day, move some of the bedding to the side of the bin, then remove the earthworms from their shipping container placing them into the center of the bin. Lightly cover the earthworms with the bedding you pulled aside.
6. Place a burlap sack or some newspapers over the top of the bedding and moisten it with a watering can. Keep the bedding moist but not soggy.
7. The container will begin to drip from the holes in the bottom, so place a tray underneath to catch the drippings. You can dilute these drippings in water and use them to water your plants!
8. Start feeding the worms slowly. If you give them more than they can eat in a twenty-four hour period, the extra vegetable waste will attract flies and heat up the bedding, which can kill the earthworms. Start feeding them soft foods like cooked veggies, bread scraps, and soups, leftover cereal with the milk, cornmeal, and coffee grounds. After a few weeks, your earthworms will be ready to handle raw vegetables. Do not give the earthworms strong foods like onions or garlic.
9. Every few weeks, add a thin layer of manure to the bin.
10. Every two weeks, turn the compost to aerate it. The earthworms will not come to the surface for a while after you turn the compost, so reduce the amount of food you give them for a few days.
11. After one month, add another two inches of bedding to accommodate the growing worm population.
12. After three months, the compost will be ready to use, but you will need to start a new bin to house the earthworms.

When you are ready to divide the existing box, cover a large table with a plastic sheet and dump the bedding and worms onto your workspace. Heap the compost into a pile in the center of the table. Pick out the rocks and put them back into the bin. Any worms exposed to the light will burrow into the center of the pile. Scrape the top of the pile of the bedding into a bucket and wait ten minutes while any exposed worms burrow deeper. After several scrapings, your worms will be at the bottom of the pile, making it easy to put them into the new bin you have made.

Problem Solving

The main concern for most gardeners who compost, especially first-timers, is the odor that comes from your compost pile. Too much nitrogen material (green material) in the pile or a wet pile will cause the bad odor. The best way to make the odor disappear is to turn the pile and add in more carbon material (brown material) as you restack it. This will help to balance the high nitrogen content. To keep the odor from coming back, make sure you add in the same amount of green and brown material and cover them both with a thin layer of soil.

If the pile is too wet, it lacks air. Turn the pile and add in more carbon material. This material will help absorb some of the excess moisture. If you live in a rainy climate, make sure your compost bin is covered.

FACT

Compost can be used to control certain plant diseases, especially fungus. Spreading compost around the base of plants that have fungus diseases or are susceptible to fungus disease is a great way to prevent it from spreading or forming. If you do not have a lot of compost, make a compost tea to water the plants.

If your compost pile looks like nothing is happening or has not sunk down at all, it is probably too dry. A properly moistened compost pile should shrink by 30 percent over a month or so. If this is not happening, assume you need to give the pile more water. The best way to do this is to turn the pile and add in water as you restack it. If this is too much trouble, you can turn on your hose at a drip and leave it on top of the pile so the water will soak into it. If you are expecting rain, leave the pile uncovered and let nature do the work for you.

If you are making compost in the spring or fall and the weather is reasonably warm, the center of your compost pile should be warm or even hot to the touch. If it is not very warm, the pile may be too dry. If the moisture level is correct, the pile may be too small to get hot enough. It should be at least three feet by three feet. If this is not the problem, the pile may not have enough nitrogen (green material) in it. To correct these problems, turn the pile and add in more green material.

If you live in a climate with cold winters, the low temperatures may inhibit the decomposition process. The compost microorganisms are inactive if the temperature in the pile goes below freezing. To keep the pile warm during the cold months, cover it with clear plastic, which will trap the sun inside and heat up the pile. If the pile still freezes, wait for the decomposition process to start up again once the weather warms up.

ESSENTIAL

If you have a large garden or grow vegetables commercially, invest in a good shredder. By shredding large pieces of compost such as brassica stocks, corn stalks, and twigs, you will be able to make good quality compost much more quickly. Smaller materials will decompose much faster!

If you have tiny black fruit flies or houseflies around your compost, it is a sign that you have not made your pile correctly or have not maintained it well. The best way to prevent flies is not to attract them in the first place. It is important to cover your pile with equal amounts of green and brown materials, then cover them both with a thin layer of soil or manure. If you have flies, try turning the pile and add in whichever matter is lacking.

Animals digging in your compost can make the area messy. Dogs, cats, raccoons, and rats are common culprits. If you have critter problems, choose or build a bin that will keep the animals out. For rats, you need a metal mesh bin with tiny holes around the whole compost. To keep out larger animals, make sure the bin is closed on all sides with wire or wood, or do your composting in a sturdy plastic compost container.

CHAPTER 15

Easy Ways to Water

Your vegetable plants need water to grow, mature, and produce fruits, pods, or seeds for you to enjoy. The amount of water each plant requires depends hugely on your climate, your soil, and the type of vegetable. All of these variables make watering a complex subject. In this chapter you will learn about the benefits and disadvantages of the various ways you can water your garden. We will discuss hand watering, overhead watering, and drip irrigation and explain how to watch for signs that your plants may be in trouble.

Hand Watering

Hand watering is done by using a container such as a watering can or a hose connected to a water source to water individual vegetable plants. When choosing to hand water, it is important that your water source is nearby. The main benefits of hand watering include your ability to direct where the flow of water goes and to control when and how much water you give the plants. It also gives you the valuable opportunity to observe your plants. And the equipment you need is inexpensive to purchase.

Any kind of container that will hold water can be used to water your plants, but watering cans are probably the most common and are all fairly inexpensive. There are several different kinds of watering cans you can choose from, but the nozzle is the most important component. Each nozzle has a different number and size of holes, which can affect how much and how quickly the water comes out. If you are watering tiny seedlings, you want a nozzle that will give a light spray of water—a Haws watering can is great for this. If you are watering larger plants, the holes can be bigger to give a heavier spray of water.

If you choose to water with a hose, you must again consider the nozzle. Choosing one that has a variety of spray options is best. That allows you to give a light or heavier spray depending on what kind of plant you are watering. Making sure your hose easily reaches all areas of your garden site will make is easier for you to water regularly.

ESSENTIAL

Water is crucial for seed germination and seed growth, so it is important to keep your seedbed moist until the seeds have germinated. When setting out your transplants, make sure the seedlings are moist when planted and water again after planting. Young seedlings have very shallow roots, so you do not want the soil to dry out.

Some plants do better if you hand water them. For example, containers are best hand watered and there is less waste than using a sprinkler. Larger vegetable plants such as broccoli, cabbages, and cauliflower do better with hand watering; if you use an overhead sprinkler to water them, the leaves can keep the water from reaching the roots. Other plants like tomatoes, squash, and carrots attract pests and disease more readily if their leaves get wet, so hand watering can be one way to keep them healthy.

Hand watering your vegetable garden can take up a lot of time, which is one definite disadvantage. It can take up to an hour to water a ten-foot-square garden and do it well. Plants often do not get enough water when they are hand watered because gardeners rush through the task. Some gardeners enjoy this aspect of growing vegetables and find it relaxing, but others do not have the patience to do it. Also consider that if you hand water your vegetables, you'll have to find someone you trust to take over for you if you want to take a vacation.

Overhead Watering

Using an overhead sprinkler is probably the easiest and most common way most gardeners water their vegetable gardens. Depending on how large your garden is, all you have to do is set up your sprinkler in one area and turn it on. Everything gets watered all at one time. It takes approximately one hour of sprinkling (depending on water pressure) for the water to soak into the soil several inches.

BENEFITS OF USING AN OVERHEAD SPRINKLER
- Simple to set up and use
- Equipment is inexpensive to purchase
- Saves time
- Timers and automatic equipment are easy to use
- Can be easily moved around your garden
- Can be used to keep plants cool in warm weather

Lettuce, spinach, salad greens, and Swiss chard all benefit from overhead watering. The leaves are kept cool while the water on the leaves evaporates, lowering the temperature of the plant and preventing plants from wilting or being scorched in hot temperatures.

DISADVANTAGES OF USING AN OVERHEAD SPRINKLER

- A lot of water can be wasted through evaporation or watering areas that do not need water.
- Moisture on the leaves of some vegetable plants can cause diseases.
- Leaves of larger vegetable plants can keep moisture from reaching the plant roots.

Tomatoes, squash, and carrots do not do well if their leaves get wet. Wet leaves make these plants more susceptible to diseases such as mildew and blight. Plants with large leaves such as broccoli, cabbage, cauliflower, and corn are not good candidates for overhead watering. The leaves can prevent enough water from reaching the roots, which can cause the soil to dry out.

FACT

One good weekly watering is much better for the plants and more effective in the soil than frequent light watering. Plant roots seek out water, and the moisture deep in the soil encourages the roots to grow deeper, which gives them access to more nutrients.

Choosing to use or not to use an overhead sprinkler is a personal choice. If time is a factor, then overhead watering may be the simplest solution. It is also important to look at the vegetables you will be growing and the effects overhead watering may have on those plants. You will have to find out which method will work best in your situation. If you have a large garden, you may be able to have the best of both worlds. You can water certain areas by hand and use overhead sprinklers for the rest.

Drip Irrigation

In drip irrigation, water seeps slowly into the soil. Gardeners use a hose that has many little holes in it or flat plastic tubing that has slits on one side. Both are laid on the ground along the base of your plants, allowing water to reach the roots. The soaker hose has the same attachments as a regular hose and is usually used in a small area where it can be easily attached to a water tap.

The flat plastic tubing needs more setup to work and is common in large commercial vegetable gardens. You need irrigation connectors, attachments, and water pipe in order to attach the tubing to your water source. With good water pressure, both the soaker hose and plastic tubing can give your garden soil up to an inch of water in approximately fifteen minutes, so drip irrigation is a very efficient way to water your vegetable garden.

ADVANTAGES TO USING A DRIP SYSTEM
- Very little water is lost to evaporation, so you don't waste water.
- Moisture reaches the roots where it is most needed.
- It adds moisture to the soil slowly, allowing it to soak in over time; this allows the roots to utilize it better.
- Soil is watered evenly and thoroughly.
- Hoses or equipment can be easily moved.

ESSENTIAL

You can recycle an old, leaky hose to make a drip irrigation system of your own! Simply punch more holes into the hose every few inches to make your own soaker hose. It's an effective way to reuse equipment you would otherwise throw into the garbage.

Make sure you have enough soaker hose or plastic tube length to cover your garden area. You can lay the hose out when you plant an area and pull it up after harvesting. For easier setup, lay it out along your beds as you plant your seeds or set out your transplants. The hose and plastic tubing can be mulched or just left on top of the ground. But be aware that both can deteriorate over time if left exposed to the sun.

DISADVANTAGES OF DRIP IRRIGATION
- It takes time and some effort to set up and to take down the equipment and hoses.
- The tubing can be easily punctured by a rake or hoe.
- Equipment can become very costly if you have a large garden area, though it will last for a long time if handled properly.

The system using irrigation tubing is best utilized if you have a large garden or are growing commercially. It can be costly and labor intensive, and therefore is not necessarily the best choice for a small backyard vegetable garden.

Every garden site has different needs and every gardener has a different outlook, so you need to choose the watering style that best suits you and your garden. Most gardeners use a combination of all the watering options to best meet the needs of all their vegetable plants. The most important part of watering your vegetable plants is to make sure they are not getting too much or too little water. Proper watering is needed for your plants to grow and produce an abundant harvest for you.

Signs of Underwatering

A plant's roots must continually grow for the plant to stay healthy and produce its fruit, seeds, or buds. The roots draw the nutrients from the soil up into the plant to make it grow. Water allows the nutrients in the soil to be absorbed into the plant. If there is too little water, the roots cannot draw in the nutrients. As a result, the plant will not grow and mature as it should. You can water the surface or even the top several inches of your soil, but the plant roots need to go deeper into the soil to get more nutrients. This is why it is essential for regular deep watering when growing vegetables.

Wilted plants are one sign that you're not watering enough. If the plant can draw enough water to replace the amount that is evaporated from its leaves, it will remain upright and strong. If the plant is not getting the water it needs, it will quickly collapse. This causes severe stress to the plant and often death. It is important to water a plant that is wilted as soon as you can.

ALERT

Deep roots make plants more tolerant to drought conditions. If you have to ration water, know which plants have the deepest roots. Beets, asparagus, tomatoes, and brassicas can do with a bit less water. Never stop watering celery, lettuce, cucumbers, squash, and peppers, because they are very sensitive to drought conditions.

It is important to take time every day to observe your plants so you can find and quickly fix potential problems. Your plants should appear strong, have a bright color, and look healthy. If you have young transplants, you need to give them a drink of water every day because their roots are very shallow and the top few inches of your soil can dry out very quickly. Too little water can lead to poor root development, which will make for an unhealthy plant. Once your vegetable plants have begun to mature, watering them once a week is usually sufficient. For some plants, it is best to stop watering them altogether once they have matured. For example, onions and potatoes need less water as they get close to maturity.

SIGNS THAT YOUR PLANTS NEED MORE WATER

- The plants appear small and very slow growing.
- The vegetable plants are not producing very many fruits, seeds, or buds and the ones being produced are often misshapen.
- Your plants are diseased.
- The plants are yellowish or pale in color.
- Your plants are wilting. Some natural wilting may occur in the heat of the day, but if your plants do not perk up by late afternoon you have a problem.

Signs of Overwatering

Most gardeners go to great lengths to make sure they add enough nutrients to their garden beds. When the soil is moist, the water helps hold the nutrients to rock particles in the soil so the plant roots can absorb them. If there is too much water in the soil, a process called *leaching* occurs. The water drains lower into the soil and takes a lot to the nutrients with it.

Vegetable plant roots grow to different depths, but most do not grow below two and a half feet. If the excess water has washed away the nutrients, there is less nourishment available for the roots to absorb. Without proper food, the plant will not grow and mature as you may expect it to.

Plants also need good air circulation to breathe. If the soil is saturated with water, there isn't any room left in the soil for air circulation. If the air supply is cut off for any length of time, the plant roots will rot, killing the plant. That's why it's crucial to know your own soil conditions. Keep a record of rainfall and regularly check the moisture in your soil either with a moisture meter or by digging into the soil with your hands or a small shovel to see how far down the moisture is. Water when needed. If you are a novice gardener, it can take time to get to know your soil and climate, so initially it is important to observe and jot down some notes so you can refer back to them the following season.

ALERT

To make digging easier, use the heel—not the ball—of your foot to push the spade into the ground. To help prevent back strain or injury, slide the dirt off the spade or shovel rather than throwing it off.

Combating Drainage Problems

You need a fertile, well-drained soil to grow great vegetables; however, most gardeners are not blessed with perfect soil or the perfect garden site.

How do you make your soil healthier and get proper drainage if you live in a rainy climate or you have soggy soil? What do you do if you have the opposite problem—a sandy soil that does not hold any amount of water? How do you increase the amount of moisture in this type of soil?

Adding organic material is the solution to both problems. It will help lighten heavy soil so the water can drain better, and it will add more organic material to the sandy soil to help hold the water in. Aged animal manure, compost, or well-drained topsoil will help. Add in as much as possible— several inches if you can get enough. It is important to add in organic matter every year because you inevitably lose soil through erosion and the process of harvesting your plants. Mulching is another way to protect your soil from being blown away or nutrients from being leached out.

ALERT

The best time to water your vegetable plants is in the morning. This gives the plant leaves time to dry off and remain cool when the sun hits. Plants—especially young seedlings—do not like to be cold, so it is best to water while the temperature is increasing during the day.

If you have an extreme problem with drainage, call a landscaper to assess the situation for you. Underground drainage pipes can help remove any excess water you may have in your garden site. A well-drained soil helps keep the plant roots from becoming waterlogged, allowing them to absorb the nutrients and oxygen needed to grow and mature. A poorly drained soil leaves your vegetable plants more susceptible to root rot and soil-borne diseases, so get help with drainage if this is a problem in your garden site.

CHAPTER 16

Controlling the Weeds

A weed is just a plant that grows where it is not wanted! It is important to keep your garden beds weeded when your vegetable plants are small so your plants get a good start. Weeds compete for the nutrients in the soil, often taking over and leaving your veggie plants without the valuable food they need to grow and mature. In this chapter you will learn different techniques to help keep your garden weed-free—or at least to help you keep them under control.

Know Your Weeds

Weed seeds are introduced to your garden by birds, the wind, and on the bottom of your shoes. If a soil will not support weeds, it will not support your vegetables, so weeds are a sign that your soil is fertile. Seeds are brought to the surface by digging or tilling the soil. Once they are exposed to the light, they start growing. Some weeds can grow very fast, stealing the light, nutrients, and space from your vegetable plants.

There are three types of weeds—annuals, biennials, and perennials. Annual weeds live for only one season, but they produce thousands of seeds to ensure their survival. They germinate in the spring, produce seeds in the summer, and die in the fall. The best way to control annual weeds is to pull them out or cut them off with a hoe before they go to seed. Annual weeds grow quickly, so you need to be on top of these weeds so they do not spread their seed. Some examples of common annual weeds are knotweed, pigweed, purslane, lamb's quarters, and chickweed.

A biennial weed grows the first year but does not produce a flower or seeds until the second year of growth. The best way to control these weeds is to remove them from your garden in the first year of their growth so they have no chance of spreading their seeds. Common biennial weeds include burdock, mullein, and Queen Anne's lace.

QUESTION

How do I get rid of poison ivy?
The best way to get rid of poison ivy is to rake it out. Using a sturdy rake, carefully tug at the ivy, making sure the whole plant—including the roots—comes out. Make sure you clean your rake and wash your hands well; the oil in poison ivy can be harmful.

Perennial weeds live for years. Some produce seeds and others spread by their roots or bulbs. Perennial weeds often have deep roots that creep underground, making them difficult to eradicate. To control them, dig them out, removing as much of the root as you can. You often have to pull these weeds on a regular basis in order to get all the root system. Some common perennial weeds are dandelion, thistle, bindweed, chicory, plantain, wild sorrel, and dock.

Woody perennials include poison ivy, kudzu, morning glory, and Japanese honeysuckle. These are often invasive and are spread mainly by birds that love the seeds of these plants. Some of these plants need only a piece of stem to come in contact with soil to begin growing, so they can multiply quickly. Grasses are another invasive perennial weed. These can make some of the worst weeds because they produce a lot of seeds and the plants are difficult to uproot. Quack grass and some varieties of bamboo are common grasses that are considered weeds, especially in the vegetable garden. These plants produce underground roots and stems, and new plants pop up several yards away from the parent plant, making them difficult to remove.

What Weeds Can Tell You

You can learn a great deal about your soil by observing the weeds that grow in your garden. They can point to soil imbalances such as poor drainage, lack of water, low fertility, lack of aeration, and nutrient deficiency. Certain weeds only grow in poor soil, which gives you an indication that you need to add more amendments and fertilize your garden area if you want to grow a successful vegetable garden. Correcting the imbalances in your soil often means you will be able to eradicate certain weeds.

WEEDS THAT INDICATE POOR SOIL
- Jersey or scrub pine
- Mullein
- Oxeye daisy
- Scrub or bear oak
- Wild carrot

WEEDS THAT INDICATE HEAVY ACIDIC SOIL WITH POOR DRAINAGE
- Creeping buttercup
- Docks
- Horsetail
- Thistles
- Wild sorrel
- Yarrow

Creeping buttercup

Wild garlic

Dandelion

Common vetch

WEEDS THAT INDICATE SANDY SOIL

- Bindweed
- Mustards
- Ragweed
- Stinging nettles
- Wild garlic

WEEDS THAT INDICATE INADEQUATE NITROGEN LEVELS

- Clover
- Medic
- Vetch
- Wild peas

WEEDS THAT INDICATE INADEQUATE ESSENTIAL NUTRIENTS

- Dandelions

WEEDS THAT INDICATE GOOD FERTILITY

- Chickweed
- Chicory
- Lamb's quarter
- Groundsel

Taking your time to observe what weeds are growing in your garden area can be especially important if you are planning to start a new garden in a certain area, or if you are looking for some property to purchase with the intention of growing your own food or growing to sell.

Weed Your Garden

Spring brings new growth to your vegetable garden. The seeds begin to sprout and the transplants start to grow—and so do the weeds. Spring is the time to pay attention to your weeds. Weeds often grow faster than your vegetable plants, so they can overtake them and steal the sunlight and nutrients your veggie plants need. It is easier to kill the weeds when they are small and the soil is moist rather than later when the soil is hard and dry. Always remove the weeds before they go to seed!

As you become more familiar with your garden site and the weeds that grow there, it will get easier to distinguish weeds from your vegetable plants. As a new gardener, it can be confusing to decide what you should pull and what you should leave. Some plants look similar, especially when they are small. Lamb's quarter looks like a radish at first and wild sorrel looks like spinach when it first starts to grow. If you aren't sure what weeds look like, delay the weeding until you see your row or the pattern of your vegetables coming up. This is another important reason to mark the area where you have planted your vegetable seeds.

ESSENTIAL

If your vegetable garden creeps onto your lawn, put in an edging between them. You can purchase plastic edging from most garden centers, or you can use wood or metal as an edging. Stone is not the best because the grass can creep in between the sections. The edging will help prevent the grass from growing into your garden site.

Getting on your hands and knees and pulling weeds (getting the roots if you can) is probably the best way to get rid of weeds in your vegetable garden. This can be time-consuming, but if you set aside time each week to do a patch, you will be pleasantly surprised that it can be easy to stay on top of them. Do not avoid weeding! Weeding is often a gardener's downfall because weeds can grow rapidly, and they can take over a garden before you know it. It is important to allot time every week all season long for your weeding. It is often the last thing on a gardener's list, but it should be on top. A healthy garden needs to have more veggies growing in it than weeds. If you have missed a few weeks of weeding and some of them have gone to seed, carefully pull out the plant and immediately put it into a plastic garbage bag. This will prevent some of the seeds from spreading.

Hoeing is a great way to keep the weeds in check. Get into the habit of hoeing your garden beds even if there are no weeds; this will prevent any seeds that may be in the soil from germinating. Scrape the hoe over the top inch of the soil. It is easier to hoe when the soil is moist, so do your hoeing after watering your garden or after a rainfall. By scraping the top of the soil, you will slice off the tops of the weeds, preventing the weed from going to seed. Depending on the type of weed, it may grow again or the roots may decompose. Keeping your hoe blade sharp will make this job easier to accomplish.

Mulch: Does It Work?

After hoeing or weeding your garden bed, add mulch to the area. Weed seeds need light to germinate and grow, so the main function of mulch in weed control is to prevent light from reaching the seeds. Cover the area completely with up to four inches of mulch, leaving a few inches around the base of the plant stem clear. You'll often have mulch materials handy from your own garden. Two common materials are leaves and grass. Raking leaves and then running the lawn mower over them to shred them makes great mulch. Collecting your grass clippings in a mower bag is another mulch that costs no money and is easy to get. Just make sure you do not use pesticides on your lawn; you do not want to contaminate your vegetable patch.

FACT

Tough perennial weeds will often show up when you do not have the time to deal with them. Placing boards over invested areas of quack grass, Bermuda grass, or Johnson grass will slow down their growth for a few weeks until you have the time you need to dig them out.

You can also make organic mulch out of newspaper, cardboard, straw, hay, bark mulch, compost, and animal manure. Nonorganic mulch materials include crushed rock, black plastic, and landscape fabric. These usually need to be purchased and can be expensive. Choosing the type of mulch you want to use can depend on what is readily available or how much you care about your garden's appearance. Either way, mulch is helpful in controlling the weeds in your vegetable garden.

But mulch has many other benefits to your garden. Mulch can reduce evaporation of water so the soil will stay moist longer. It can help by either warming up the soil or keeping the temperature cool. The organic mulch will decompose over time, adding organic matter and nutrients into your garden soil. Earthworms like the darkness it provides and will thrive under a thick bed of mulch. Mulch can offer some protection to fruiting plants; it keeps their fruit from lying directly on the ground, which can help prevent pests and diseases.

However, mulch also has its disadvantages. Mulch can promote fungus and disease, especially if it keeps the soil too damp and cold. Slugs and mice love mulch, so only use mulches sparingly if you live in an area where these are a problem. Using certain types of mulch can cause deficiencies in your soil. For example, pine needles are very acidic and may make it more difficult to grow your vegetables in a soil that is already acidic. Sawdust uses up nitrogen to decompose, which it does at the expense of your plants. It is important to understand what materials are best for your garden site and the reasons you are using mulch.

Other Ways to Control Weeds

One great way to prevent weeds is not to bring them into your garden. Keep any tools you work with clean. Remove any weeds that have gone to seed from your garden. When shopping for plants, make sure there are not any weeds in the containers. When you bring in hay or straw to your garden, make sure it is from a weed-free source. If it is not weed-free, you may soon find hay growing in your garden beds! Animal manures can have lots of weed seeds in them, so make sure you know what kind of bedding was used and what the animals were fed. All of these small things can make it easier to keep your garden free of weeds, or at least make sure you are not introducing new weeds to the area.

Growing a cover crop can smother weeds. By growing a cover crop you can enrich your soil as well as control weeds. Cultivate or dig the area and then sow the green manure crop thickly. Turn the green manure over before the weeds you are trying to control have a chance to set seed. To be most effective, you will need to grow and turn two or three cover crops in succession. By growing vegetables close together, you can reduce the number of weeds by shading any area from the sun. Grow your lettuces close together so they overlap each other or grow your squash under your corn to prevent weeds from getting any light.

Applying heat to weeds is another effective way to kill them. This is most useful in your pathways, driveway, or sidewalks. Heat will kill your vegetable plants as well, so don't use this method in your vegetable garden. You can purchase a handheld flamer, which basically burns any weeds the flame touches. To kill weeds in small areas such as the crevices of a stone patio, pour boiling water over the weeds. This will keep your patio or sidewalk weed-free.

ALERT

Clean your gardening tools after using them. Weed seeds and diseases can be easily carried from one area to another, attached to your hoe, spade, or even your shoes. Make sure you give all your tools a good rinse whenever you are finished working with them for the day to prevent infecting other areas.

Planting a windbreak will help prevent weeds from blowing from another area into your garden. This can be very effective, especially if your garden borders on a wooded area or a wild meadow area where there are many different weeds. You cannot usually mow or keep these areas cut back, so a windbreak keeps the seeds from reaching your garden. Cedar and laurel hedges make good windbreaks. Both grow quickly and are fairly dense when mature. A fence could also work as a windbreak, blocking unwanted seeds from coming through.

The Benefits of Weeds

Weeds do have some benefits to your garden as well. Many perennial weeds are deep rooted, which helps bring nutrients to the surface so your vegetable plants have access to them. The deep roots also aerate the soil, which can be helpful, especially if you have drainage problems in your garden site. Weeds will grow when most other plants will not and are beneficial for preventing soil erosion and for preventing leaching of nutrients due to heavy rainfall. Many weeds are a great food source for bees, butterflies, birds, and beneficial insects, which all help control unwanted pests and disease in your vegetable garden.

Stinging nettle

Chickweed

White clover

WEEDS THAT ATTRACT BUTTERFLIES

- Clover
- Milkweed
- Nettles
- Thistles

WEEDS THAT ATTRACT SONGBIRDS

- Chickweed
- Lamb's quarters

WEEDS THAT ATTRACT BENEFICIAL INSECTS

- Corn spurry
- Queen Anne's lace
- Wild mustard
- White clover

Weeds can be composted so long as they have been pulled before they go to seed. If you have only pulled a few weeds, you can leave them to dry in your pathway; however, if you have a whole bucketful of weeds, it is best to remove them from the garden, because they can attract pests. Place them into your compost instead; they are a good source of green matter.

Most gardeners consider comfrey and stinging nettles to be weeds, but they can be added to your compost or used to make a nitrogen-rich fertilizer tea. Both of these plants draw up and store nitrogen in their leaves. When they are composted or made into teas, the nitrogen is released.

ALERT

Use quack grass to kill your slugs! Slugs avoid areas where this weed grows. Put some quack grass in your blender with some water to make a solution you can spray on your plants. Test the spray on a few plants; it may act too strongly on young seedlings and kill them.

There are many edible weeds that you can harvest to use in cooking. Stinging nettles, dandelion greens, purslane, lamb's quarter, and burdock are all edible. It is important to do the research and know exactly what plant you are harvesting before you eat it. However, once you know what weeds are edible, you will have a whole new outlook and even more choices to add to your dinner table—and the weeds grew without any work on your part!

CHAPTER 17

Pests and Diseases: What Do I Do?

Having healthy soil and a healthy garden environment is the best way to prevent pest infestation and diseases. In this chapter, you will get advice on how to make your soil healthy and how to implement good gardening practices. No garden is without pests and diseases, but the important thing is to control them before they become a problem. The secret is taking the time to observe your garden. You can keep your plants healthy by using natural controls and promoting beneficial insects.

Find the Problem

Take the time every day or at least once a week to walk through your garden just to observe the plants. Ignore the weeds and do not stop to harvest; just take a few minutes to turn leaves over, check inside the cabbage leaves, and look closely at any insects or pests you may see. Doing this on a regular basis will allow you to catch problems early on. Is a certain plant looking less healthy than it did last week? Are those new holes in the leaves? Is something eating my spinach? Are those cabbage flies around my brassica plants? Do my tomatoes have spots or are they split? By observing the changes to your plants you can determine whether there is a threat to the plant and act quickly. If the problem is not obvious, you will need to be a detective to find out what could be wrong.

QUESTIONS TO ASK
- ❑ Is the problem affecting the whole plant or just part of it?
- ❑ Is the problem on one plant or on several plants?
- ❑ Is there a pattern to it or is the problem random?
- ❑ Is only a certain area of the garden affected?
- ❑ Are only young plants affected?
- ❑ Is there anything unusual on the underside of the plant leaves?

If you can see an insect or pest but do not know what it is, try to take a sample of the problem to your local nursery to see if they can identify the problem for you. A healthy plant will be able to fight a lot of problems, so give the infected plant a little more care and attention. Does it need more or less water? Has it been fertilized recently or is it overdue? If the plant is too damaged, pull it out and immediately place it into a garbage bag and remove it from your garden site so as not to spread the problem to other areas.

ALERT

Ladybugs are a gift to any vegetable garden. They eat unwanted pests like aphids, mealy bugs, spider mites, thrips, and whiteflies. To attract them to your garden, plant marigolds, goldenrod, or butterfly weed. They can also be purchased at most garden centers or from seed catalogs.

Keeping a journal of any problems you have had in your garden this season will help you to plan for next season. You can use the successes and failures as a jumping-off point for tackling problems in future seasons.

Start with Healthy Soil

Having healthy, fertile garden soil is the best way to keep pests and diseases away. First, find out what kind of soil you have and correct any imbalances. Healthy soil will produce healthy vegetable plants. Healthy vegetable plants will not be stressed and will be less vulnerable to pests or diseases. Nutrient deficiencies, overwatering, and underwatering can make your vegetable plants more susceptible to pests and diseases.

If you till your soil when it is too wet or too dry, you can harm living organisms and earthworms in the soil. You can also change the soil structure, which can cause drainage problems, leaching of nutrients, and an overall unhealthy space for your plant roots to grow. Most gardeners are raring to go in the spring and want to get the garden going, but it is important not to till too early. Take the moisture test before you till in the spring. Squeeze a handful of soil. If it forms a firm hard ball, it is too wet; if it crumbles into dust, it is too dry. Soil that is just right will keep some shape but easily crumble when you squeeze it.

eV FACT

Most vegetables do best in soil with a pH between 6.0 and 6.9. Brassicas, spinach, and lettuce like it to be on the higher side. Tomatoes, peppers, eggplants, and most root crops can take the lower end. Squash, peas, beans, and onions prefer the pH to be right around 6.5.

Tilling or digging your soil in the fall will expose insects, larvae, and eggs to the elements, which can help destroy them. After you harvest an area you are going to leave bare, dig it up and let it sit for a week or so. Then either mulch the area or plant a green manure. Mulch will help keep the soil from getting too wet and will prevent leaching if you live in a rainy climate. On the flip side, mulch can also be a haven for pests such as slugs and can encourage mold and disease, so regularly check under the mulch for any larvae or eggs during the winter and spring.

Growing green manures is another way to keep your soil healthy. They are grown in the fall and help keep the soil from being blown away by the wind. Green manures also prevent erosion and leaching of nutrients. It is tilled under in the spring, which adds organic matter and nutrients to the soil, making it more fertile and healthier.

Good Gardening Practices

Maintaining a clean vegetable garden will go a long way to keeping it free of pests and disease. Trash, garden debris, and diseased plants can be a haven for many pests and diseases. Remove weeds from the garden after they are pulled out. They can be put in the compost bin or the trash if they have gone to seed. If you have any diseased vegetable plants, make sure you put them into a garbage bag immediately after pulling them so you don't spread the problem into other areas of your veggie garden.

If you find any pests, kill them on the spot by squishing them with your shoe or between your fingers. A good way to kill slugs is to cut them in half with your shovel. If you just place a pest on the ground or move it to another spot, it will be back! If you are squeamish about killing them, place them in a garbage bin and make sure they are not left on site. If the insect is too small to pick off and kill by hand, a good sharp spray of water can do the job. Spray infested leaves with an insecticidal soap or make your own insect spray to kill or deter harmful insects.

QUESTION

How do I make an insect spray?
Place the following ingredients in a blender: 1 garlic bulb, 1 small onion, 1 tablespoon cayenne pepper, and 1 quart water. Blend together and let the mixture steep for a few minutes. Mix in 1 teaspoon liquid nondetergent soap. Use immediately or keep up to a week refrigerated.

When harvesting, make sure all the fruit is removed from the garden. If there are any moldy fruits, place them into the compost rather than leaving them on the ground. When a plant is matured and no longer producing, pull it out and place it into your compost. Debris that is left in your garden beds or in the pathways can easily become a home for many pests and diseases.

Always have clean, sharp tools. Take the time at the end of each day to clean your tools. Scrape off any mud or dirt from each tool and give it a good spray of water to clean it. This will remove any pests. This is especially important if you have been working with diseased plants or in an area infested by pests. Every few weeks, take a little more care and wash the blades thoroughly with soap and water and then sharpen and oil them. A clean, sharp tool will make your life easier when working in the garden and will ensure you are not spreading pests and diseases around your garden.

FACT

To preserve the wooden handles on your garden tools, coat them with boiled linseed oil. This type of oil is thicker and dries quicker than the edible linseed soil. Simply rub the oil into the handle, allow it to sit for five to ten minutes to penetrate the wood, and rub off any excess oil with a clean, dry cloth.

Crop rotation is another essential practice to ensure a healthy garden. By growing your veggie plants in a different area each year, you will discourage pests and diseases in your soil. Each vegetable plant or family of plants requires different nutrients and attracts different pests and diseases. These pests usually live in the soil right where the plant was, so by moving your plants to a new area of the garden they will be less likely to survive. A good rule of thumb is not to plant the same vegetable or family of vegetables in the same area for four years.

Companion planting is another practice that can help to keep pests and diseases away from certain plants. In this method, certain plants are grown together so that they help each other. One plant may attract beneficial insects that will eat common pests, keeping the plants nearby healthier. Another plant may deter a pest, keeping the plant beside it healthier.

Keep Your Plants Healthy

To have healthy vegetable plants, you need to start with healthy seeds and transplants. Buy your seeds from a reputable seller or—even better—save your own seeds, especially if you find a certain variety that does well in your garden! A reputable seller should be willing to answer all your questions, provide you with information on where and how the seeds were grown, and give you growing tips. If your garden site is susceptible to certain pests or diseases, try to find seed varieties that are resistant to the problem. Seed catalogs have valuable information regarding different varieties of seeds. Choosing the right varieties of vegetable plants for your garden will help keep the soil and plants healthier.

When you purchase plants or transplants, make sure they are healthy. Many gardeners have unknowingly brought pests and diseases into their gardens via transplants. Look closely at any transplants you are planning to bring home. Check for any insects in the soil or on the undersides of the leaves, holes in the leaves, and evidence that insects have chewed the leaves. These are all signs that the plant may be infested. Make sure the plant looks healthy. The stem should be strong and thick, the leaves should be well formed and bright green, and the plant should not be root bound.

ESSENTIAL

To quickly transplant your seedlings, use a bulb planter to make the holes. The hole is just the right size for individual plastic cells. Gently drop each seedling into the hole and cover it with the soil you pulled out. Firm the soil around the base of the plant.

When you set out your transplants or weed around them, make sure you do not damage the plant roots. Injured roots are more likely to attract pests and diseases, and a stressed or damaged plant will be less likely to fight off problems.

When planning your garden layout, make sure you calculate how many plants you will need. Most gardeners purchase too much and then think they have to squeeze all the plants into their garden. Plants need a certain amount of space to grow well, so be careful not to overcrowd them. Vegetable plants will grow better with good air circulation, which will help prevent mold or fungus on the leaves or fruit. Keeping fruit off the ground will also keep the plant and fruit healthier; if the fruit is touching the wet soil, it will often rot before it is harvested.

Correct watering is another important aspect to keeping your plants healthy. Most vegetable plants need at least one inch of water each week, although this will vary depending on the specific plant and your climate, rainfall, and soil conditions. Plants that get either too much or too little water will be more likely to attract pests and diseases.

Regularly fertilizing your vegetable plants will help keep them healthier as well. Record how much and when you fertilize them so you don't give them too much or too little.

Use Natural Controls

Okay, you have kept your garden clean, your tools clean, and you have tried to keep your plants healthier, but you still have some pest and disease problems. Do not fret—a few problems don't mean you have to throw it all in and quit. There are some easy ways to control any problems you may have. It is important to observe your garden on a regular basis so you can catch any potential problems early on; problems are much easier to handle if not too many plants are infected.

Larger pests or animals can cause a lot of damage in vegetable gardens. Deer, elk, raccoons, squirrels, opossum, skunks, gophers, and bears like vegetables just as much as we do. Take the time to observe what kind of animal is entering your garden. They often come out and feed at dusk or dawn. If it's not a wild animal, maybe your neighbor's dog or cat is sneaking in and digging up your plants. Keep watch to see what is causing the problem.

If you need to set physical traps to stop insects and other animals, consider the following:

- Set mouse traps.
- Put out a dish of beer to attract slugs or lay a board for them to crawl under and then destroy them.
- Use cutworm collars around the base of the plant to prevent the cutworm from climbing up the stem.

- Set out sticky yellow flytraps, which will attract the flea beetle. The flea beetle sticks to the trap and dies.
- Use row covers to prevent flea beetles, carrot rust flies, or cabbage flies from reaching the veggie plants so they can't lay their eggs on them.
- Build a fence to keep out dogs, cats, raccoons, bear, and deer.

Attracting predators that will eat your pests is another natural way to keep the cycle in your garden healthy. Grow flowers, herbs, and certain vegetable plants to attract birds, ladybugs, honeybees, and lacewings, which will keep a lot of your pest problems under control.

Harmful Pests Versus Beneficial Insects and Animals

When you first begin to garden, there is a lot to learn about which bugs are good for your garden and which ones are harmful. It takes time to get to know what is living in or entering your garden, and each year may bring a new problem. Learn by asking fellow gardeners, reading books, checking out the Internet, or asking questions at your local nursery or garden center. Vegetable gardening is a new experience each season because you cannot predict what will happen. Do not be afraid to experiment with new plant varieties and try out different natural controls. Stay away from pesticides when it comes to your vegetable garden; they will not make your soil healthier and will kill the beneficial insects as well as the pests. Attracting and keeping beneficial animals and insects in your garden brings you closer to having healthier plants and a more abundant vegetable harvest.

Birds, bats, toads, and snakes are all animals you want in your garden. They will keep slugs, snails, and many insects under control. All these animals need food, water, and shelter. Your unwanted pests give them all the food they need, but you may need to supply water and shelter for these animals in order for them to stick around. If you do not have an existing water pond or fountain, place some water bowls around your garden and keep them filled. Place a birdhouse in at tree near your garden. A bat house looks like a flattened birdhouse with a thin slot for the entrance; they can also be kept in trees. Use a clay flowerpot with a chipped rim as a toad house. Place the pot upside down near a water source. Snakes will live in a pile of rocks or a pile of sticks; just leave a bit of space in between for them to crawl into. Making a home for these animals will help control the ones you do not want!

FACT

Birds will keep harmful insects under control but will also eat your corn seedlings and strawberries. If the birds are eating the seeds, cover your seed beds with bird netting until the seeds have sprouted. Some gardeners tie colored tape to tree branches and fences, which can be effective in keeping the birds out of your garden.

There are as many beneficial insects as there are harmful ones. Each garden site has a variety of different insects and soil animals.

COMMON BENEFICIAL INSECTS
- Ground beetles
- Honeybees
- Lacewings
- Ladybugs
- Praying mantis
- Spiders
- Syrphid flies
- Tachina flies
- Wasps
- Yellow jackets

Planting flowers among your vegetables or letting some of your vegetable plants flower rather than pulling out the plant is another way to attract beneficial insects to your garden. The flowers add color to your garden, some are edible, and they can make your garden more attractive overall.

Lemon balm

FLOWERS THAT ATTRACT BENEFICIAL INSECTS
- Broccoli flowers
- Calendula
- California poppy
- Celery flowers
- Dill flowers
- Lemon balm
- Marigolds
- Nasturtiums
- Parsley flowers
- Sunflowers

Having a healthy ecosystem in your vegetable garden lets nature take care of things for you. Start with healthy soil, plant healthy seeds and plants, and create an environment that will keep everything in your garden in balance.

Common Diseases

You can physically see a pest or insect, but it is more difficult to diagnose a plant disease because the symptoms can be similar to those caused by other factors like excessive heat or cold, nutrient deficiencies in the soil, or poor drainage. Having healthy soil, giving your plants proper water and fertilizer, and maintaining good garden practices minimizes your plants' vulnerability to many diseases. If you do have a recurring problem, it is important to learn what it is and try to correct the cause.

There are four main types of pathogens that cause disease in vegetable plants—bacteria, fungi, nematodes, and viruses. They all attack plants in different ways but have some common symptoms such as wilting, yellowing, and stunted growth. The pathogens can be spread in various ways. They can be blown around by the wind or carried in water. Animals, humans, garden tools, and other equipment can also transfer them from plant to plant. Insects can carry a pathogen in their saliva and transfer it from plant to plant. When you are trying to diagnose a disease, it is important to learn the life cycle of the pathogen so you can avoid spreading it.

Before any disease can occur, three elements must be present in your garden: a susceptible plant, a pathogen, and favorable conditions for the pathogen to survive. To control or manage plant diseases, you need to remove one or more of these elements. A disease cannot develop if one of these elements is missing. Planting disease-resistant varieties of vegetables can remove a susceptible plant from this equation. Pulling out and destroying the infected vegetable plant removes the pathogen. You can make it difficult for pathogens to survive by creating an environment that is not compatible for them. For example, avoid overhead watering or take time to trellis a plant so it has better air circulation. Both of these measures make it more difficult for the pathogen to survive.

ALERT

Aphids can easily spread viral and bacterial diseases. Controlling aphids often helps you stop the spread of the disease. Control aphids by attracting braconid wasps, hoverflies, lacewings, and ladybugs to your garden. An alternative is knocking the aphids off the plant with a strong stream of water.

The best way to keep your vegetable garden free of pests and diseases is to have healthy soil, to give your plants the proper amount of water, to use crop rotation, and to keep your garden and tools clean. A healthy plant will be better able to fight off anything that comes its way. No vegetable garden will be totally free of all pests or diseases, and remember that you want beneficial insects and animals to stay around.

CHAPTER 18

Harvesting Your Bounty

Picking and eating your own veggies is definitely the reward for all the hard work you have put into your garden. Some vegetables will mature more quickly than others, some will produce fruit or pods over several weeks, and others will provide only one harvest. In this chapter you will learn how to recognize when your plants are ready to be harvested, which vegetable plants will keep producing for you, how to store your veggies, which veggies will freeze well, and which veggies are best for canning.

Harvesting Tips

We are usually impatient to have our fruit, pods, and seeds ripe enough to eat. Harvesting is one of the best things about vegetable gardening. The taste and crunch of freshly picked veggies is one of life's little pleasures.

Harvested veggies

TIPS FOR AN EASY HARVEST

1. Observe your vegetable plants to see if they are ready to be harvested. When you plant, make a note in your garden journal of the plant's maturity day. It is best to pick vegetables when they are at the peak of ripeness. For most vegetables, the "pick and taste" method is probably the best test to see if your veggies are ready to be harvested.
2. If you harvest too early, your veggies may lack sweetness, size, and flavor. If you wait too long, many vegetables lose their flavor, develop a starchy taste, and toughen. Peas and corn become starchy tasting with age. Beans become stringy and zucchini become too large and taste dry if they are not harvested on time.
3. Some plants, such as peas, beans, and zucchini, need to be harvested regularly so the plant will keep producing. If the pods or fruit are not harvested in a timely way, the vegetables plants will take that as a signal to stop producing and they will start forming their flowers and seeds.

4. For best taste and flavor, harvest the vegetables just before eating or preserving them so you will get the full benefit of the vegetable's nutritional value.
5. Harvest early in the morning when there is still dew on the plants. This is especially beneficial for leafy vegetables like lettuce or other greens. They will keep longer if the leaves are kept moist.
6. Use sharp tools to harvest your veggies. Some fruit can be easily pulled or broken off, which can damage the plants and prevent them from producing anything more.
7. When harvesting root crops, have a bucket of water handy to wash off the dirt on the vegetables. Remember to water your other veggie plants with the muddy water!

Harvesting can be a fun way to get your family together. Taste as you pick and make it an event. If you have lots of veggies, get your neighbors involved and share the pickings. Give away raw veggies, host a meal, or have a canning party.

ESSENTIAL

If you are planning to overwinter some of your root crops, put a layer of leaves over the veggies, cover the leaves with plastic, and add another heavy layer of leaves. The plastic will keep the first layer of leaves from freezing, which makes it easier to dig out your vegetables during the winter.

By making a note of your vegetable varieties, their planting dates, and their maturity dates, you'll have some indication when your veggies should be harvested. If you know the plant is supposed to mature in fifty days, you can mark that on your calendar and then start observing the plant before the fifty days are up. Maturity dates are only guidelines; the growth of your vegetables can vary depending on your soil conditions, weather, rainfall, sunlight, and a host of other conditions.

Knowing When to Pick Vegetables

Different vegetables are harvested at different times and in different ways. Certain vegetables need to be harvested on a regular basis to keep the plant producing more. Some only produce one veggie, which is harvested at the peak of ripeness, while others will produce a second, smaller crop.

Salad Stuff

Lettuce, spinach, Swiss chard, oriental vegetables, and salad greens can be harvested by individually cutting baby leaves or mature plants. Baby greens, which are used in salads, can be cut when they are two to three inches high. You can usually get two cuttings before they stop producing or start tasting bitter. For a mature plant, check the seed packet to see how long they are supposed to take to mature. Most plants do not grow much higher than twelve to sixteen inches.

A mature plant can be cut off at the base of the plant or individual leaves can be cut as well. If the root is not disturbed, the plant will grow again, usually producing a smaller head. For salad stuff, pick a leaf. If it has a sweet, fresh taste, it is ready for your dinner plate! The plant is finished when the leaves start to taste bitter. Let the plant flower so you can collect the seeds or pull it out and plant something else in its spot.

ESSENTIAL

To keep lettuce longer, moisten a clean kitchen towel and wrap it around the lettuce. Place this into a plastic bag and put it in the refrigerator. Do not seal the bag, as it will keep better with air circulation. The lettuce will keep for up to two weeks stored this way.

Brassicas

Cabbages, broccoli, and cauliflower usually produce one good-sized head, although some will produce smaller heads once the main one has been harvested. These vegetables can be harvested with a sharp knife once the head reaches approximately four to eight inches in diameter. For cabbages, look for a firm head. They can be harvested on the small size or left until they get larger. If the head begins to split, you know it is getting on the old side. After the main cabbage is cut from the plant, smaller heads will form if the plant is left in the ground.

For broccoli, harvest the head when it is a bright green color and still firm. Once it starts to open, it is beginning to flower and will be less flavorful. Broccoli will produce side shoots off the main stem. These will be considerably smaller in size, so cut them regularly because they will go to flower quickly.

Cauliflower will produce only one head. Make sure the head it filled out and firm before harvesting it.

Peas, Beans, and Squash

These veggies are best picked on the early side because they are usually sweeter and more tender when small. Pea pods should be full, easy to open, and sweet tasting. Once they get older, the pods become wrinkly and the peas taste bitter and starchy. It is easy to miss a few pods when you are picking them, so leave the ones that have gotten old on the vine for harvesting for next year's seeds. Once your peas are ready for harvesting, do so every few days or the plant will stop producing. Hold the plant with one hand while gently pulling off the pod with the other. This will help minimize the damage to the plant.

The same goes for beans. A fresh green bean is best picked when it is slender and about three to four inches long. As beans get older, they become stringy and less sweet. If you are growing beans for the seeds, you want the pod to fill out as much as possible and dry on the vine.

FACT

African slaves brought black-eyed peas to America. They were first planted mainly as animal feed and are now a very popular food for many Americans. They are sometimes also called *cowpeas*, and if the eye is yellow they are know as "yellow-eyed peas."

Zucchini summer squash needs to be harvested regularly, starting when the squash is four to eight inches long. Tiny zucchini are a delicacy for many chefs. They are tender and taste best when small. They can grow several inches overnight, so check on them every few days. If you happen to miss one and it grows too large, harvest it anyway so the plant will produce more. The larger zucchini can be used for a stuffed zucchini recipe or in baking. For winter squash, it is best to leave the fruit on the vine as long as you can. Prick the skin with your fingernail to see if they are ready. If it leaves an indentation, it is not ready. If it does not leave a mark, the skin is hard and the fruit can be harvested.

Root Veggies

Root veggies can be left in the ground. After they mature, they will just grow bigger and most will keep their flavor. The advantage to growing root crops is that you can harvest them as you need them rather than having to eat them up as soon as they mature. Carrots, beets, rutabagas, and potatoes can be harvested as small as you want them to be. Pulling baby carrots or beets helps make room for the other plants to grow larger. For new potatoes, dig with your hands around the base of the plant and pull out the ones you can feel. This leaves the plant to produce more potatoes. Most root crops can be left in the ground over winter so long as the soil does not get too wet and the plants are well mulched so they do not freeze.

A good garden fork is invaluable. Gently loosen the soil around the area where the plant is growing and then use your hands to pull up the tubers or the root. Be careful not to pierce you potatoes or break the carrots when digging them. If you happen to pierce or break a potato, use it as soon as possible.

Heat-loving Veggies

Specific traits tell you whether your heat-loving veggies are ready for picking. The tomato is easy. It starts out a green color and then turns red, orange, or black as it ripens on the vine. If left on the vine too long, the tomato will become soft and mushy and will fall to the ground. The bell pepper can be harvested at pretty much any size, usually when it is three inches or so in diameter. It is often harvested when it is green, but if it is left on the plant it will turn red, orange, or yellow depending on the variety. It can take several weeks for a pepper to fully change color once it reaches its full size.

FACT

The secret to a healthy pepper with good color and flavor is adequate water and fertilizer. The pepper plant does not need a lot of nitrogen; this will promote leaf growth but not fruits. Keep the plants mulched with grass clipping to keep the soil moist and free of weeds.

Eggplants should be firm and have a shiny skin before harvesting. A dull color means the fruit is getting old. You can harvest cucumbers at pretty much any size depending on the varieties you have planted. Pick the English variety once they are about a foot long and approximately two inches in diameter. The peeling varieties are best harvested at about eight inches before they become too big. If a cucumber gets too large, it will become seedy and bitter tasting.

All the heat-loving vegetables will keep producing over several weeks if you continue to harvest the fruit. The exception is corn. Each stalk will produce only one or two cobs. Before you harvest corn, you want the cob to be filled out and firm to the touch. Gently pull away some of the husk and see if the kernels are a bright yellow (some varieties are white or a mix of yellow and white). If they look fully formed and are a good color, gently prick the kernels with your fingernail. If a milky liquid shoots out, they are ready to be harvested.

Storage Tips

You cannot buy vegetables with the kind of flavor and nutrition you get from growing and harvesting your own. Since gardening is largely a seasonal activity, it is great to be able to keep some vegetables for the off-season. If you want to feed your family with your fresh veggies all year long, it is important to start at the planning stage. Make sure you estimate how much you will eat fresh and how much you would like to store, freeze, or can and then plant accordingly. By storing vegetables, you can slow down the aging process of the vegetable. Vegetables will eventually rot if left alone, so it is important to store then properly.

ESSENTIAL

To make limp celery crispy again, cut off the end of the stalk and stand it upright in a jar or vase of cold water. Place it in your refrigerator and leave it in the water until it becomes crispy again. Then store it in a sealed plastic bag or airtight container in the refrigerator.

Salad greens have a very short life and need to be refrigerated. It is not possible to store these for long periods of time. Other vegetables, like winter squash, potatoes, and onions, will store for several months if cured properly.

VEGETABLES TO USE ASAP
- Artichokes
- Asparagus
- Broccoli
- Greens
- Eggplant
- Okra
- Peas
- Radishes
- Tomatoes

VEGETABLES TO STORE IN A COOL, DAMP AREA
- Beets
- Brussels sprouts
- Cabbage
- Carrots
- Cauliflower
- Celery
- Leeks
- Parsnips
- Peppers

- Potatoes
- Rutabagas/Turnips
- Summer squash

VEGETABLES TO STORE IN A COOL, DRY AREA
- Garlic
- Onions

VEGETABLES TO STORE IN A WARM, DRY AREA
- Pumpkins
- Winter squash

You will need to have a proper storage space for the types of vegetables you want to store. If you are lucky enough to have an existing root cellar, use it to store your veggies. Root cellars are usually cool, dry, and dark. A cool, dry area in your basement or pantry will work just as well.

Freezing Veggies

Freezing your veggies to use during the winter months is a great way to save money and eat healthy all year long. When planning your garden, make sure you plant a sufficient amount so you can freeze some of your harvest. Freezing and canning are great ways to store a bumper crop so it does not go to waste. Freezing will preserve the nutrients and flavor of the vegetables.

When you are planning to freeze your produce, pick it and freeze it the same day. Pick it in the early morning when the temperature is lower. Choose the freshest and most tender veggies. Keep the vegetables cool until they can be put into the freezer. If left at room temperature for more than two hours, the vegetables start to lose their nutrients.

Blanching, also known as scalding, destroys enzymes in your vegetables. Enzymes will affect the color and flavor of your vegetables if they are kept frozen for any length of time. If you plan to eat your frozen veggies within a month, you do not have to blanch these items. Any veggies that will be stored longer than a month should be blanched.

▼ **BLANCHING VEGETABLES**

Vegetable	Blanching Time
Asparagus	2 minutes
Broccoli	3 minutes
Brussels sprouts	3 minutes
Carrots (whole)	5 minutes
Carrots (sliced or diced)	3 minutes
Cauliflower	3 minutes
Corn (whole)	4 minutes
Corn (kernels)	1 minute
Greens	2 minutes
Peas	1 minute
String beans	2 minutes
Tomatoes	1 minute
Zucchini	1 minute

To blanch your harvested vegetables, fill a pot with water and bring it to a fast boil. You can add a few teaspoons of lemon juice or salt to help offset discoloration. Use a wire rack to hold the vegetables and lower them into the boiling water. Start timing immediately and closely watch the time; just one minute over will give you mushy vegetables. Remove the vegetables from the boiling water and plunge them into ice-cold water for the same amount of time to stop the cooking process. Drain the vegetables and then place them on a tray or cookie sheet and put them in the freezer for an hour. After that time, you can portion them into bags or containers and return them to the freezer. This prevents any water crystals from forming in your bags or containers.

ALERT

Your vegetables will not improve in quality when frozen, so avoid freezing produce that has been sitting around for a few days or produce that was old when it was harvested. This is why you should choose the freshest vegetables to freeze!

Labeling is an essential part of freezing your vegetables. Use a felt pen and write on the bag or container, purchase peel and stick labels, or get really creative and color code each type of vegetable. Label the top of the container if you have a chest freezer and the front if you have an upright freezer.

Canning Veggies

Families used to can vegetables each fall, and those vegetables would become a family's only source of vegetables during the winter. With so much fresh and canned foods available at the local supermarket, canning has waned in popularity. However, preserving has experienced a bit of a resurgence over the last few years. It is a great feeling to open a jar of pickles from your pantry in the dead of winter knowing you grew those cucumbers!

Make sure you choose the best quality vegetables. You want to harvest and can the veggies within a few hours if at all possible so the vegetables retain their freshness and nutrition. Wash the vegetables thoroughly; even a little dirt can contain bacteria. Wash vegetables individually under running water. If you are preserving a large number of veggies it may be easier to place the vegetables into a large container and change the water several times to make sure they are clean. (However, soaking the vegetables in water will cause them to lose flavor.) After you've washed them, let them drain. You do not want to can bruised vegetables, so handle them gently.

ESSENTIAL

To open a jar lid that just will not budge, try using rubber gloves to get a better grip. You can also try placing a wide rubber band around the rim of the jar. This method allows you to grasp more firmly and open the jar more easily.

Most vegetables can be canned raw (cold pack) or precooked (hot pack). Try both and decide which method you prefer. For cold packing, fill your jars with the vegetables and pour boiling water over them. In hot packing, precook the vegetables, then pack the jars and pour the cooking liquid or boiling water over them. With either method, the jars will need to be processed in a pressure cooker.

GREAT CANNING VEGETABLES

- Artichokes
- Beans
- Beets
- Cabbage (sauerkraut)
- Carrots
- Cauliflower
- Corn
- Cucumbers (pickles)
- Onions
- Peas
- Peppers
- Squash
- Tomatoes (sauces, whole, ketchup)

Store your canned goods in a cool, dry, dark place. Dampness will erode the lids, which can cause leaking. Warmth can affect the quality of the vegetable, and freezing can crack or break the jars. Basements and pantries are great places to store your canned vegetables. Canning may take some time, but it is well worth the effort. You can pull out a jar of tomato sauce or salsa that you preserved from the veggies you grew!

CHAPTER 19

Top Gardening Tools

Planting and tending your vegetable garden is easier and a lot more fun if you are working with the right tools for the job. If you are a novice gardener, you will only need some basic tools that are usually fairly inexpensive and easy to find. This chapter details the top garden tools, tips on how to choose them, the importance of keeping your tools clean, and methods for sharpening them.

Choosing the Right Tool

In vegetable gardening, there are some basic tasks that require some basic tools. Vegetable gardening is definitely a hands-on activity, so prepare to get your hands dirty! The basic tasks start in the spring with digging the garden beds, getting them ready for planting, moving amendments and debris to and from the garden site, planting the seeds for transplants, watering, harvesting, and making compost.

Basic gardening tools can be purchased at garden centers, hardware stores, and garage sales or flea markets. If you purchase them secondhand, just make sure they are in good shape. Try to set a budget when purchasing tools; they can vary in price. Always choose the best quality you can afford! Blades should be forged from a single piece of metal and should have a solid socket construction where they meet the handle. Studies have shown that a D-shaped handle is easiest to use. Choose a handle made of wood, metal, or good quality plastic for longevity.

ALERT

Proper footwear is important in the garden, especially if you will be doing any digging. A boot with a heavy sole will make it easier to press down on a spade or shovel when digging or moving amendments or compost. If your garden is uneven, proper footwear can prevent you from tripping or falling.

When you go looking for your vegetable gardening tools, make sure you purchase the tools that are right for you. Choose the size and weight that will work best for you. You want to be able to dig, hoe, or rake without straining your back or arms. Someone who is five feet tall will need a different size tool than a person who is six feet tall in order to use it properly and with ease. Choose a handle that works for your height and make sure the circumference of the handle fits comfortably in your hand.

Shovels

You'll need a shovel for making, digging, or tilling your garden beds. There are two basic shovels—round edged and flat edged. Each has different functions, but you may only need one depending on what kind of garden site you have. A round-edged shovel is used for scooping and lifting soil. This type of shovel is great for turning your garden beds and adding in organic amendments such as compost or aged animal manure. A shovel with a flat rectangular blade is used more for prepping a garden bed. They work well for cutting edges, stripping sod, digging holes, and prying up rocks.

Choose a shovel with a smooth, rounded shoulder at the top of the blade to protect your feet when pressing down on the shovel. When using the shovel, stand up straight while digging and bend your knees when lifting. When moving material from one area to another, turn your whole body, not just your hips. This will help protect you from any back strains or injuries.

Flat-edged spade

Garden Fork

You'll need two different garden forks. One is used for digging and the other for turning your compost. The digging fork (sometimes called a *spading fork*) is used for turning over soil, mixing in soil amendments, lifting and breaking up clumps of soil, and harvesting root crops. The compost fork (sometimes called a *pitchfork*) is ideal for turning and moving compost, mulches,

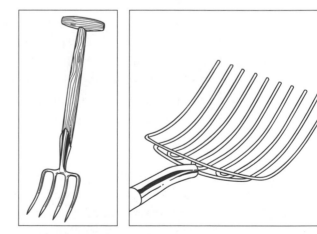

Perennial fork   Compost fork

straw, green manures, and other organic material used in or around your garden beds.

Your digging fork should have four broad, flat metal tines with V-shaped ends. You want a solid fork with a bit of weight to it so that you can easily turn soil or lift out rocks without the tines bending. The compost fork has four fine, curved tines that can easily penetrate and hold on to the organic matter. You want this fork to be lighter because you will be doing more lifting and throwing of materials with it.

When choosing a fork, make sure the size and weight are a good fit for you. Always choose the best quality you can afford.

FACT

Your computer can be a useful tool for gardening. Set up a garden chart on your computer and update it regularly with information regarding when, where, and what you planted. Keep track of how each plant did and how much you harvested. This will be a great resource to look back on when planning for next season.

Rake

The rake is used for preparing and cleaning your garden bed and for collecting organic matter like garden debris and leaves. You want a garden rake that has a long handle attached to a bar with small tines. This type of rake is used for leveling and cleaning any larger pebbles and debris from your planting bed. A fine clean bed is necessary when planting seeds like carrots, radishes, turnips, rutabagas, and salad greens.

ALERT

You've seen the slapstick comedy bit where someone steps on a rake and it swings upward and hits the person in the face. This can look funny in a movie, but it can cause serious injury to a person if it happens in your garden. Be aware of where you leave your rake and never leave it with the tines facing upward!

The garden rake can be used for raking up leaves, grass clippings, and other garden debris, but a leaf rake is much easier to work with for these jobs. The leaf rake or landscape rake has longer teeth that are arranged in a fan style. The tines or teeth are usually made of steel, plastic, or bamboo. This allows you to easily rake up a larger amount of debris.

When choosing a rake, make sure it fits your body. You want to be able to stand upright while raking so you don't injure or strain your back. If the rake it too long or too short, it will be difficult to work with.

Hoe

The hoe is used to dig up persistent and stubborn weeds. There are several different types of hoes you can purchase depending on your needs. The basic one is a gooseneck hoe, which has a flat edge that is used for digging and chopping weeds. The stirrup hoe is easier to use when weeding your garden beds because it slices the top inch or so of the soil, cutting the weeds off just below the soil surface. This motion is easier on your back and shoulders than the digging motion you make with the gooseneck hoe.

The handle of the hoe should be forty-eight to fifty-four inches long. This is a good length for working standing upright. Keep the blade sharp and slide it parallel to the soil to loosen the weeds and sever the roots. Hoe in the evening just before the sun goes down to discourage the weeds from germinating. It is easier to hoe when the soil is moist, but if it has been dry, hoeing hard soil will help it to absorb the moisture better when it does rain.

Trowel

The hand trowel is handy for digging a hole when setting out your transplants or planting garlic bulbs or seed potatoes. A hoe will do a similar job, but a trowel is easier to work with because you are generally close to the ground when you are planting your vegetables. You can also use the trowel as a measuring stick. You can purchase some trowels with the depth measurements written on the blade or you can make your own marks on one you already have. Having a measurement marker makes it easier to get the correct depth when planting your seeds, bulbs, or seed potatoes.

Using the trowel and hoe together is a great way to make a straight garden row to place your seeds. Use the handle of your hoe as a marker for the row and then use the trowel to make a trench to the desired depth.

FACT

Reuse some items around your home as tool holders. Old golf bags can be used as carts. Aprons with large pockets, wicker or plastic baskets, backpacks, and wagons can be also be used to hold items. Using a holder will make it easier to keep all the tools you need in one place.

Wheelbarrow

The wheelbarrow is an essential tool for the vegetable gardener. It is used for hauling items to and from your garden site. The wheelbarrow can be used for transporting large amounts of harvested vegetables and carrying large amounts of plant material to your compost area. You can hang your garlic or onions over the sides of the wheelbarrow and use it to easily move them in and out of the sun.

There are many different types of wheelbarrows. The most common has a single wheel with two handles for pushing. Before choosing a wheelbarrow, make sure you know what you will be using it for and how much weight you will be hauling in it. If you are going to be carrying heavy loads, then choosing a sturdy metal one is probably best. If you have a small garden and will only use the wheelbarrow for lighter loads, then a lightweight plastic or cloth type may work better for you. When purchasing a wheelbarrow, take the time to push it around in the store. If it feels heavy for you when it is empty, go for a model that is more lightweight. It will only get heavier when you fill it up!

Garden Hose

No matter how small your garden is, you will be less likely to water your plants adequately if you have to pack water. Make sure you have a water source nearby. Your garden hose should be able to reach the far end of your garden. Hoses come in different lengths and can be easily connected to make a length that works for your garden site.

Hoses come in a variety of styles and are usually a half inch to one inch in diameter. The bigger the hose diameter, the faster the water will come through, although this may vary depending on your water pressure. Choose a no-kink hose so you can easily move it around without it twisting and disrupting your water flow. Purchase the best quality hose you can afford. You can spend a lot of money on hose carriers and systems to roll them up; what you choose will depend on your garden site.

ESSENTIAL

Make up a transplanting kit with some tools from your house. Your kit should include small scissors for thinning seedlings, a teaspoon to move a tiny transplant from one pot to another, a wooden spoon for making holes for seedlings, tweezers for picking up tiny seeds, and a salt shaker for sowing tiny seeds.

Attaching a water wand or nozzle to the end of your hose can make gardening easier as well. Water wands allow you to reach the plant more easily and without straining. Buy a nozzle that has several spray options so you can water your vegetable plants in different ways.

Sharp Knife

A small sharp kitchen knife is one of the most flexible tools a home gardener can have. A simple paring knife is great for opening bags of fertilizer, cutting string, harvesting vegetables, cutting off stems of plants for composting, cutting off diseased or pest infected plants, and slicing into a tomato or cucumber to eat it! Buy one just for your garden tool kit.

Garden Gloves

Working in soil or with other organic materials can give your hands a beating. Digging or shoveling for any length of time is a sure way to give yourself a blister if you are doing it with bare hands. Weeding can be hard on the fingernails and fingertips. A good pair of gloves will help protect your hands from all these.

Make sure the gloves you choose fit snuggly but aren't too tight. If they are too large, they will fall off every time you set a tool down. Large gloves also make it harder to grip anything. Choose a pair of gloves that fits well and is made with a breathable material. Buy a couple pairs so you'll always have a spare when one pair is in the wash. If you are working in wet soil, rubber kitchen gloves are a good option for keeping your hands dry.

Garden Journal

Keeping track of information such as where you planted certain vegetables, how they grew, and what gardening methods worked or did not work is invaluable for planning and troubleshooting in future seasons. The journal can be as fancy or as simple as you want it to be. Choosing a book with some kind of binding or folder is best. Scraps of paper can be easily misplaced and are harder to look back on.

There are several types of garden journals, and all have valuable tips and information for the vegetable gardener. Making your own can save you money and allows you to customize your journal according to what you want and need.

The following are important notations you should always include in your journal:

- A drawing or map of your garden site
- A section for each type of vegetable (or family of vegetable) (List the variety you planted, where it was planted, and the maturity date. As the season progresses, jot down how well it grew, whether your harvest was successful, and whether you would grow this variety again.)
- A place to note when you fertilized each vegetable, with what, how much, and the results
- A section for maintenance notes (This is where you will detail any pest or disease problems, your remedies, and their results.)

Writing in a garden journal is one of the best habits a vegetable gardener can have. You'll forget the details of your gardening experience by the time next season rolls around, but if you keep a journal you'll be able to look back. Even little notes about the weather and how many birds or butterflies were in your garden each season are interesting to review. It is important to jot down your thoughts about what worked or did not work to make it easier to plan for next season.

Cleaning and Sharpening Your Tools

It is extremely important to clean your tools, pots, and work surfaces, especially when they have come into contact with diseased plants or soil. If you do not take the time to clean them the disease can easily and quickly spread throughout your whole garden. Even if you are not working with diseased plants, it is still a good practice to clean your tools on a regular basis. Every gardener should get into the habit of cleaning off any dirt and wiping the tool after every use.

After working in your garden, remove the tools from the garden area and scrape the soil off them. Wipe the tool clean and store it in its proper place. Brush or sweep all benches or surfaces. Clean pots or pails with a solution of a one part bleach to ten parts water.

ALERT

Having a large, well-organized garden shed is a luxury most gardeners do not have, but it is important to organize your tools and equipment in the storage space you do have. Keep frequently used items where you can easily reach them. If you have an organized space, you will be less likely to purchase duplicate tools, which will save you money!

Do a thorough cleaning of all your tools at the end the season before you put them away into storage. Rub off any debris with a cloth or burlap sack. If the dirt is dried on, use a wire brush or steel wool to scrape it all off. Then wipe any metal parts lightly with oil (car oil works well) and wipe wooden handles with boiled linseed oil. A good quality tool that is properly used and cared for can last you several decades.

Having a sharp tool will make gardening tasks easier to accomplish. All tools should be regularly sharpened, but pay particular attention to your hoe and digging tools. These should be sharpened before you start to work in the garden. When hoeing your beds, you may need to sharpen the hoe blade in the middle of the project, especially if you are working in a large area.

To sharpen your tools, smoothly draw a flat file down the blade from top to bottom. Do not go back and forth; just move the file in one direction. File the blade until all the nicks are smoothed out. When the blade is sharp to the touch, move the file over the back edge of the tool to remove any buildup on that edge.

CHAPTER 20

Troubleshooting

There are so many different problems that can occur in the vegetable garden. You have control over some, such as soil conditions or plant damage. Others, such as the weather or the amount of sunlight your garden gets, are often out of your control. You must become a plant detective to identify the problem and find a solution. This chapter gives you advice and tips on how to identify and treat common problems in your vegetable garden.

Identify the Problem

Some problems may affect your entire garden while others may affect only one type or one variety of vegetable. Plants are as different as people; some are more susceptible to problems than others. Identifying the problem can take some effort; often, the symptoms of a disease or a pest infestation are similar to those of an undernourished or underwatered plant.

Walk through your garden and observe your plants every day or once every few days. It's often easier to treat a problem you spot in the early stages before it can spread to other plants or areas of your garden. Before you make a diagnosis, inspect the leaves, blossoms, stems, roots, and surrounding soil. Look for any wilting, distortion, discoloration, holes, eggs, spots, and insects on the leaves. Check the blossoms and fruit for any discoloration, holes, spots, premature dropping, lack of fruiting, and insects or eggs. Study the stems at soil level or slightly below the soil to look for growths such as cankers or galls, wilting, stunted, or spindly growth, sticky coating, and eggs or insects on the stem or in the soil around the base of the plant. This information will help you determine if there are any pests on the plant or in the immediate area.

Attracting birds to your garden can be one way to keep the unwanted pests under control. Provide a home for birds by placing a birdhouse in a nearby tree. Offer pools of water at ground level for the birds to play in. They do not like their baths too deep; one inch of water is sufficient.

If your have a pest problem in your vegetable garden, it can often be handled by handpicking, trapping insects, or spraying plants with organic remedies. Removing an infected plant can also stop the spread of a disease. If the plant is very diseased, pull it and check the roots for discoloration, decay, eggs, distortions, and insects. Always place diseased plants into a garbage bag as soon as you pull them. This will help keep the problem from spreading throughout your whole garden.

Garden Concerns

So what do you do if you cannot see any pests or specific disease patterns? What else could the problem be?

The most common problems in a vegetable garden are often caused by:

- Overwatering
- Underwatering
- Inadequate nutrients in the soil
- Poor drainage
- Poor air circulation

If a plant is stressed by under- or overwatering or lack of nutrients, it will be more susceptible to pests and disease. Trying to combat the problem early is the best plan of action. Plants are great at letting us know there is a problem. The following section details some common concerns and what you can do in your garden planning and plant maintenance to help the situation.

Standing Rainwater

This means the water is not able to penetrate into the soil. This could be caused by poor soil structure or a hard clay soil. A short-term solution is to hoe the garden area just before a rain to break up the hard surface. This will allow the water to be absorbed more easily into the soil. In the fall or spring, add in more compost or aged animal manure to improve the soil. Doing this every year is a long-term solution to a poor drainage problem.

ALERT

Water is heavier than you think! When watering by hand, make sure you use a lightweight plastic watering container. A two-gallon watering container will weigh up to sixteen pounds when filled with water. That's why it is important to have your water source nearby.

Seeds That Won't Germinate

First, check to see if the seeds are still in the ground. A pest that you cannot see may be eating your seeds or they may be rotting. Soil temperatures that are too low or too high can cause poor or slow seed germination. Make sure you are planting the seed at the recommended time of year and at the recommended depth. Check the seed packet for the proper planting depth and replant. If your seed is old, it may not be viable and you may have to buy some new seeds.

Unhealthy Plants and Stunted Growth

Many factors can be responsible for plants that don't look as healthy as they should or are not growing as well as they should. Low soil fertility or low pH is probably the most common reason. Give the plants a boost with a side dressing of compost or a manure or compost tea. Observe what happens over the next few weeks.

Other causes include lack of sunlight, too little or too much water, and poor drainage. Most vegetable plants need at least six hours of sunlight each day and an inch of water every week. If nature isn't cooperating, you may have to step in yourself.

FACT

Wood ash is a quick fix for acidic soil. It will neutralize the soil in a few weeks, whereas limestone can take up to six months to do the same job. It is important to thoroughly till the wood ash into the soil in the fall. Use one and a quarter pound of wood ash for every one pound of lime recommended.

If you are a novice gardener, be patient with yourself. It takes practice and a lot of knowledge to diagnose a problem in your garden. It is often a process of trial and error, even for a seasoned gardener. Having a healthy, fertile garden soil goes a long way to having healthy vegetable plants, so concentrate your energy there if you're in doubt.

Signs of Nutrient Deficiency in the Soil

Vegetable plants need fertile soil to grow well. The three main nutrients your vegetable plants need are nitrogen, phosphorus, and potassium. The following table identifies nine additional micronutrients your vegetable plants need. Problems with your vegetable plants can alert you and help you identify soil deficiencies and other concerns.

▼ **TABLE 20-1: NUTRIENT DEFICIENCY GUIDE**

Nutrient	Symptom	Causes	Solutions
Nitrogen	Plant leaves are light green or yellowish in color.	Easily leaches from the soil.	Mulch or plant a cover crop.
Phosphorus	Plants are stunted and have a purplish color.	Wet, cold soil; low pH (acidic soil).	Plan to lime next spring.
Potassium	Leaves are brown and curling.	Excessive leaching.	Mulch or plant a green manure.
Calcium	Stunted plants, stubby roots, and blossom end rot on tomatoes.	Very acidic soil, excessive dry or wet soil, too high of potassium levels.	Add lime, check for drainage problems, and fertilize carefully.
Magnesium	Yellowish color on older leaves.	Very acidic soil, potassium levels too high.	Add lime and fertilize carefully.
Sulfur	Yellowish color in young leaves and stunted growth.	Low organic matter often found in sandy soil.	Add in compost and aged animal manures in the fall and spring.
Boron	Leaves are distorted, crown of the plant dies.	Soil pH above 6.8 or below 5.5, low organic matter, sandy soil.	Do a soil pH test to see if you need to add in lime for sulfur.
Copper	Yellowish leaves that become thin and elongated.	High pH (too alkaline).	Add sulfur to the soil in the spring to lower the pH.
Iron	Youngest leaves are light green or yellow colored.	High pH (too alkaline), low organic matter, and excessive phosphorus in the soil.	Add sulfur, compost, and aged animal manures in the spring and fall.
Zinc	Yellow beet leaves, rust spots on beans.	High pH (too alkaline), cool wet soil in the spring, and excessive phosphorus in the soil.	Add sulfur and fertilize carefully.
Manganese	Mottled yellowish areas on younger leaves.	High pH (too alkaline).	Add sulfur in the spring.
Molybdenum	Distorted leaves, curling at leaf edges, yellowish outer leaves.	Low pH (acidic soil).	Add lime in the spring.

A soil test can tell you the soil pH and reveal any nutrient deficiencies. The soil test will give you an idea of what nutrients are needed and how much to add to your soil to raise them to an optimum level. If you do not want to incur the expense of a soil test, closely observe your vegetable plants for indications of what they may be missing. Note the problem in your journal so you can plan to make the necessary changes or additions to your garden beds next season.

ESSENTIAL

Calcium in your soil is essential for growing crunchy cucumbers. Side dress your cucumber plants with bone meal, gypsum, rock phosphate, or dolomite lime to add in calcium. Pick the cucumbers young; the older they get, the less crunchy they are.

If you observe your plants regularly, you'll be able to tell when there's something wrong. Adding in amendments, fertilizers, or compost teas can easily correct worrying symptoms in your vegetable plants.

What's Wrong with My Plants?

The following table will help you identify what could be causing problems with your vegetable plants and offers some solutions.

▼ **TABLE 20-2: PLANT PROBLEM GUIDE**

Symptoms	Possible Causes	Possible Cures
Stunted plants with a yellowish or pale color.	Low fertility, low pH, poor drainage, insects.	Do a soil test for fertility recommendations, add lime, and add in organic matter.
Stunted plants with a purplish color.	Low temperature, lack of phosphorus.	Plant at the recommended temperature and add phosphorus to the soil.
Holes in leaves.	Insects.	Identify the insect by looking on the leaves and use appropriate controls.
Wilting plants.	Dry soil, excess water, and disease.	Irrigate if dry, drain if wet; plant resistant varieties.

Weak spindling plants.	Too much shade, too much water, too much nitrogen in the soil, planting is too thick.	Place in a sunnier location, avoid excess fertilization, thin plants to proper spacing.
Fruit not forming.	High temperature, low temperature, too much nitrogen, insects.	Plant at the recommended times, avoid overfertilization, identify insects and find the appropriate control.
Abnormal leaves.	Virus disease.	Remove infected leaves.
Spots, molds on stems and leaves.	Disease.	Identify and use appropriate controls.

Your vegetable plants hold a wealth of information about problems in the garden. They will wilt if they get too much heat or not enough water, they will turn yellow if they are not getting the nutrients they need, and they may even die if they are not taken care of properly. It takes time and knowledge to be able to read your plants and to make a diagnosis based on what you see. Over time, you will get to know your soil conditions and the natural rhythm of your garden, which will make it easier to pinpoint problems and come up with solutions.

FACT

Many vegetables are related to common weeds, so a diseased weed can spread the sickness to your vegetable plants. Mosaic virus on cucumbers is often spread by milkweed, pokeweed, or ground cherry. Horse nettle and jimsonweed can spread diseases to the nightshade family.

Every garden is different, so what may work for one gardener may not have the same effect in your garden. You have to be willing to experiment a bit and not be too concerned if you lose a plant or two to pests, disease, or improper soil nutrition. Observe, take notes, and learn from it!

Specific Veggie Concerns

Some problems affect certain vegetable plants and not others. Temperature and soil conditions are common causes of poor growth, lack of flowers, and poor fruit or pod development. Here are some common problems regarding garden veggies.

Bean Flowers Fail to Develop

Beans need warm temperatures to grow well, but flowers will not form if daytime temperatures get above 90°F. When the temperature drops, they will start flowering again.

Poor Kernel Development in Sweet Corn

Corn needs to be pollinated in order to form kernels. Plant your corn in blocks rather than rows so that the wind will help the pollen reach each plant. Choose only one variety of corn so they do not cross pollinate. If you have multiple varieties in a large garden, make sure the different varieties are spaced several hundred feet from each other.

Wilting Cucumber Plants

When a cucumber plant gets poor air circulation, mosaic virus is a common problem. The leaves start to wilt and die in some areas. The best way to prevent this is to trellis your cucumber plants so air circulates easily around them. Lack of water can also cause the plant to wilt and produce bitter-tasting fruit. Keep the soil around your cucumbers moist.

Lettuce and Spinach Quickly Go to Seed

This is a normal occurrence when the temperature rises. Both lettuce and spinach grow best in the spring and fall when the weather is cooler. Consider planting varieties that can withstand more heat if you live in a hot climate.

Small Onions

Onions that are smaller than expected may not have gotten enough water during the early growing stage. Onions need regular watering early on and then no water once the tops start dying back. The plants could also be overcrowded; they should be spaced at least six inches apart. Onions like a fertile soil but do not like hot manure, so make sure you add any amendments to the onion bed in the fall rather than in the spring.

FACT

Onions are one of the oldest known vegetables. They belong to the Alliaceae family, which includes more than 280 species of bulb plants, such as garlic, leeks, and shallots. There are hundreds of cultivated varieties, which vary in size, appearance, taste, and storing qualities.

Pea Plants Stop Flowering

Peas need cooler weather to grow well, so your peas will stop producing flowers or pods once the summer heat arrives. It is best to plant peas as early as you can in the spring so you get a good harvest before the summer heat.

Greenish Potato Tubers

Sunburning, also called *greening*, is caused when light reaches the tubers. Hilling soil along rows of potato plants is necessary to keep the tubers well covered with soil. The green part of the potato is still edible.

Tomatoes, Peppers, and Eggplants Are Not Forming Fruits

Extremely hot or cold temperatures are usually to blame when vegetable plants fail to produce fruit. If the nighttime temperature falls below 65°F or if daytime temperatures go above 100°F, the plants will not form fruits. The fruits that do form can be rough and misshapen. It is important to protect your heat-loving plants from the cold and make sure they get good ventilation if they are grown in a greenhouse during hot weather.

Vegetable Pest and Disease Identification

When you find an insect or bug on your plant, look at it closely. Once you have identified it you will be able to use the proper control to destroy it or prevent it from spreading to other plants. The following chart has a list of vegetables and some common symptoms that can help you identify the pest or disease.

▼ **TABLE 20-3: VEGETABLE PEST AND DISEASE CHART**

Vegetable	Symptoms	Pest or Disease	Organic Control
Asparagus	Distorted spears.	Cutworm.	Plant tansy between rows.
Beans	Seedpods and leaves are damaged.	Mexican bean beetle.	Handpick and destroy; plant marigolds near beans.
Beans	Withered and discolored leaves.	Leafhopper.	Remove harvest debris from garden immediately; treat leaves with insecticidal soap; use floating rows to keep infestation from spreading
Beets and Chard	Small, round spots on leaves.	Leaf spot.	Use crop rotation.
Brassicas	Holes in leaves.	Cabbageworm or cabbage looper.	Handpick and destroy by putting them in hot water.
Brassicas	Curled and discolored leaves.	Aphids.	Remove with a blast of water and spray with insecticidal soap.
Brassicas	Wilting plants.	Cabbage maggot.	Use crop rotation.
Brassicas	Stunted growth and large, thick swelling on roots.	Club root.	Avoid planting in infested soil for up to five years; use crop rotation.
Carrots and Turnips	Roots have black spots and holes.	Rust fly.	Cover young plants with row cover.
Carrots and Turnips	Root and stem boring.	Carrot weevil.	Use crop rotation.
Carrots and Turnips	Brown or black spots on leaves.	Leaf blight.	Use crop rotation, avoid excessive watering, and keep garden clean.
Corn	Silks and ears are damaged.	Earworm.	Put 2 or 3 drops of mineral oil into each ear when the silk first appears; encourage birds in your garden.
Corn	Collapsed tassels, single hole at the tip or base of ear.	Corn borer.	Handpick worms each day; destroy stalks when plant is harvested.
Cucumbers and Squash	Curled and wilted leaves.	Squash bug.	Handpick beetles, destroy eggs, and plant nasturtiums near vegetable plants.
Cucumbers and Squash	Wilted or crinkled vines.	Squash or vine borer.	Plant late or early as eggs come out in July, handpick, and clean up vines after harvesting.
Cucumbers and Squash	Chewed leaves.	Striped or spotted cucumber beetle.	Handpick; plant nasturtiums or radishes near plants.

▼ **TABLE 20-3: VEGETABLE PEST AND DISEASE CHART—*continued***

Vegetable	Symptoms	Pest or Disease	Organic Control
Eggplants, Peppers, and Tomatoes	Small pinholes in leaves.	Flea beetle.	Plant late, trap beetles using yellow sticky traps, and cultivate after harvesting.
Eggplants, Peppers, and Tomatoes	Plants severed at the base of the plant.	Cutworm.	Wrap a collar of stiff paper or tin around the plant base; keep the garden clean and weed free.
Eggplants, Peppers, and Tomatoes	Dark blemish at blossom end of fruit.	Blossom end rot.	Soil is too acidic; add lime.
Eggplants, Peppers, and Tomatoes	Chewed fruit and leaves.	Tomato hornworm.	Handpick and destroy worm; grow fennel or dill near plants; cultivate after harvesting to destroy pupae.
Eggplants, Peppers, and Tomatoes	Wilted and curled leaves.	Aphids.	Remove with a spray of water; plant garlic or garlic chives among plants.
Lettuce	Rot at base of plant.	Bottom rot.	Caused by poor drainage; grow in raised beds.
Lettuce	Virus disease.	Leafhopper.	Plant early, grow in a more sheltered area, and use disease resistant varieties.
Onions and Leeks	Shriveled, unusable bulbs.	Onion maggot.	Do not use fresh manure where planting; allow soil to dry out occasionally; use good garden sanitation.
Onions and Leeks	Leaves are withered and have white spots.	Thrips.	Interplant with marigolds or spray with a soap solution.
Peas	Seed fails to germinate and rots.	Dampening off.	Soil too wet and cold.
Potatoes	Damaged leaves.	Colorado potato beetle.	Handpick beetles and crush egg clusters; mulch with 3 inches of hay or straw when plant first emerges.
Potatoes	Tubers have black spots and holes.	Wireworm.	Till soil in the fall; use crop rotation.
Radish	Roots have gouges and appear tunneled.	Root maggot.	Use crop rotation; plant early.
Spinach	White tunnels on leaves.	Leaf miner.	Handpick, use crop rotation, and remove weeds.

Crop rotation is one of the best ways to prevent and control pests and disease in your vegetable garden. Crop rotation will help prevent problems and will build better soil, which will make for a healthier plant and harvest.

FACT

The best way to attract beneficial insects to your garden is to provide them with plants that have nectar. Some useful plants are flowers and herbs such as nasturtiums, calendula, cosmos, basil, fennel, dill, caraway, and parsley. Planting them around your vegetable garden will help bring in beneficial insects.

Companion planting is another way to help keep the pests and disease out of your garden or at least under control. Intermix flowers and herbs among your vegetables to help ward off harmful insects and attract the beneficial ones.

CHAPTER 21

Organic Versus Nonorganic Vegetable Gardening

You've already learned the basics for growing healthy organic vegetables. You know when and where to plant your vegetables, how to space out your plants, and what to feed them. But it's worth discussing organic growing methods—and nonorganic alternatives—in more detail. Organic gardening uses practices that help restore and maintain harmony with nature, which include feeding the soil. Nonorganic or conventional practices use chemicals and pesticides to help plants grow. In this chapter, we will discuss the differences between growing your vegetables organically versus nonorganically.

What is Organic Gardening?

Gardening without using synthetic fertilizers and pesticides can be considered organic gardening. In organic gardening, the motto "feed the soil, feed the plant" is the basis for growing your vegetables. This means bringing in a minimal amount of off-site additions into your garden. Making your own compost and growing cover crops when your garden is idle are two easy ways to accomplish this.

ESSENTIAL

Overall, there are not many disadvantages to organic growing, but it can take a lot of planning and can be labor intensive. Sustaining good soil fertility takes work and commitment. It can take time to identify the source of infestations and find natural ways to deal with them, which obviously takes longer than simply spraying a chemical to kill them.

The restoration, preservation, and enrichment of the soil are the cornerstones of organic gardening. All plants need four basic requirements to grow: warmth, moisture, food, and light. Your garden soil provides the first three and the sun provides the fourth! The soil is a living system that needs care and attention to remain in a healthy enough state to provide plants with the nutrients they need to grow and produce vegetables.

Maintaining a healthy, fertile garden soil is extremely important to having a successful vegetable garden. Building good soil starts with knowing what soil type you have and how fertile it is. You then need to regularly use certain methods, such as adding amendments every season, rotating your crops, and growing cover crops to enhance your existing soil. If your existing soil is poor, it can take several years to get your garden beds to a state of high fertility and good structure, but do not let that discourage you. Some very successful vegetable gardens started out with sandy or rocky soil!

In nonorganic or conventional methods, synthetic chemicals and pesticides are used to enhance the growth of the plant and to promote fruit or pod production. Nonorganic growing methods emphasize feeding the plant, not the soil. Using these artificial forms will make your vegetables grow, but they also deplete and will not enhance the soil fertility or soil structure. Most conventional growers have dead soil; there are no replenished nutrients in the soil for the plants to draw from. Relying on something outside your soil to grow vegetable plants creates a vicious circle. You have to purchase more and more chemicals and pesticides in order for the crops to grow each season.

FACT

Earthworms will gradually make an acidic soil less acid and an alkaline soil less alkaline by passing the soil through their bodies. They will eventually bring soil that is out of balance back to the neutral pH range. Most vegetables grow best in a pH range of 6.0 to 6.9.

The Organic Principles

The International Federation of Organic Agricultural Movements has laid out a list of principles of organic farming. It emphasizes growing high quality food, considering the social and ecological impact of organic food production, promoting natural biological cycles within the farming systems, optimizing the long-term soil fertility, minimizing pollution, and using water resources responsibly.

Most gardeners grow vegetables so they can eat them. Everyone wants to get the best possible harvest from their seeds or transplants. The best way to do this is to try to copy what nature does as closely as you can. The forest is a perfect example of how plants remain healthy and vibrant without any outside additions. In the forest, the seasons and the natural relationships between plants and animals create a healthy soil. With a vegetable garden, you have to work a bit more in order to get the same results. You can accomplish this by feeding the soil compost, animal manures, leaves, and other organic matter.

When growing in your backyard, it is important to consider other living creatures in the area. For example, encouraging birds, wasps, and bees will help deter pests. You can assist the natural cycle of life by including plants that encourage and attract certain insects in your garden.

You are helping the environment and minimizing pollution by growing your own vegetables. For every vegetable you grow and eat yourself, you are saving fuel that would be used to bring that item to you. By composting your kitchen scraps or garden waste, you support the environment by not adding to landfills. Most waste is either burned or buried, and both methods affect our environment.

ESSENTIAL

Aquatic animals such as toads, box turtles, and frogs love to eat insects, so encourage their presence in your garden. For a shelter, place a clay flowerpot upside down in your garden and chip the side to make a little space for them to enter. Make a pond or fill a shallow container with water to give them a source of water.

Another principle in organic gardening is creating a harmonious balance between vegetable production and animal husbandry. Chickens and larger animals such as cows, pigs, and sheep are a fabulous complement to vegetable gardening. And you don't have to live in a rural area to take advantage of this balance. Chickens are allowed in backyards in some cities, so check your local regulations.

Animal manures are a great amendment to any garden soil. Chicken manure is especially high in nitrogen, which your vegetable plants need to promote healthy green leaves. Just make sure you let the manure age for at least six months before adding it to your garden bed or it will burn your vegetable plants. If you do have animals either as pets or for slaughter, it is important to treat them humanely. They deserve to have proper food and shelter.

ALERT

There are 115 species of snakes in North American, and only four are poisonous. Most of the ones you find in your garden will only bite if you pick them up or step on them, and their bites are largely harmless. The common garter snake, eastern ribbon snake, western terrestrial snake, green, and brown snake will eat slugs, snails, and insects.

Encouraging certain wildlife to enter your garden site is probably not the wisest choice. One deer or elk can devour a whole garden in a single night. Ensure that these animals stay wild by erecting a proper fence to protect your garden and still allow them access to the grass and weeds nearby.

Maintaining and promoting a healthy use of water is another one of the organic principles. Using proper methods for watering your vegetables will produce healthier plants without depleting our water resources. Gardeners often give their plants more water than is necessary, so take the time to check the soil to see if it really needs water. Use drip irrigation or soaker hoses rather than sprinklers to save on the amount of water that is wasted through evaporation.

The Benefits of Eating Organic

There are many reasons to choose to grow and eat organically grown vegetables. Organic food is healthier than food grown with pesticides and chemicals. It has higher levels of vitamin C and other minerals such as calcium, iron, chromium, and magnesium. Organic vegetables are normally harvested when ripe and are therefore tastier, more flavorful, and more nutritious.

Organic foods that are processed do not contain any food additives or artificial hormones, which contribute to health problems such as migraines, heart disease, and obesity. Children are much more susceptible to chemicals and pesticides added to vegetables and other products. Choosing to grow and eat organically grown vegetables is one way to keep your family healthier.

ALERT

Foods that meet the U.S. Department of Agriculture's requirements for organic production will have a USDA seal. To obtain the seal, foods must be 95 percent organic. Foods using only organic products and methods may also state "100% organic" on the packaging. A lower level of organic certification is available for foods that are 70 to 95 percent organic. These foods can be labeled as "made with organic ingredients."

In conventional or nonorganic growing, vegetables are routinely sprayed with more than 400 chemical pesticides. They harm the person who eats the food and the person who grows it. They do nothing to replenish the soil to help it stay healthy and remain fertile. Genetically modified organism (GMO) crops are not allowed under organic standards but are commonly used in nonorganic or conventional growing methods. These seeds have not been tested on humans, so the long-term effects of eating them are still unknown.

Choosing to grow your own vegetables and committing to growing them using organic principles and methods will give you the assurance of knowing what you are eating. It is also becoming more popular to purchase vegetables, fruits, and other products that are grown and made in your local community or area. Because of this new trend, there are more small growers—even some backyard gardeners are growing extra vegetables to sell at farmers' markets or gate sales. If growing veggies is something you love to do, you might be able to earn a living doing it. If you have the desire and time to grow vegetables, the extra money is a huge bonus—as is the satisfaction of selling fresh produce that others will enjoy.

ALERT

Maximize a small space by interplanting a variety of vegetables within a certain area. Grow combinations of fast-growing varieties with vegetables that take longer to mature. Grow lettuce with corn, peas, or tomatoes. Grow beans with carrots, corn, or cucumbers. Grow radishes with onions, peas, or carrots.

The Transition

If you are a gardener who has not been growing organically and has decided to make some changes, there are a few easy ways to make the transition. A vegetable garden can take a fair amount of care and attention. If you are transitioning from nonorganic to organic growing, be patient with yourself and your garden. Change can be difficult on all living things—remember, your soil and plants are living organisms. Commit to using the organic method, and when the process seems difficult, remember that you are enhancing the health of your family and the planet. You will soon see positive results with happier vegetables, fewer pests, and more beneficial insects and birds to enjoy.

Commit to Organic Gardening

First, make the commitment to growing using organic methods. If you are hesitant to change, start with a small area and transition more space each year. If you have decided to go organic right now, the first thing you must do it throw out any pesticides or chemicals you may have in your garden shed or garage. Take them to a place where they can be disposed of responsibly. Check with your local waste management site for the best way to destroy them.

Start with Soil Investigation

Get a soil test to check the current nutrient amount and fertility of your soil. Research the organic fertilizers that are available at your local garden center. Look for blood meal, alfalfa meal, bone meal, kelp, rock phosphate, and greensand. These are all excellent products to add to your soil in the spring a few weeks before you start planting.

Start a Compost Pile

Compost is one of the foundations of organic gardening. Use your kitchen waste, garden waste, leaves, and grass clippings. Rather than throwing them into the garbage, use them to make an excellent amendment for your garden soil.

ALERT

Steep slopes where rainfall can wash away soil are not the best place to plant your vegetable garden. A slight slope will work if you plant your rows across the slope. On level ground, run your rows north to south to maximize exposure to the sun.

Collect Organic Matter

No matter how fertile your soil is, you will always need to add in organic matter on a regular basis as the plants use up the nutrients in the existing soil. Your garden soil will always need to be replenished. Contact local farms that may have animal manure for you to use. Some may charge for it, others may give it away, and still others will give it away if you come and clean out the pens! Try to get as much as you can.

Plan Your Crop Rotation

Planting your vegetables in a new area each year is an important aspect of organic gardening. This helps prevent pests and disease and keeps your soil healthier.

Plant Cover Crops

Cover crops are an inexpensive way to add organic matter to your garden soil. These are green plants that are usually planted in the fall and turned under in early spring. The green tops and plant roots add the organic matter to the soil. There are a variety of crops you can grow depending on what type of soil you have and what you want the crop to ultimately do for the soil. They can be used to add nitrogen to the soil, prevent weeds from growing, or just to add in lots of organic matter, which will decompose into a rich humus material. Check with your local garden center or any seed catalog for the varieties that are available for your area.

ESSENTIAL

Even in a small garden, leave space between your garden rows so you can walk and work between them. In large vegetable gardens, make paths and leave enough space at the end of rows so you can easily turn a cultivator and wheelbarrows.

Use Mulches

Mulches are used in organic growing to help protect the garden soil from getting too wet, becoming too dry, and eroding. Straw, hay, shredded leaves, and grass clippings are all common mulch materials. These items are all organic matter, which will decompose over time and add to the fertility of your garden soil. If your cover crop gets too high (more than six inches), cut or mow it before tilling it under and use the green matter as mulch in another area of your garden.

CHAPTER 22

Plan for Next Season

Planning is one of the essential elements of a successful vegetable garden. Knowing what worked and did not work will help you plan and avoid the same problems. Take time during the year to document what happened. At the end of the season, you can evaluate what worked well and what you would like to do differently. Apply the questions in this chapter to your own vegetable garden and your experiences.

Did You Choose a Good Garden Site?

Go over the questions you answered in Chapter 1 to start your garden. Do you still agree with your reasons for starting a garden or have they changed? What did you like about the site you picked? What would you change about it? If the site did not work well, evaluate different sites or different gardening methods. If you chose to grow in your backyard but found you preferred to grow in containers, maybe you can plan to use more containers next year. Were you satisfied with all of your vegetables? Would you like to grow different vegetables? More vegetables? Fewer vegetables?

ALERT

There is always something new to learn about your garden site and growing vegetables. Take a course at your local community center, go on gardening tours, take a seminar, or join a gardening club. These are all fabulous ways to learn more and connect with fellow gardeners.

If you reinvented an old site or grew in an existing garden what worked and what did not? What would you need to do to make it even better next year? Gardening is always a work in progress. Plants grow and die back, some do better than others in your soil conditions, the weather and sunlight affect how plants grow, and unexpected problems always crop up. By taking the time to revisit your gardening season, you can write down ideas and plans for next season. We all think we will remember, but more often than not the small details are what can make your gardening life easier. Those little things are what you need to write down!

Did Your Plants Get Enough Sunlight and Rainfall?

Most vegetable plants need an average of six hours of sunlight a day and one inch of water every week to grow their best.

Did your site get the amount of sunlight you thought it would? If not, can you move your garden to another area? What other changes can you make?

The sun shifts over the season, so what was in full sun in the spring may not have been in the summer and fall months. Do you need to plan your vegetable plantings to take advantage of this? If you know part of your garden is going to be in shade in the hot summer months, perhaps your lettuces will do better in a given spot than your tomatoes. Take time to re-examine your garden rotation.

FACT

Gardening can be a very creative pursuit. Designing and planning your vegetable garden layout each season can be a way to express your creativity. Use your creative or artistic abilities to create structures, sculptures, or use garden ornaments to make your garden special for you and your family.

Water, like sunlight, is essential for growing vegetables. Did you take into account the amount of rainfall you did or did not get? When you watered was it an easy or a difficult process? Do you need to make changes on how you watered your veggies? How you water certain vegetable plants can affect how they grow and what pests or diseases they may attract. Now is the time to make a list of any new hoses, water wands, or nozzles you have or may want to purchase for next season. The best sales are often in the fall, when you do not need to water!

Was the Garden Too Large or Too Small?

Novice gardeners in particular find it challenging to assess the resources they need to plant, grow, maintain, and harvest a vegetable garden. How did you do? If you struggled to keep the area you had in reasonable shape, do not feel bad about scaling back a bit. If you started out small and feel you can easily go larger, then take the time to see how best to expand your garden site.

Weeds are often easy to control in a new garden site. When an area is newly tilled, weed seeds are often killed off. In other cases, the soil may not be as fertile, so the weeds do not grow as well. But beware. In the second or third season, weeds often seem to get out of control. Take that into consideration if you want to expand your garden. Once you start adding compost and amendments to your garden soil, both your veggies and your weeds will grow faster and bigger. If you can't decide whether to expand, try growing in the same-size area for a second season and then make your decision.

FACT

You can make money vegetable gardening! Some gardeners garden as a hobby, but there are others who earn a living by growing and selling vegetables. If this is something you want to pursue, check out your local farmers markets or roadside stands to see what others are doing and talk to them to see how they got started.

The fall is a great time to change the size of your vegetable garden. If you need to till a larger area, do it in the fall, adding in as much compost and aged animal manure as you can get your hands on. Plant a cover crop if you have time or add in some mulch to keep the nutrients from leaching out. In the spring, you will have a fertile garden bed ready to be planted! On the other hand, if you find you have taken on more than you can handle, the fall is a perfect time to plant some grass seed or perennial flowers and shrubs into the vegetable garden beds you won't use again next year.

Did You Have Too Many or Too Few Vegetables?

Did you and your family eat what you grew? Did you plant too much or too little of any vegetables? Were you surprised about what grew really well or did poorly? Did the family like something you tried as an experiment? Jot down notes so you remember what you want to plant next season.

ALERT

Growing healthy, safe food is a priority for some gardeners. Because there are more food scares and more product recalls, it is more important than ever to know where your food is grown. If you can grow your own vegetables and fruits, you will create a healthier life for yourself and your family.

Be careful not to mistake a bumper crop for overplanting. The perfect soil conditions and the perfect amount of water, sunlight, and heat can give you an overabundance of a certain vegetable. If you planted four cucumber plants and had too many for your use, think about scaling down to three plants. If you still have too many cucumbers the second season, perhaps you have the perfect garden for cucumbers! You can then scale back a bit more. However, remember that each year may bring different challenges, so plant at least two of everything to ensure you will have some veggies to eat.

Is there anything you can do to improve the growing conditions of the veggies that did not do so well? Not every vegetable will grow well in every site. Certain vegetables need more warmth, sunlight, or protection from the elements than others. Would certain plants do better in a container on your front patio than in the backyard? Do you need a greenhouse or cold frame to give your plants that extra warmth they need? If a vegetable plant consistently does not do well in your garden, try growing it in another way or acknowledge your site is just not what that plant needs. It does not mean anything about you as a gardener!

Did You Have Pest Problems?

It never fails. You finally feel you have vanquished the pests in your garden and something new shows up! No garden is pest-free—nor do you necessarily want it to be. There are beneficial and harmful insects and organisms and they both need to coexist for a healthy vegetable garden.

ESSENTIAL

Gardening can be a very pleasurable experience. Having a vegetable or flower garden in your backyard, patio, or balcony can add beauty to your home. Plants can attract wildlife, birds, butterflies, and other insects that are beautiful to watch and enjoy. Take the time to really experience your garden.

What is important is to document your problem pests, what you did to prevent or get rid of them, and your results. This is valuable information to have for the seasons to come, although not every season will have the same problems. If something worked one season it will probably work again. If, however, something did not work, you do not want to waste your time doing the same thing again next season!

Tilling your garden beds is one way to expose any insects and larvae to the elements, which will make it harder for them to survive. Planting a cover crop or using mulch will keep your soil healthy. Keeping your plants healthier makes it easier for them to fight off any harmful pests. Once the garden is winding down in the fall, put up new fences or fix the ones that were not working to keep out any unwanted animals.

Were Certain Diseases a Problem?

If your vegetable plants have a certain disease one year, they will most likely get it again. Diseases that affect plants are often soil-borne diseases that are very difficult to get rid of. But there are ways to prevent or at least minimize the effect they have on your vegetable plants. If you have diseased vegetable plants, try to identify the problem and research its cause. The more information you can get on the disease, the better equipped you will be to prevent it next season.

Some gardeners feel intimidated and disheartened if they have problems in their vegetable garden. Rather than letting the problem ruin your gardening experience, see it as a learning experience or an adventure. If your garden site is susceptible to a certain disease, try growing varieties that are resistant to that particular problem, or do not grow that vegetable at all. Gardening will be more fun if you are not fighting the same issue every year!

Gardens can offer a spiritual connection for some people. Your vegetable garden can be a tranquil retreat where you can escape from the outside world. Take a stroll around your garden to lift your spirits and release the stress or anxiety you may be holding onto. Sit and take in the peace and beauty all around you!

Keeping your garden clean is one of the best ways to prevent disease. In the fall, make sure you clean up any debris in and around your garden beds.

Either plant a cover crop or mulch the area to prevent any soil erosion and leaching of the nutrients in the soil. If you have veggies growing all winter long, make sure you take care of them so you won't invite problems for next season.

Did You Have the Tools You Needed?

As a new gardener, good quality tools can be expensive. Buying a good tool every season may be the most economical way to get everything you want. Now that you have a growing season under your belt, you can make your list of what you need and a separate wish list. Proper tools for the job and the proper fit for the gardener can make vegetable gardening more fun and easier on the body.

The fall is a great time to make your list and catch some sales. It is also very important to take care of the tools you already have. Keeping tools clean all season long is a habit every gardener should have. Tools also need to be stored properly for the winter. If you do not have a garage or garden shed, find another protected area to store them—under a patio, under your front steps, attached to a wall that has an overhanging eave, or even under a large tree covered with a tarp to keep them somewhat protected from the weather.

ESSENTIAL

Use your garden to expand your social circle. Gardening is a great way to meet your neighbors and get involved in your community. Give extra vegetables to the local food bank or soup kitchen or organize a neighborhood party. Have everyone bring a dish of food made from something they grew in their backyard!

What Do You Want to Try Next Season?

Imagine your perfect vegetable garden. What do you see in your perfect garden next season? What steps do you need to take to make it that way? Review what worked or did not work and choose to make changes that will make it more of what you want. Small and inexpensive changes can make a huge difference in how your garden looks and how well the vegetables grow. It is fun to experiment with planting vegetables that may not be common to your area or trying a new variety.

Trying something new can renew your interest if the garden is becoming a bit stale or your interest is waning. If you have a wild area and prefer a manicured garden, it may take some money and effort to make it happen, but it can be done. If you have recently moved into a new home and the garden is not quite to your taste, now is the time to make plans to change things. It may take several seasons, but it all starts with a dream and then a plan of action.

FACT

Most of us have childhood memories about food or gardening. Gardening is a fun way for the family to spend time together and for children to learn how to grow vegetables. Gardens are where memories are made.

Adjust the garden to changes in your life. If you have welcomed a new child, taken on a more demanding job, or retired, reassess how much time, energy, and money you'll be able to put into your garden. Be realistic, and you'll have a more enjoyable gardening experience.

Did You Have Fun?

There are many reasons to have a vegetable garden. Gardening can give you food, exercise, and pleasure. It can help you can meet your neighbors, make money, be creative, relax, and establish family time. These are all wonderful reasons, but you also need to have fun and enjoy the tasks involved in growing a successful vegetable garden. Gardening can be hard work and there is a lot to learn, especially as a beginner. The best advice is to start small. Start with a tiny patch that you can easily handle and cannot wait to get back to every spring.

Web and Book Resources

The following websites and books were inspirational during the research and writing of this book. If you want more information, they are helpful resources for vegetable gardening.

Web Resources

YOUR-VEGETABLE-GARDENING-HELPER.COM
This site has some great how-to steps and some garden design books to help you to have a fabulous vegetable garden.
www.your-vegetable-gardening-helper.com

GARDENING KNOW HOW
All kinds of gardening information can be found on this site.
www.gardeningknowhow.com

GARDENWEB
A listing of gardening sites, vegetable gardening information, and more.
www.gardenweb.com

FOOD-FROM-THE-GARDEN.COM
Learn how to grow your own food.
www.food-from-the-garden.com

Book Resources

Abraham, George "Doc," and Katy Abraham. *Raise Vegetables Fruits and Herbs without a Garden* (Newbury, UK: Countryside Books, 1974).

Ball, Jeff, Robert Kourick, and Susan Lang. *Easy Composting* (San Francisco: Ortho Books, Chevron Chemical Company, 1992).

Better Homes and Gardens. *Vegetables & Herbs You Can Grow* (Des Moines: Meredith, 1978).

Coleman, Eliot. *The New Organic Grower: A Master's Manual of Tools and Techniques for the Home and Market Gardener* (White River Junction, VT: Chelsea Green Publishing, 1995).

Denckla, Tanya L. K. *The Gardener's A-Z Guide to Growing Organic Food* (North Adams, MA: Storey Publishing, 2003).

Edwards, Jonathan. *Greenhouse Gardening: Step by Step to Growing Success* (Wiltshire: Crowood Press, 1988).

Herriot, Carolyn. *A Year on the Garden Plan: A 52-Week Organic Gardening Guide* (Victoria, BC: Earthfuture Publications, 2005).

Jeavons, John. *How to Grow More Vegetables* (Berkeley, CA: Ten Speed Press, 1979).

Jesiolowski Cebenko, Jill, and Deborah L. Martin, eds. *Insect, Disease & Weed I.D. Guide: Find-It-Fast Organic Solutions for Your Garden.* (Emmaus, PA: Rodale, 2001).

Minnich, Jerry, Marjorie Hunt, and the editors of *Organic Gardening* magazine. *The Rodale Guide to Composting* (Emmaus, PA: Rodale Press, 1979).

Moore, Bernard. *Vegetable Gardening with Bernard Moore* (Vancouver, BC: Intermedia Press, 1980).

Schwenke, Karl. *Successful Small-Scale Farming: An Organic Approach* (North Adams, MA: Storey Publishing, 1994).

Solomon, Steve. *The Complete Guide to Organic Gardening West of the Cascades* (Seattle: Pacific Search Press, 1983).

Sunset Books. *How to Grow Vegetables & Berries* (Menlo Park, CA: Lane Publishing, 1982).

Sunset Books. *Vegetable Gardening* (Menlo Park, CA: Lane Publishing, 1973).

Yeomans, Kathleen. *The Able Gardener Overcoming Barriers of Age and Physical Limitations.* (Williamsburg: The Book Press, 1992).

APPENDIX B

Glossary of Terms

acidic soil
Soil that has a pH of less than 7. See pH.

aeration
Free movement of air through the vegetable plant root system; prevented when soil is compact or waterlogged.

alkaline soil
Soil with a pH above 7; often called *sweet soil*.

annuals
Plants that live one year. During this time the plant grows, flowers, produces seeds, and dies.

blanching
Preventing light from reaching the plant to reduce the green color, as in celery.

blood meal
Dried animal blood used as an organic soil fertilizer. It has high nitrogen content.

bolting
This is when a vegetable plant goes to seed prematurely, often caused by high temperatures.

bone meal
Finely ground animal bones used as an organic soil fertilizer. It is used to add phosphorus to the soil.

cold frame
A small unheated, covered structure used to grow and protect young vegetable plants in the early spring. The top is covered in plastic or glass, allowing sunlight to reach the plants.

companion planting
Plants that have an influence on each other, either beneficial or harmful.

compost
Decayed plant material such as vegetable scraps, leaves, grass clipping, garden waste, and animal manures. It is a valuable amendment for garden soil.

cool crops
Vegetables that grow and produce better in cooler weather, such as peas, lettuce, spinach, and cabbage.

crop rotation
Growing annual vegetable plants in a different location in the garden each year. This helps to control insects, improves soil fertility, and helps to prevent soil erosion.

crown
This is the growing point of the plant where the new shoots or top develops.

fertilization
The union of pollen from the male flower with the female flower in a plant to produce seeds. This is essential in producing edible parts in corn, squash, and tomatoes. Also, the application of nutrients to the soil such as nitrogen, phosphorus, and potassium.

fertilizer tea
A mix of organic materials intended to bolster the health of growing vegetable plants.

germination
Sprouting of a vegetable seed and the beginning of the plant's growth.

green manure
Crops such as legumes or grasses grown in the fall to be plowed under in the spring. Used to increase the organic matter in garden soil, which will improve the soil structure.

greensand
A sea deposit containing iron, potassium, and other elements used as a organic fertilizer.

hardening off
Adapting vegetable plants to outdoor conditions by gradually moving them out of a cold frame, hothouse, or greenhouse. This helps the plant to survive when transplanted outdoors.

heavy feeder

Vegetables that use large amounts of soil nutrients to grow to maturity. These include leafy greens, corn, cucumber, cauliflower, and tomatoes.

heavy soil

Soil that usually contains a large amount of clay. It has a tendency to retain moisture, should not be cultivated when wet, and needs to be improved by adding organic matter regularly.

humus

Decomposed organic material that improves the structure, texture, and fertility of garden soil.

inorganic

Refers to fertilizers that are produced chemically. Material not arising from natural growth.

insecticide

Natural ingredients used to control insects either on contact or through ingestion.

interplanting

Planting to get maximum production from your garden. This is done by planting vegetables that mature early in the season alongside plants that mature later in the season.

irrigation

Applying water to the garden soil using sprinklers, drip irrigation, or hand watering.

K

Symbol for potassium, also know as "potash."

leaching

Loss of soluble fertilizers such as nitrogen by the action of water running downward through the soil.

leggy

Weak stemmed and spindling vegetable seedlings. This is usually caused by too much heat, too much shade, crowding, or overfertilization.

legume

A plant that produces pods and is often grown for its ability to pull nitrogen from the air with the nitrifying bacteria that live in certain plant roots.

light feeders

Vegetables that require smaller amounts of nutrients to grow to maturity. Some examples are root crops.

light soil

Soil that is usually made up mostly of sand. It is easy to cultivate, retains little moisture, and needs organic matter added to it regularly.

lime

A compound containing calcium and magnesium. It is applied to garden soil to reduce acidity.

loam

Soil that consists of a mixture of sand, silt, and clay. It is an ideal garden soil for growing vegetables.

manure

Animal waste used as a soil amendment and fertilizer. You want to use aged manures in order not to burn the vegetable plants.

microorganism

A microscopic animal or plant that may cause disease or may have a beneficial effect when a plant is decomposing.

mildew

Plant disease caused by fungi. It is recognized by the white cottony coating on vegetable plant leaves.

monoecious

Vegetable plants that have a male and female sex organ on different plants, such as cucumbers and squash. You need to have a male and female plant in order to produce fruits.

mulch

Organic or inorganic materials used to cover the soil surface to conserve moisture, maintain an even soil temperature, and control weeds. Some examples are straw, leaves, newspaper, or black plastic.

nitrogen
One of the essential nutrients a vegetable plant needs for growth and to give it a green color.

organic matter
A portion of soil that is a result of decomposition of plant and animal residue. It helps maintain good soil structure and promotes microorganisms in the soil.

P
Symbol for phosphorus.

peat moss
Partially decomposed plant life that is removed from bogs and used as a soil amendment or rooting medium.

perennial
A plant that normally lives for more that two years. Some examples of perennial vegetables are asparagus and artichokes.

pH
A chemical symbol use to identify the level of acidity or alkalinity in garden soil. The scale ranges from 0 to 14, with 7 being neutral. Readings of less than 7 indicate acidic soil and readings of about 7 indicate alkaline soil.

plant residue
Plant parts such as leaves, stem, and roots that remain after a crop has been harvested. These parts can be used to make compost.

phosphorus
One of the three major nutrients needed by vegetable plants; designated by the letter P.

pollen
A reproductive material produced by the male part of a flower. It is usually dustlike in appearance.

pollination, open
This is the transfer of pollen from the flower of one plant to the flower of the same plant or a different plant by means such as the wind or bees.

pollination, self
This is the transfer of pollen through direct contact from the male part of one flower to the female part of the same flower or to another flower on the same plant.

potassium
One of the three major nutrients needed by vegetable plants. Same as potash.

ripe
The stage of maturity at which the fruit of a vegetable is ready to be harvested.

rock phosphate
This is finely ground rock powder used as an organic fertilizer. It is used to add phosphorus to the soil.

rust
A plant disease caused by a fungus and characterized by a round red or yellow lesion. May be found on beans or corn.

seed bed
The garden soil after it has been prepared for seeding or setting out transplants.

seedling
A very young vegetable plant.

short-season vegetables
These are vegetables that are ready for harvesting after one or two months following planting.

side dressing
Applying compost, fertilizers, or aged animal manures on the soil surface around the base of a plant so cultivating or watering will carry the nutrients to the plant roots.

silt
Soil particles that are between the size of sand and clay.

soil

This is the upper layer of the earth's surface. It is composted of organic matter, minerals, and microorganisms, all making it capable of supporting plant life.

soil aeration

The mechanical loosening of the soil to help water absorption and air movement.

sour soil

Same as acid soil. It has a pH below 7.

staking

Using materials like wood, bamboo, or plastic to provide support to vegetable plants.

succession planting

Planting a new crop of vegetables every few weeks so as to get a continuous harvest throughout the growing season.

thinning

Pulling out young plants from the soil in order to leave others at the proper spacing so they will grow to maturity.

variety

Closely related vegetable plants forming a subdivision of a species that have similar characteristics.

virus

This is a pathogenic organism too small to be seen with a magnifying microscope. It is capable of causing plant disease. The disease is often spread from infected to healthy plants through pruning or handling of plants or by sucking insects such as aphids or thrips.

wood ash

Residue from burned wood. It is used as an organic fertilizer or soil amendment. This is used to add phosphorus to the soil. Make sure it is well tilled into the garden bed.

APPENDIX C

Vegetable Garden Recipes

Mediterranean Potato Salad

This potato salad works for all different varieties of potatoes.
It's especially good if you've grown multiple varieties in your garden.

INGREDIENTS | SERVES 4

2 pounds assorted potatoes, cooked and cooled

1 bunch scallions, thinly sliced

1 cup grape tomatoes

2 hard-boiled eggs, quartered

1 cup chopped Italian flat-leaf parsley

¾ cup pitted Niçoise olives

3 tablespoons bacon bits

2 tablespoons mayonnaise

2 tablespoons buttermilk

1 tablespoon olive oil

1 teaspoon smoked paprika

Salt and freshly ground black pepper to taste

1. Cut the potatoes up until they are of a uniform size. Put them into a salad bowl and add the scallions, grape tomatoes, eggs, parsley, olives, and bacon bits.

2. Mix together the mayonnaise, buttermilk, olive oil, smoked paprika, salt, and pepper. Whisk together until well mixed. Dress the salad, tossing gently to coat all the ingredients. Serve.

Country Corn Cakes

Good for either breakfast or supper, these corn cakes may be served with melted butter and maple syrup, fruit syrup, or applesauce.

INGREDIENTS | SERVES 4

1 cup buttermilk

1 egg, lightly beaten

2 tablespoons melted butter

1 cup uncooked grits or coarse cornmeal

1 cup all-purpose flour

1 cup corn kernels, preferably fresh

1 cup cooked black-eyed peas

1 tablespoon baking powder

1 teaspoon baking soda

Salt and freshly ground black pepper to taste

Vegetable oil for pan-frying

1. Combine the buttermilk, egg, and butter in a large mixing bowl. Stir in the grits, flour, corn kernels, black-eyed peas, baking powder, baking soda, salt, and pepper; the batter will be thick.

2. Heat about 2 tablespoons vegetable oil in a large skillet or on a griddle over medium to medium-low heat. When the surface is hot, spoon about ¾ cup of batter per cake onto the surface, and when the bottom has browned, carefully turn the cake over to cook the second side. Be sure the skillet does not overheat, or the cakes will burn. Repeat until all the batter is used up, adding more oil as needed. Serve hot.

About Black-Eyed Peas

If you live in the South, you know the tradition: eat black-eyed peas on New Year's Day to bring good luck for the rest of the year. But these delicious legumes, also known as "cow peas," should be enjoyed often. These "peas" (they are actually beans) are rich sources of calcium, potassium, protein, and vitamin A.

English Garden Pea Soup

Pair this soup with a salad and fine artisan bread for a hearty and satisfying meal.

INGREDIENTS | SERVES 2

1 tablespoon olive oil

2 cloves garlic, thinly sliced

1 leek, thinly sliced

2 cups garden peas

1 cup white wine

3 tablespoons plain yogurt

3 tablespoons heavy cream, optional

Salt and freshly ground black pepper to taste

Snipped chives for garnish

Garlic croutons for garnish

Bacon for garnish

Tarragon leaves for garnish

1. Heat the olive oil in a saucepan over medium heat and sauté the garlic and leek for 3 to 4 minutes.

2. Spoon this mixture into a blender or food processor. Add the peas, white wine, yogurt, and heavy cream if using. Purée until smooth. Season with salt and pepper. Pour into soup bowls and garnish as desired.

Rinsing Leeks

Because leeks are raised in mounds of sand, the grains of which seem to trickle freely between its tightly furled leaves in the stalk, they are notoriously gritty and require a thorough rinsing in cold water. One way to get rid of the sand is to slice from just above the root end (leave the root intact for this) and, using a very sharp knife, slit the leek in half lengthwise. Then swish the leek and its separated leaves through a sink filled with water. When the sand is gone, slice off the root and use.

Veggie Frittata

Versatile and adaptable to whichever veggies are in season, this wholesome dish starts the day with a bang, and it makes a good light supper, too. It's easy to increase quantities to feed larger groups, so judge the size of your crowd. Made too much? This is delicious packed up for lunch.

INGREDIENTS | SERVES 4

3 tablespoons olive oil

2 red potatoes, diced

6 asparagus spears, trimmed and cut into 2-inch lengths

½ zucchini or yellow summer squash, diced

2 teaspoons minced garlic

1 teaspoon seasoning salt

1 teaspoon smoked paprika

6 large eggs

1 cup shredded Cheddar cheese

½ cup chopped Italian parsley

What's Smoked Paprika?

A Spanish seasoning made from slowly oak-smoked and ground pimentón, a variety of Spanish red pepper, smoked paprika imparts an earthy, woodsy taste to an infinite number of savory dishes. It's readily available in well-stocked supermarkets, specialty food stores, and online mail-order sites.

1. Preheat the broiler.

2. Heat the oil in an 8- or 9-inch skillet over medium heat. Add the potatoes and sauté for about 3 minutes or until the cubes begin to brown. Add the asparagus, zucchini, garlic, and seasonings and cover the skillet, cooking for 2 to 3 minutes.

3. Meanwhile, beat the eggs until foamy. Stir in the cheese and parsley and pour the egg mixture over the vegetables. Using a spatula, lift up the edges of the eggs and tip the skillet to all sides, allowing the uncooked eggs to flow underneath the vegetables and cook.

4. When the eggs are almost firm, slide the skillet under the broiler and cook until the top is bubbly and brown. Serve hot sliced in wedges; the cheese should be melted and runny.

Super-Hero Wrap-Up

This is such a versatile carry-all for nutrients that you can switch filling ingredients around depending on what you have on hand. While the filling ingredients are only suggestions, try to stick to the amounts suggested, or the wrap may spill out all the goodies.

INGREDIENTS | SERVES 1

1 tablespoon olive oil

1 tablespoon minced garlic, or to taste

3 ounces chicken strips

¼ red onion, thinly sliced

1 10-inch flavored wrap

3 tablespoons plain yogurt, preferably the thick Greek yogurt

2 tablespoons chopped fresh dill weed

½ cup julienned cucumber

½ cup julienned red pepper

1. Heat the oil in a large skillet over medium heat. Sauté the garlic, chicken strips, and red onion for 3 to 4 minutes or until the onion wilts slightly. Set aside to cool.

2. Heat the wrap for 30 to 40 seconds per side in a nonstick skillet or according to package directions. Set aside.

3. Toss the "chicken" mixture with the yogurt, dill weed, cucumber, and red pepper. Spread the wrap out flat and top with this mixture. Roll up as desired.

About Wraps

You may use any kind of flat bread to make these portable sandwiches, from pita bread to lavash, but most supermarkets stock flat breads—plain or flavored—that resemble tortillas but are larger around. You must soften these first before using, otherwise they may tear when you roll them up. Follow package directions for rolling and folding, or simply roll the sandwich up like a tube and enjoy.

Artichokes Stuffed with Couscous

Garlic mayonnaise is good for dipping the leaves and seasoning the artichoke bottoms after the couscous is eaten.

INGREDIENTS | SERVES 2

½ cup pomegranate juice

1 teaspoon butter

1 cup uncooked couscous

¾ cup toasted pine nuts

10 dried apricots, coarsely chopped

½ cup cilantro leaves

Pinch salt

2 very large globe artichokes, trimmed and cooked

1. Combine 1 cup water and the pomegranate juice in a saucepan and heat to boiling, then stir in the butter and couscous. Remove from the heat and cover; set aside for 5 minutes.

2. Meanwhile, in a mixing bowl, combine the pine nuts, apricots, cilantro leaves, and salt, stirring well. Fold in the couscous.

3. Part the artichoke leaves to expose the center. Using a spoon, scoop out the central thistles, or choke, and discard. Spoon the couscous mixture into the artichokes, mounding it up to fill them completely. Serve hot or at room temperature.

Southwestern Sprouts

This recipe kicks Brussels sprouts up a notch with seasonings and texture.
You'll want to serve these often.

INGREDIENTS | SERVES 4

1 pound Brussels sprouts, trimmed and halved

1 tablespoon olive oil

1 tablespoon taco seasoning or to taste

½ cup crushed spicy taco chips

½ cup spicy or mild salsa

½ cup shredded Cheddar cheese

½ cup sunflower seeds, optional

1. Preheat the oven to 350°F.

2. Toss the sprouts with the oil and taco seasoning and put them in a roasting pan. Cook for about 30 minutes or until the sprouts become tender.

3. Put them in a serving bowl and toss with the taco chips, salsa, cheese, and sunflower seeds if using. Serve hot.

Sautéed Mixed Greens with Kielbasa

*Bursting with flavor and nutrients, this greens medley suits a casual dinner;
offer this with a toasted baguette.*

INGREDIENTS | SERVES 4

2 tablespoons olive oil

1 large onion, thinly sliced

1 (12-ounce) package Kielbasa, thinly sliced

1 bunch chard, rinsed and coarsely chopped

1 bunch collards, rinsed and julienned

½ cup grated Parmesan cheese

1. Heat the oil in a large stockpot over medium heat and sauté the onion and sausage slices until the onion turns golden.

2. Add the greens and a sprinkling of water, cover the stockpot, and steam the greens until they are wilted and tender. Sprinkle the greens with the Parmesan cheese and serve.

Baked Spinach Tart

Popeye loved his spinach from a can,
but you will love it fresh with its bright flavor and color.

INGREDIENTS | SERVES 4 TO 6

2 large eggs

1 cup plain nonfat or whole milk yogurt

1 cup feta cheese

1 cup shredded mozzarella cheese

1 bunch fresh spinach, well rinsed, wilted, and chopped

½ cup chopped onion

Salt and freshly ground black pepper to taste

1 (9-inch) unbaked deep-dish pie shell

½ pint grape tomatoes

1. Preheat the oven to 350°F.

2. Beat the eggs until foamy. Stir in the yogurt, feta cheese, mozzarella cheese, spinach, and onions, mixing well until combined. Season with salt and pepper.

3. Spoon the mixture into the pie shell and push the tomatoes into the top of the mixture.

4. Bake for about 40 minutes or until the mixture is firm to the touch. Let it cool slightly before slicing and serving.

Spinach Salad

You'll find dozens of recipes for spinach salads, but this particular dish has some unexpected flavors. A rich Thousand Island dressing mixed with salsa to taste accents the flavors well. Leftovers are great.

INGREDIENT | SERVES 4

About 6 cups fresh baby spinach, well rinsed and dried

3 hard-boiled eggs, quartered

1 (15½-ounce) can navy beans, drained and rinsed

½ to 1 red onion, diced

½ cup bacon bits

½ cup toasted pumpkin seeds

1 to 2 jalapeños, thinly sliced

Commercial salad dressing, as desired

Combine the spinach, eggs, beans, onion, bacon bits, pumpkin seeds, and jalapeños in the salad bowl. Dress as desired and serve.

Turkish-Style Stuffed Pepper

You can easily double or triple this recipe to serve more people, but it's so easy to prepare, it's fine just for one. For added texture, add a tablespoon or two of toasted pine nuts.

INGREDIENTS | SERVES 1

1 large red bell pepper
Olive oil for rubbing
½ cup cooked brown rice
¼ cup bacon bits
2 tablespoons raisins
2 tablespoons chopped dried apricots
2 tablespoons chopped fresh mint
2 tablespoons chopped parsley
2 tablespoons plain yogurt

1. Preheat the oven to 400°F.

2. Cut the top off the pepper and clean out the seeds and membranes. Rub the pepper inside and out with the olive oil.

3. Combine the rice with the bacon bits, raisins, apricots, mint, parsley, and yogurt. Carefully spoon the mixture into the hollow pepper. Prop the pepper upright in a baking dish.

4. Bake the pepper for 30 minutes or until tender. Serve.

Peck of Peppers Tart

For this colorful entrée, mix and match the colors, sizes, and heat quotient of the peppers you select. If you don't want it too piquant, go easy on the hot chilies. Otherwise, live it up.

INGREDIENTS | SERVES 6

2 tablespoons olive oil

1 tablespoon minced garlic

About 2 cups coarsely chopped peppers of your choice

4 eggs, well beaten

1 cup milk

1 cup shredded Swiss cheese

1 to 2 teaspoons smoked paprika

Salt and freshly ground black pepper to taste

1 (9-inch) deep-dish piecrust

1. Preheat the oven to 350°F.

2. Heat the oil in a large skillet over medium heat and sauté the garlic. Add the peppers and sauté for 2 to 3 minutes.

3. Meanwhile, mix the eggs, milk, cheese, paprika, salt, and pepper together until well combined. Stir in the peppers and pour the mixture into the piecrust.

4. Bake the tart for 30 minutes or until the center is firm and the top browns. Serve hot.

Roasted Asparagus with
Mixed Summer Squashes and Peppers

INGREDIENTS | SERVES 4

¼ cup olive oil

3 tablespoons balsamic vinegar

1 tablespoon minced garlic

1 pound asparagus, stem ends trimmed

1 pound mixed summer squashes, thinly sliced

1 pound sweet peppers, stemmed and sliced in half lengthwise

2 to 3 hot peppers, or to taste, chopped

Seasoning salt to taste

1. Preheat the oven to 400°F.

2. Mix the olive oil, balsamic vinegar, and garlic together and set aside.

3. Place the vegetables into a large roasting pan, mixing them together so the flavors will mingle. Pour the olive oil mixture over top, lifting and gently mixing the vegetables so they are all coated with oil. Sprinkle the vegetables with seasoning salt.

4. Roast the vegetables uncovered for about 45 minutes or until they begin to darken; stir occasionally. Serve hot.

Index

Standard U.S./Metric Measurement Conversions

VOLUME CONVERSIONS

U.S. Volume Measure	Metric Equivalent
⅛ teaspoon	0.5 milliliters
¼ teaspoon	1 milliliters
½ teaspoon	2 milliliters
1 teaspoon	5 milliliters
½ tablespoon	7 milliliters
1 tablespoon (3 teaspoons)	15 milliliters
2 tablespoons (1 fluid ounce)	30 milliliters
¼ cup (4 tablespoons)	60 milliliters
⅓ cup	90 milliliters
½ cup (4 fluid ounces)	125 milliliters
⅔ cup	160 milliliters
¾ cup (6 fluid ounces)	180 milliliters
1 cup (16 tablespoons)	250 milliliters
1 pint (2 cups)	500 milliliters
1 quart (4 cups)	1 liter (about)

WEIGHT CONVERSIONS

U.S. Weight Measure	Metric Equivalent
½ ounce	15 grams
1 ounce	30 grams
2 ounces	60 grams
3 ounces	85 grams
¼ pound (4 ounces)	115 grams
½ pound (8 ounces)	225 grams
¾ pound (12 ounces)	340 grams
1 pound (16 ounces)	454 grams

OVEN TEMPERATURE CONVERSIONS

Degrees Fahrenheit	Degrees Celsius
200 degrees F	100 degrees C
250 degrees F	120 degrees C
275 degrees F	140 degrees C
300 degrees F	150 degrees C
325 degrees F	160 degrees C
350 degrees F	180 degrees C
375 degrees F	190 degrees C
400 degrees F	200 degrees C
425 degrees F	220 degrees C
450 degrees F	230 degrees C

BAKING PAN SIZES

American	Metric
8 x 1½ inch round baking pan	20 x 4 cm cake tin
9 x 1½ inch round baking pan	23 x 3.5 cm cake tin
1 x 7 x 1½ inch baking pan	28 x 18 x 4 cm baking tin
113 x 9 x 2 inch baking pan	30 x 20 x 5 cm baking tin
2 quart rectangular baking dish	30 x 20 x 3 cm baking tin
15 x 10 x 2 inch baking pan	30 x 25 x 2 cm baking tin (Swiss roll tin)
9 inch pie plate	22 x 4 or 23 x 4 cm pie plate
7 or 8 inch springform pan	18 or 20 cm springform or loose bottom cake tin
9 x 5 x 3 inch loaf pan	23 x 13 x 7 cm or 2 lb narrow loaf or pate tin
1½ quart casserole	1.5 litre casserole
2 quart casserole	2 litre casserole